Veith Kilberth, Jürgen Schwier (eds.)
Skateboarding Between Subculture and the Olympics

D1665004

body cultures

Veith Kilberth, born 1976, blends his Sports Sciences diploma from the University of Cologne with experience as a former professional skateboarder. Currently a doctoral candidate at the Europa University Flensburg, he plans and realizes skate park projects as a partner in agency Landskate. He specializes in the fields of youth marketing, trend sports, skateboarding and skateparks.
Jürgen Schwier is a professor of sport pedagogy and sport sociology at the Europa University Flensburg and co-leader of the master-programme »Leitung frühkindlicher Bildungseinrichtungen«. His research focus includes sports communication, youth (sub-)cultures and the development of alternative sports.

Veith Kilberth, Jürgen Schwier (eds.)

Skateboarding Between Subculture and the Olympics

A Youth Culture under Pressure from Commercialization and Sportification

[transcript]

Bibliographic information published by the Deutsche Nationalbibliothek
The Deutsche Nationalbibliothek lists this publication in the Deutsche Nationalbibliografie; detailed bibliographic data are available in the Internet at http://dnb.d-nb.de

Cover concept: Kordula Röckenhaus, Bielefeld
Cover illustration: © Axel Flach
Printed by Majuskel Medienproduktion GmbH, Wetzlar
Print-ISBN 978-3-8376-4765-5
PDF-ISBN 978-3-8394-4765-9
https://doi.org/10.14361/9783839447659

Contents

Quo vadis Skateboarding?

Jürgen Schwier & Veith Kilberth

Skateboarding is a worldwide movement culture that traditionally seems to be particularly attractive for male teenagers as well as for young adults. This movement culture, however, is perceived by numerous skateboarders of every sexual orientation and gender identity as an expression of a special attitude to life and as an idiosyncratic lifestyle which, depending on the degree of personal involvement, can permeate almost all areas of their everyday lives. At the same time, since its beginnings as so-called asphalt surfing in the 1950s, skateboarding has undergone both various technical developments as well as cultural develop-ments.[1] Over the past few decades, skateboarding has experienced several waves when it comes to the number and typology of participants. That is, in Europe and North America, skateboarding has faced several phases of commercial highs and lows.

With regard to its historical development, skateboarding – in the form of practice that has prevailed to this day – has, on the one hand, been created in the environment of Californian surf culture. On the other hand, the trends in the US still retain a certain pioneering function for the rest of the world. This applies in particular to the longer-term process of change that, according to Lombard (2010), has led to the fact that skateboarding, which only a few decades ago was labelled either as a form of play for children or as a purely underground activity, has gradually become a valued field of action for youth marketing and sports sponsoring as well as an object for state programmes to promote open youth

---

1   The close connection between surfing and skateboarding is reflected, among other things, in surf skating, which attempts to transfer the feeling of movement of surfing to skateboarding in concrete bowls and on asphalt surfaces (cf. www.carver-skate boards.com, www.curfboard.com or www.landlockedboards.com).

work or to revitalise public spaces (cf. for example, Beal, 2013, pp. 106-107; Beal et al., 2017; Borden, 2001, pp. 229-237; Borden, 2018, 2019; Vivoni, 2018).

Not least due to its playful approach to spaces, objects and social forms, this movement practice is, so to speak, an experimental laboratory for innovative forms of physical expression and youthful self-empowerment (cf. Schwier, 1998, pp. 24-38). In skateboarding, the mastery of driving techniques and tricks, driven by self-directed learning processes, pre-supposes regular, lengthy and sometimes painful practice, during which one has to get used to the unusual, overcome resistance, pass individual tests and deal with the risk of injury.

Overall, this adventurous aspect underscores the need for a genuine commitment to body capital, vitality and free time – or that which adolescents tend to have in abundance. In addition, risk is one of the style elements that initially make skateboarding – true to the motto 'skate and destroy' – a distinctive practice in the first place.

In this context, it should be noted that skateboarders do not normally travel alone with the board and carry out their own manoeuvres. There is simply something like a casual compulsion in skateboarding to form informal groups of like-minded people. In principle, social co-existence is the focus of and is anchored in this social and cultural practice. Community experience, mutual recognition and respect for the individual members of the scene and their movement action play a central role in this (cf. for example Butz & Peters, 2018; Schwier & Kilberth, 2018a).

Since the 1970s, at the latest, urban skateboard scenes have also emphasised sub-cultural attitudes (cf. Borden, 2001, pp. 137-139) and do not view skateboarding as a regular form of sport at all but rather as a rebellious movement practice or as a creative movement art and logically distance themselves both from the system of organised sport and from the usual social conventions. From this perspective, skateboard communities tend towards self-marginalisation – which can certainly include a 'coolonialist' resistance myth (Butz, 2014, p. 172) – and, with their anti-authoritarian basic attitude, are located on the fringes of the urban or municipal order: "The loud takeover of city streets by skateboarders unearths the potential redefinition of urban space for pleasure and protest" (Vivoni, 2018, p. 121; cf. e.g. Bradley, 2010; Németh, 2006).

At the same time, skateboard communities are increasing continuously for quite some time. Beside older skateboarders (beyond the age of 30) and queer skaters, young women and girls who skate, in particular, are increasingly drawing attention to their practice and developing their own networks and projects.[2]

Public skateparks, whose construction and maintenance are mostly financed by cities and municipalities, are not to be underestimated with regards to the development of this movement culture in German-speaking countries. Skateparks are purpose-built spaces that were initially created as a reaction to the general demand and the almost uncontrollable appropriation of urban spaces by young skaters. Part of the skate community thinks that such facilities, on the one hand, contribute in to the 'domestication' of the actual sub-cultural action practice, to which the idea of an isolated sports space has traditionally been alien (cf. Howell, 2008; Peters, 2016, p. 153).[3] On the other hand, the parks are assigned an important social function as playgrounds for communal self-presentation, as places of local scene formation and as places of shared aesthetic values (cf. Beal, 2013, pp. 100-102; Bradley, 2010; L'Aoustet & Griffet, 2003).

There is, however, an ongoing discussion within the skateboard community about its own identity, as a response to the commercialisation and its role as a sport, most notably through the construction of skateparks, an increase in contests and competitions, and an increase in marketing and sponsorships. For some time now, this movement practice has been permeated by exploitation and marketing processes that not only seek to appropriate the skateboard culture for their own purposes from the outside, as it were, but at least, partially, also emerge from the scene itself. Due to the fact that skateboarding will at least temporarily be an Olympic sport in the near future, this debate about the commercialisation and development into sport of rollerblading has undoubtedly gained additional momentum. With the inclusion in the Olympic Program 2020, skateboarding reaches the interim peak of progressive development into a competitive sport. From the point of view of the scene, the identity of skateboarding is at stake. The Olympic perspective increases tensions between sub-culture and consumer culture, between a continuation of the stylistic forms of expression of an alternative movement culture, the objective quantification in the sense of the (performance) sports system and the commercialisation through the influence of brands and

---

2   Cf. for example, www.indiegogo.com/projects/carving-space#/; www.goerlsrocknroll-skateboarding.com; www.suckmytrucks.de; www.geezerskate.co; www.facebook.com/groups/skatersover50/about/.

3   A striking reaction to the worldwide renaissance of skateparks is certainly the DIY movement, whose popularity is also reflected in the fact that videos about local DIY skate spots on platforms such as YouTube generate up to 1.8 million hits (www.youtube.com/watch?v=-P18nCQIA0g&t=1s).

media (cf. Schwier & Kilberth, 2018b). For skateboarding as an adapted, conformist sport represents something quite different from the non-conformist habits of skateboarding, which presumably inspired many actors to opt for this practice in the first place (cf. Beal, 2013; Beaver, 2012, p. 25).

Another aspect of the Olympic debate concerns gender relations in skateboarding culture. As already mentioned, skateboarding is globally regarded as a male-dominated movement practice in which different concepts and stagings of masculinity and femininity can be found but there are still noticeable barriers to access for girls and young women (cf. Atencio, Beal & Wilson, 2009, pp. 18-19; Sobiech & Hartung, 2017, pp. 214-219). Against this background, the question arises whether and to what extent the tendencies towards commercialisation and development into sport not only create more jobs and role models for female skaters but also – in the long run – favour equal participation for all genders in skateboarding.

This anthology therefore focuses on the current discussion about the inclusion of skateboarding in the programme of the 2020 Summer Olympics in Tokyo from various cultural and social science perspectives and gathers ten contributions on current developments in the context of skateboarding. It begins with a contribution by Jürgen Schwier, who is intended to introduce the problem area and, in a first step, portrays skateboarding as a youthful movement (sub-)culture. Subsequently, the tendencies towards commercialisation and development into sport will be traced and possible effects of participation in the Olympic Games on the further development of skateboarding culture will be discussed.

Eckehart Velten Schäfer addresses the Olympics by reconsidering the assumption that skateboarding has undergone several fundamental developments over the last sixty years. Within the framework of these development and transformation processes, he distinguishes 'sport-hostile' and more 'sport-compatible' movement culture formats. In this context, Schäfer tries to clarify which forms of skateboarding stand closer to or further removed from the classic (competition) sport.

Veith Kilberth analyses the terrain of the Olympic skateboard disciplines, which have re-configured themselves several times in the past. Using the reconstruction of the Olympic terrains 'Park' and 'Street', he works out developmental patterns and constellations that make visible an interplay between development into sport and skateboarding's sub-cultural origins. Suggesting a possible scenario for the future, Kilberth shows how the involved actors can secure commercial advantages for themselves, while at the same time preserving their non-conformist identity.

Iain Borden explores the key aspects of the global renaissance of skateparks over the last two decades, tracing inter alia the manifold usage options of such urban movement spaces. Borden argues that skateparks not only generate new forms of community, but – within certain limits – can also stimulate social change and processes of self-empowerment in challenging places (for example, social aid projects in neglected neighbourhoods or war-torn countries).

As documented by previous research, the debates around 'authentic' ways of being a skateboarder illustrate power dynamics within skateboarding. Becky Beal and Kristin Ebeling argue that the notion of authenticity as embodied by a risk-taking, creative, cisgendered male was fostered through the industry in the 1980s and reinforced throughout much of its history since. They consider how this version of authenticity has served to marginalize other groups of people, especially females and queer folk. The inclusion of skateboarding in the Olympics is one of the key shifts in the evolving narrative of authenticity, especially the inclusion of women as legitimate participants. Beal and Ebeling explore other key moments that have disrupted the traditional narrative and created spaces for gender inclusion.

The resilience of skateboard culture is the central theme of Sebastian Schweer's contribution. Using the example of the Swedish skateboarder Pontus Alv and his Polar Skate Company, Schweer claims that the heterodox skateboarding style popularised by Alv can be understood as a reaction to the sportisation of the scene. He describes this as a form of resilience. Schweer concludes his remarks by referring to Hartmut Rosa's resonance theory at the level of society as a whole.

Katharina Bock explores the role of online media content for skateboarding culture and examines how these digital media formats (e-zines, video portals, websites, skate-videos and tutorials) affect the scene. She concludes that online media (co-)created by the scene document the scene, whilst contributing to the production of knowledge and meaning. Starting from the historic description of skateboarding as an art form, Antoine Cantin-Brault sketches the dialectical process of how the practice is developing into a sport, which will reach its provisional endpoint with the appropriation by the Olympic Games. With reference to Jean-Paul Sartre's existentialism, he argues that skateboarding currently runs the risk of gambling away the last remnants of its own autonomy.

Tim Bindel and Niklas Pick ask whether skateboarding can ever be an appropriate subject for (sports) education. They suggest that skateboarding in the context of schools necessarily differs from street skating on the road. A qualitative study at its core, this chapter explores the central challenges associated with a corresponding educational process in the context of school sport – along the categories of teacher involvement, the teaching-learning problem and the spatial theme.

Skateboarding is taking place at the 2020 Summer Olympics, but don't expect skateboarders to assimilate with all the other 'real' athletes. What would happen if skateboarders defied the strict rules and behavioural expectations of the International Olympic Committee and manifested the intrinsic values of skateboarding at the Games instead? Known as the author of the thought-provoking manifesto 'The Skateboarding Art' (2012), skateboard writer Tait Colberg imagines an Olympic debut true to the values of self-expression, international camaraderie, and DIY-initiative in his colourful essay. Watch out Olympics – you can take the skateboarders out the streets, but you can't take the streets out of skateboarders...

We would like to thank many people: to Tine Kaphengst for the manuscript design; to Sander Holsgens and Dirk Vogel, for helping during different stages of the project; to Alex Flach for providing us with the extraordinary and impressive skateboard photography on the book cover, to the Department of Sport Science at the Europa-University Flensburg for supporting our work as researchers and finally to LNDSKT skatepark design office for supporting the project.

REFERENCES

Atencio, M., Beal, B. & Wilson, C. (2009). Distinction of risk: Urban skateboarding, street habitus, and the construction of hierarchical gender relations. *Qualitative Research in Sport and Exercise* 1, 1, 3-20.

Beal, B. (2013). *Skateboarding. The Ultimate Guide*. Santa Barbara, Denver, Oxford: Greenwood.

Beal, B., Atencio, M., Wright, E. & Mc Clain, Z. (2017). Skateboarding, Community and urban politics: shifting practices and challenges. *International Journal of Sport Policy and Politics* 9, 1, 11-23.

Beaver, T. D. (2012). By the Skaters, for the Skaters. The DIY Ethos of the Roller Derby Revival. *Journal of Sports and Social issues* 36, 1, 25-47.

Borden, I. (2001). *Skateboarding, Space and the City. Architecture and the Body*. Oxford: Berg Publishers.

Borden, I. (2018). Another Pavement, Another Beach. Skateboarding and the Performative Critique of Architecture. In Butz, K. & Peters, C. (Eds.), *Skateboard Studies* (pp. 246-266). London: Koenig Books.

Borden, I. (2019). *Skateboarding and the City: A Complete History*. London: Bloomsbury.

Bradley, G. L. (2010). Skate Parks as a Context for Adolescent Development. *Journal of Adolescent Development* 25, 1, 288-323.

Butz, K. (2014). 'Coolonialismus'. Wie das Skateboard nach Schleswig-Holstein kam. *Pop. Kultur und Kritik* 3, 5, 162-173.

Butz, K. & Peters, C. (Eds.) (2018). *Skateboard Studies*. London: Koenig Books.

Colberg, T. (2012). *The Skateboarding Art*. Washington: Lulu.com.

Howell, O. (2008). Skatepark as Neoliberal Playground: Urban Governance, Recreation Space, and the Cultivation of Personal Responsibility. *Space and Culture* 11, 4, 475-496.

L'Aoustet, O. & Griffet, J. (2003). The experiences of teenagers at Marseilles' skate park: emergence and evaluation of an urban sports site. *Cities* 18, 413-418.

Lombard, K.-J. (2010). Skate and create/skate and destroy: The commercial and governmental incorporation of skateboarding. *Journal of Media & Cultural Studies* 24, 4, 475-488.

Németh, J. (2006). Conflict, Exclusion, Relocation: Skateboarding and Public Space. *Journal of Urban Design* 11, 3, 297-318.

Peters, C. (2016). *Skateboarding – Ethnographie einer urbanen Praxis*. Münster: Waxmann.

Schwier, J. (1998). *Spiele des Körpers. Jugendsport zwischen Cyberspace und Streetstyle*. Hamburg: Czwalina.

Schwier, J. & Kilberth, V. (2018a). Zwischen Vereinnahmung und Unabhängigkeit. Jugendliche Bewegungs- und Sportkultur Skateboarding. *Schüler 2018: Sport* (pp. 48-51). Seelze: Friedrich Verlag.

Schwier, J. & Kilberth, V. (Eds.) (2018b). *Skateboarding zwischen Subkultur und Olympia. Eine jugendliche Bewegungskultur im Spannungsfeld von Kommerzialisierung und Versportlichung*. Bielefeld: transcript.

Sobiech, G. & Hartung, S. (2017). Geschlechtsbezogene Körper- und Raumaneignung in urbanen (Spiel-)Räumen am Beispiel Skateboarding. In Sobiech, G. & Günter, S. (Eds.), *Sport & Gender – (inter-)nationale sportsoziologische Geschlechterforschung* (pp. 207-221). Wiesbaden: Springer VS.

Vivoni, F. (2018). City of Social Control. Skateboarding and the Regulation of Public Space. In Butz, K. & Peters, C. (Eds.), *Skateboard Studies* (pp. 110-127). London: Koenig Books.

Skateboarding between Subculture and Olympic Games

Jürgen Schwier

INTRODUCTION

Skateboarding, along with surfing, is one of the first movement activities that, since the 1950s, have produced an unconventional alternative to the standardised world of modern sport and alternative interpretations of moving. From a sports, sociological and economic perspective, both skateboarding and surfing can also be described as long-term niche trends which, in terms of their attractiveness and circulation, now exhibit several wave movements. Beyond these 'ups and downs', the shared creation and awareness of differences in youth and body culture with the system and routines of organised sport stimulate the formation of a particular style. The practice of skateboarding always hangs in the air, so to speak, because it is not set in stone. Rather, it is produced and further developed through action (cf. Schwier, 1998).

When people are asked why they regularly and passionately ride a board with two axles and four wheels, there are certainly a variety of possible answers. Skateboarders of all genders are after the perfect trick and the perfect way to ride, perennially looking for uncommon (bodily) experiences or physical adventures. They seek to experience control where even the slightest control proves impossible. Skateboarders want to present themselves, develop their own style, strive for an intense yet fleeting experience, appreciate the community of like-minded people, and embrace the feeling of freedom. The rationale for skateboarding can therefore be as diverse as the intensity and forms of individual engagement. The scientific knowledge about motives and motivations mentioned above is still as incomplete as the entire state of knowledge about the practice of skateboarding, whereby in recent years, in German-speaking countries, there has been a significant increase in corresponding publications.[1] However, since the majority of these qualitative studies deal with local street-skate scenes, their findings can only be generalised to a limited extent.

Against this background, this article examines the tension between the commercialisation and 'sportisation' of skateboarding on the one hand, and its potential as a creative, recalcitrant and subversive youth culture on the other. To approach this tension field, skateboarding will first be characterised as a youth culture, whilst the ongoing trends towards commercialisation and 'sportisation' of this practice will be covered afterwards. Further argumentation then deals with the opportunities and risks connected to the inclusion of skateboarding in the programme of the 2020 Summer Olympics, as well as with the already perceptible counter-movements.

SKATEBOARDING AS A YOUTH CULTURE

Skateboarding is a form of motion, a social practice and a form of cultural expression, whereby interrelations between culture and (motion) practice are shaped differently by different scenes, and in individual development phases. Like other lifestyle sports, skateboarding not only articulates an understanding of sport open to manifold readings, but its sometimes risky forms of body thematisation also stress the reckless character and the subcultural-hedonistic aura of activity. Moments of improvisation and exuberance are as much a part of the game as the immediate joy of moving unaided and an orientation towards personal challenges. Since its early days, skateboarding has been a youth culture with a massive male over-representation. But within the last ten years "female skater crews are also coming onto the scene" (Atencio et al., 2018, p. 14).

Youth cultures in the field of action sports unfold an ensemble of meanings, actions, aesthetics, rituals and strategies that mutually refer to each other, shape a style perceived as authentic by actors, and set the culture apart from other juvenile scenes. In a certain sense, they are thus always and also cultures of expression, which set their own signs with the body, design action spaces, produce a shared stock of knowledge, but at the same time show instances of the unfinished, fluid and changeable (cf. Schwier, 2008, pp. 272-274). The practice of

---

1   See e.g., Bock, 2017; Butz, 2012; Butz & Peters, 2018; Eichler & Peters, 2012; Peters, 2011, 2016; Schäfer, 2015a, 2015b; Schäfer & Alkemeyer, 2018; Schweer, 2014; Schwier & Kilberth, 2018; Tappe, 2011.

skateboarding thus requires an inescapable ability to move, albeit not only on wheels; as a lifestyle, in fact, it encompasses large parts of actors' everyday life. Everyday practice – similar to surfing – includes both visual signs (from clothing to board brands) and an invisible system of distinctive features and hedonistic values, which is permanently in flux. Therefore, anyone who wants to lead a skateboarder's life must go through a learning process which, according to Peters (2016, p. 172), results in a complete involvement, includes competent handling of scene-typical rituals and clothing, as well as special forms of dealing with pain and injuries.

Would-be skateboarders learn what makes this style special by visiting meeting points and participating in motion practice and scene life. In skateboarding, however, the orientation of scene life (cf. Hitzler & Niederbacher, 2010, p. 16) does not follow a uniform pattern, but unfolds in the everyday practice of local communities, cliques or factions that keep the competition for style going (cf. Schwier & Erhorn, 2015, pp. 180-182). And it can also be in-style to warn against overdoing it among skaters, or to set individual accents. Still, striving to find the most accurate form of embodiment does not seem to be worth the effort; rather, in street or vert skating, the individuality of actors, their independent character and devotion to the cause must remain perceptible. Basically, style questions in the community are also regarded as rather insecure terrain on which you better tread cautiously: you cannot always say exactly what it means to do the right thing in a certain situation (or to refrain from doing it), and you cannot always say why a certain skateboarder embodies the style almost ideally.

Style skills combine motor skills, movement skills, willingness to improvise and take risks with coolness, interaction competence, connoisseurship (music, fashion, scene language, locations, Internet videos, etc.), as well as a demonstration of identity. Irrespective of age, gender and ethnicity, being a skateboarder ultimately involves an attitude that Stern (2010, p. 261) has described as a total commitment to new sports practices, which knows no clear boundaries between sport and everyday life. Against this background, the following explanations – deliberately neglecting other characteristics of the "style culture" (Stern, 2010, 2011) of skateboarding – concentrate on the forms of community and special space appropriation techniques.

Without a doubt, the community and the communicative construction of scene culture play a key role in skateboarding (cf. Bock, 2017, p. 197). Skaters seek the closeness and respect of like-minded people, as well as exchange and stimulation in the scene. In fact, riding solo is only an option if you want to practice a new trick, which you intend to present to the group once properly mastered. At first glance, skateboarding on the street or in a skatepark certainly ap-

pears to be an 'individualistic sport', since skaters ride by themselves and acquire new skateboarding techniques and tricks through informal, predominantly
self-directed learning processes.

Concurrently, other riders on site constantly observe, reflect and evaluate riding techniques, the tricks and the manifold facets of the mutual style competence. Successful tricks or cool actions without a board are rewarded by attending skateboarders by 'giving props'. This formulation, borrowed from hip-hop
culture, means that one shows 'proper respect' to others. Common forms of such
respectful expressions are a simple handshake, applause and the 'high five' gesture, whereby two people stretch one arm upwards and clap their hands. But it is
more than skateboards that we see on roads or in skateparks; conversations unfold and videos are shot, riders move whilst browsing the Internet, or simply
chill together.

In informal sports, however, the desire for social integration and community
results – as revealed by an ethnographic study by Bindel (2008, pp. 143-161) –
among other things in an unconstrained compulsion to negotiate various interests
and interpretations of needs, as well as in the gradual development of one's own
social order patterns (such as positions, role expectations or definitions, interaction rituals, behavioural norms). The ongoing work on the communicative fram-
ing usually ties in with familiar motion-cultural language and dress codes, requires an ongoing negotiation processes, and implies a "training of equal relationships" (Bindel, 2008, p. 155), the balancing of recognition relationships, as
well as a playful handling of status.

Since there are no 'gate keepers' at the spots – or at least no 'gate keepers'
recognisable to novices – interested young people must seek access to the respective skater group on their own initiative, which first requires a precise observation of interactions, language, rituals or clothing and music preferences in
this seemingly loose network of skaters (cf. Peters, 2016, p. 189; Schwier, 1998,
p. 39; Tappe, 2011, p. 235). Still, the process of deciphering style resources and
practicing the skateboard culture can only lead to successful access if riding
skills meet certain minimum standards.

The development of youth cultures in the field of alternative, non-traditional
sport is also closely linked to the use or reinterpretation of urban and near-
natural spaces, whereby – according to Derecik (2015, pp. 15-18) – the meaningful self-motion of young people can be described ideally along five dimensions
of appropriation.

Firstly, appropriation as an extension of motor abilities firstly arises from
handling certain items (e.g. the skateboard), and refers to accompanying motion
learning (e.g. the acting appropriation of a new trick) processes.

Appropriation (2) as an extension of the action space and (3) as a change of situations refer to the linking and temporary re-purposing of (local) spaces (e.g. a car park, a schoolyard or a shopping arcade as a skatespot).

Fourthly, appropriation as the connection of spaces mainly represents the ability to link different geographical and virtual spaces with one another, or to be present simultaneously in different spaces (e.g. the skatepark and a social network or a video platform on the internet).

Finally, appropriation as "spacing" – in the sense of Löw's relational spatial model (2001, p. 160) – illuminates the physical stagings of skateboarders on inner-city stages chosen by themselves, i.e. the "independent creation of spaces" (Derecik, 2015, p. 17; cf. Borden, 2018, pp. 248-249), as an extended form of appropriation. In this context, self-determined appropriation means the active contention with usage options, as well as readings of urban or virtual spaces, and can equally be an expression of individual freedom. Appropriation thus requires the actors' proactive action (cf. Deinet & Reutlinger, 2004, pp. 7-9). The creation of space in skateboarding is therefore mostly intentional and follows its own subcultural conventions, which are sometimes inconsistent with intended uses and specifications. Therefore, street skateboarding can be characterised as an urban practice:

"Street skateboarding happens without the spatial and material framings that classic skate-specific spaces such as indoor and outdoor skate parks and street plazas designed for skateboarding provide. Its natural habitat is the street; it takes place in the public space of the city [...]. Street skateboarding thus autonomously occupies its spaces and venues in the public realm and in praxis constitutes them as skate spots." (Peters, 2018, p. 202; cf. Chiu, 2009; Peters, 2011; Woolley & Johns, 2001)

In the most widespread variant of street skating, actors continuously 'scan' inner-city spaces (public squares, transit spaces, sidewalks, shopping streets, parking lots, backyards, city parks) for their 'skatability', acquire suitable spaces temporarily, make them suitable through their "staging work" (Löw, 2001, p. 208) into a scene of youth self-empowerment, where local items and structures (railings, curbs, stairs, flower pots) are reinterpreted via resistant action. According to Peters (2016, pp. 140-141), during participation in street skating, there will also be a training of awareness on the nature of hitherto unknown inner-city areas.

On the one hand, the (re-)use of the respective urban spots gives individuals plenty of room to implement creative ideas and express their emotions (cf. Schwier & Erhorn, 2015). On the other hand, it connects street skaters with each other and largely follows uniform stylistic ideals (cf. Eichler & Peters, 2012, p. 151). Spaces and the meaning creation processes directed at them ultimately play a non-negligible role in the creation of an independent style. The meaning of skateboarding also emerges on the background of the respective spatial structures, and the actors' collective syntheses (processes of perception, imagination and memory), decisively so in the context of repeated physical performances.

"Whether on planned or found spaces, street skateboarding more closely embodies a politics of resistance and social inclusion. Practitioners of this style skate over distinctions between human-made and natural surfaces through spatial tactics of appropriation that transform the city into a playground." (Vivoni, 2018, p. 125; cf. Löw, 2001, p. 224; Schwier, 2008, pp. 272-273)

In a sense, street skateboarding becomes a perfect example of the rebellious and resistant practices of spatial production as described by De Certeau (1984, pp. 91-110), which counter the concept of the planned city – aimed at extending social control – with clever reinterpretations, subversive appropriation of space, and 'guerilla tactics'. For actors on skateboards, urban space is a place with which to do something (cf. De Certeau, 1984, pp. 91-110, 1990 pp. 292-295). Last but not least, the do-it-yourself (DIY) skateparks, which have been built in many places by 'locals' for some time, are unauthorised and, in the truest sense of the word, irregular. Within certain limits, they can be regarded as a remarkable result of such tactics (cf. e.g. Borden, 2016; Lombard, 2016b; Peters, 2018; Schäfer, 2015b; Stratford, 2002).[2]

For some time now, beyond the more or less subcultural life in the skateboard scenes outlined here, a commercialisation and 'sportisation' of this youth culture, in which at least a part of the skateboarding community actively participates, has been emerging.

---

2 The philosopher, historian and cultural theorist Michel de Certeau (1984, pp. 30-42, 1990) uses the term tactics in opposition to the term strategy. In contrast to the term strategy – which is linked with corporations, governments and other public or private institutions – he understands tactics as an art of making-do (in the sense of 'bricolage') and as a form of creative resistance in daily practices: "In short, a tactic is an art of the weak. [...] Power is bound by its very visibility. In contrast, trickery is possible for the weak, and often it is his only possibility" (De Certeau, 1984, p. 37).

COMMERCIALISATION AND 'SPORTISATION'

Skateboarding, which for decades has been an economically interesting niche market, undergoes cyclical fluctuations and is considered difficult due to the unpredictability of skaters regarding equipment and fashion. This niche market now comprises all common segments of sports markets: besides sporting goods (clothing, shoes, hardware) and sporting events (from fun sports fairs to the Titus-only Locals Competition and Street League Skateboarding), we find sponsoring (e.g. of contests and company teams), event marketing (e.g. Vans Shop Riot), media formats (from X Games to magazines; from films and video clips to the video game series Tony Hawk's Skateboarding), sports tourism (e.g. skatecamps), digital platform economy (e.g. skateboarding in social networks), social services (e.g. skateboarding in the child and youth work sector), as well as education and training formats (training, workshops, license acquisition).

The commercialisation of skateboarding can hardly come as a surprise on closer inspection, since alternative sport practices do not embody an idyllic special world, isolated from capitalist society, but – even if they adamantly deny this from time to time – also belong to the system. Among the first beneficiaries of commercialisation in this case are those (male) skateboarders who, for the first time, succeeded in turning their passion and intrinsically motivated commitment to skateboarding into a profession (as a sponsored rider, shop owner, skatepark designer, hardware or clothing manufacturer). But in a certain way the professional skateboarder, shop owner or skatepark designer still more or less represent the subcultural values and the rebellious image of skateboarding. Professional skateboarders seem to have less stress in competition because they view themselves not just as athletes "who happen to ride skateboards, but are 'skaters', expected to participate in a lifestyle associated with involvement in the sport" (Honea, 2013, p. 1255).

This could be one reason why companies founded and/or managed by skateboarders still enjoy high respect in the scene, and are usually perceived as more credible and authentic. One example is the company 'Titus' founded by the German skateboard pioneer Titus Dittmann, which concentrates on event management, franchising and mail order business. Like other companies that have emerged from the scene, the skateboard supplier presents itself on its website (www.titus.de) as a respectful and sincere promoter of skateboard culture and, further to actual products, offers a wide range of text resources, images and sounds. In addition to the web shop, the online presence includes blogs and wikisites that provide news, stories and interviews from the scene, competitions, illustrated information on company teams and skate parks in Germany, as well as video clips – from skatepark renovation to team riders and product promotion. Of course, the Titus Skate Camp with accommodation in the Skate Hostel is also advertised. Every activity on the board or in online media simultaneously refers to other skating areas in the World of Titus, and should ensure the lasting attention of the young players.

It should also be noted that the distance to the market leaders in the sporting goods sector, which was notable in the 1990s, has dwindled. Skateboarders with shoes from the Nike SB collection can now be seen at almost every spot – and not only in Germany. Through the organisation of skateboarding contests and events (Go Skateboarding Day), as well as the construction of skatehalls and skateparks (e.g., Nike SB Shelter), the industry giant has apparently demonstrated its willingness to do something for skateboarding in a target-group-oriented manner, and has gradually gained brand notoriety.[3] Nike, Adidas, Red Bull and other brands bind themselves to contemporary skateboard culture, illustrate their fascination content, sometimes create new spaces for action and strive to represent values associated with the so-called "sporting counter-culture" (Bouchet, Hillairet & Bodet, 2013, p. 99).

Red Bull in particular follows a marketing logic that goes far beyond sponsoring contests or riding teams in various trend sports, by also creating innovative and complex productions to capture as much of the young audience's attention as possible (see Schwier, 2016, pp. 114-115). Above all, multimedia productions for social media are intended to deliver previously unseen images of skateboarding at locations that have never been used for this purpose (e.g. jam sessions in front of the historic backdrop of the City of London, skateboarding in an abandoned indoor swimming pool, in a museum or a former military base in the middle of the North Sea). To some extent, Red Bull tries to create singular breath-taking episodes, which seem to be unique and different to any other action sports event. Such spectacles attract attention and are an occasion for discussion in the local communities, the special promotion of which is consistently integrated into Red Bull's marketing concept.

The view that skateboarding is a self-willed youth culture and, in any case, more than a sport, is not only indisputably part of the self-conception of the skater communities, but also probably forms a core of the marketing messages formulated by the world of goods and consumption.

---

3   In addition, social media platforms (www.youtube.com/user/nikeskate-boarding) and audio-visual media – like the Nike SB Chronicles (see e.g., www.youtube.com/watch ?v=l9ohmfKkkCk) – play a significant role in Nike's marketing communication mix.

Next to brands, audio-visual media are the main driving force behind the commercialisation of youth cultures in the field of action sports. After a previous decline, the X Games – produced by the US cable channel ESPN – established skateboarding as a television sport in the mid-1990s, promoting its popularity worldwide and initiating a new round in the commercialisation of this motion culture. Rinehart (2004), for example, regards this TV-compatible preparation, spectacularisation and (self-) marketing of trend sports as a form of appropriation by the established (media) sports system (cf. Lorr, 2016, pp. 139-141; Schäfer, 2015a, pp. 162-164); among other things, because of the commercials specifically produced for the X Games, the comprehensive sponsoring and merchandising, or the games and apps available as downloads.

In this context, the fact that the sports television channel ESPN has succeeded in unfolding a motion and body-oriented meta-language with the generation of peculiar codes, patterns, themes and myths of its X Games, which, according to Rinehart (2004, pp. 319-320), remains open for both dominant and oppositional readings, is probably jointly responsible for the continuing commercial success. On the one hand, the ambiguity of the media staging of skateboarding leaves enough room for diverging readings and recalcitrant interpretations. On the one hand, it stimulates the viewer's attachment to the X Games, which is what the producers are striving for.

Against this background, Cantin-Brault (2015), among others, believes that the X Games and, above all, Street League Skateboarding (SLS; held since 2010) have been developed for cross-media marketing and fundamentally transformed the idea of contests – which has always belonged to skateboard culture – and alienated it from its origins. In this view, such event spectacles are mainly used to tame street skateboarding, which is increasingly turning into a commercial sport:

"But in this present reification we have come to see the apparition of what has been called 'mega'-contests, in which the participants have lost control over the format of the contests they participate in: participants, vert skaters but now also street skaters, who are being shown in the casing of a spectator friendly environment, have lost their freedom in being sold and advertised as things. […] These contests, and perhaps especially the SLS, are mimetic attempts to make skateboarding an organised sport." (Cantin-Brault, 2015, p. 63)

The fact that a youth culture, like skateboarding, is gradually becoming sports-oriented is not a singular process, but can be traced in the historical context, of (among other things) the 'sportisation' of games (cf. Bernett, 1984). 'Sportisation' means first of all that, at least in some areas of skateboarding culture, there is an intensification of the physical practice (in the sense of the Olympic motto 'Citius, Altius, Fortius'), where the agonal performance comparison with success thinking gains importance and institutionalisation processes begin. What remains largely unclear is the relationship between 'sportisation' and the rebellious nature of skateboarding and the pure joy of riding. Schweer's argumentation (2014, p. 115) now suggests that skateboarding has long since become a 'normal' sport, in which competitive sport orientations, competitions, the promotion of young talent or sponsoring are here to stay, and where no a priori resistant component can be found.

The founding of skater clubs and associations, the provision of courses at skateparks for a fee, as well as the holding of national and international championships can certainly be cited as further evidence of the trend towards 'sportisation'. With Street League Skateboarding, there is now also – as already mentioned – a global format that makes use of common staging patterns of (media) sport (cf. Atencio & Beal, 2016, pp. 110-113; Schweer, 2014, pp. 117-125). Skateboarding has undoubtedly been moving towards the field of sports for some time now, with which it shares an aesthetic experience pattern anyway, and which Gumbrecht (2017, p. 131) describes as "practicality without purpose", with reference to the intrinsic motivation of the actors and the lack of function of sporting movements for the actors' lifeworld.

And yet there is still a difference: the atmosphere at a skateboard contest, the interactions of players, and the applicable evaluation standards are noticeably different from, for example, a match in the Premier League. In football, the party that scores more goals always wins; in skateboarding, however, having performed more or particularly spectacular tricks does not always lead to a victory.

Style does not play a major role on the soccer field. For example, a long-range shot from thirty metres into the goal angle does not count more than a ball slowly rolling into an empty goal, by chance, from two metres away. In addition, matches in lower football leagues are only played because a federation divides these leagues up, sets appropriate criteria for membership to a certain league, trains and licenses referees and coaches of both sexes, coordinates the use of referees, issues player passes, manages seasonal tables, monitors the enforcement of internationally valid rules and guarantees a sports jurisdiction. Such a degree of regulation is neither imaginable nor even remotely necessary for skateboarding. Recreational skaters simply ride the streets when and where they want, participate only partially in local contests and largely ignore the victory-defeat logic of sports, stressing instead the expressive dimension of body and motion. Skaters rarely join a club. And if they do, it hardly follows reasons regarding sport, but the assumption that this association represents the interests of the scene vis-à-vis the local or municipal administration.

Besides the interlinked trends towards the commercialisation and 'sportisation' of skateboarding there is still "a proximity to activist scenes", at least in Europe (Schäfer, 2015a, p. 166). Due to the extremely fragmentary empirical findings, however, it is unfeasible to issue general statements on the influence of commercialisation and sports processes on the (sub)culture of skateboarding in Germany, or other European countries.

WHO NEEDS THE OLYMPICS?

The reasons why skateboarding will be included in the circle of Olympic sports at the Tokyo 2020 Summer Games are undeniably of an economic and sports policy nature. Ultimately, the reform efforts of the International Olympic Committee (IOC), bundled in the so-called Agenda 2020 (see www.olympic.org/ olympic-agenda-2020), have seen the Tokyo Summer Games' programme include, for the first time, several alternative, non-traditional sport cultures (BMX freestyle, skateboarding, surfing and streetball). With a total of forty recommendations in this reform package, the IOC wants to make its premium product more flexible, increase the transparency of decision-making processes, enforce the principles of good corporate management, increase the rights of the respective host to influence the selection of competitions, and position the games on the (media) markets for the future.

With some delay, the Olympic Movement is continuing the successful format of the X Games, and is increasingly turning to activities that are popular with young people and youth marketing. To put it bluntly: Olympia must rejuvenate itself within certain boundaries, be trendy and stage itself differently to retain its mega-brand status. BMX, skateboarding, streetball and surfing are therefore taking part in the medal hunt to increase the attractiveness of the Olympic Games for the important target group of teenagers and young adults. The International Olympic Committee has to bring action sports to the youth and the Games need the trendy factor of non-traditional sport cultures. Therefore, IOC President Bach told the press: "With the many options that young people have, we cannot expect any more that they will come automatically to us. We have to go to them" (IOC, 2016).

Against this background, some prominent voices from the national and international skate community confidently emphasise that skateboarding is more important for the Olympic Games than participation in the Games for skateboarding. It remains unclear why skateboarding should then be put at the service of the International Olympic Committee, and what profits are envisaged for skate culture when around eighty female and male skateboarders compete in the street and park disciplines in Tokyo 2020. On the other hand, Olympic participation is out of the question for other parts of the scene since skateboarding is not a competitive sport for them. They reject the IOC as an institution, because they perceive such 'sportisation' as a bureaucratisation of their practice, or because they expect a further boost in commercialisation.

On this point, however, both proponents and opponents of Olympic skateboarding agree: the Olympic Games' global show is expected to attract even more attention to skateboarding, generate more sponsorship, brand communication and marketing, and bring significant sales growth to the skate industry.

While the proponents interpret the expected commercialisation boost – especially in times when the number of skateboarders worldwide is likely to decline slightly – as a positive impulse for the further development of the skate culture, for the 'NOlympia movement', it probably represents the last nail in the coffin for the idiosyncratic subversive skateboard culture (cf. Cantin-Brault, 2015, p. 65). Furthermore, the inclusion in the programme of the Summer Olympics also affects gender relations in this traditionally masculine practice (cf. Atencio et al., 2016, pp. 189-190), since skateboarders in particular hope that the equal participation of both sexes in the competitions will lead to a permanent upgrade of their practice and thus increased sponsorship for professional female riders.

On the new level of functionaries that emerges with a more sporting approach, however, the informal networks of the 'Old Boys' appear to be gaining ground across the board at first, while the few established female skateboarders may not have sufficient social and symbolic capital (following Atencio, Beal & Wilson, 2009) to be adequately taken into account when filling functional roles. The nine-member executive committee of the national German sports commission (SK SLB Sportkommission Skateboard/Longboard) responsible for the Olympic preparation consists of only one female member, the current national women's coach, and there is only one female skateboarder among the fourteen specialist attendants.

Incidentally, it should be noted that the for-and-against discussion that had been going on in the scene for some time, would hardly have been conceivable in this moderate form around twenty years ago, because the mere presentation of Olympic skateboarding at the time would have triggered either exuberant cheerfulness or sheer horror at the supposed sell-out of all ideals. It is also noteworthy that two levels can be distinguished in the debate on the Olympic Games: on the one hand, it is about who can be the legitimate representative of skateboarders.

On the other hand, Schweer (2014, p. 128) rejects this question as a matter of principle, as representation of skateboarding is unthinkable. With this in mind, the skate community is trying to square the circle by initiating the necessary organisational steps for participation in the Olympics. First of all, it is indeed completely unclear who (and for what reasons) can speak for skateboarding (see also Brixey, 2012; Schweer, 2014, pp. 127-138). Given that a generally accepted umbrella organisation is lacking and processes of democratic decision-making within the multi-faceted community are difficult to set in motion, but at the same time contact partners for organised sport must be promptly identified, there is a need for functioning networks that quickly demonstrate their willingness to participate, appoint independent expert observers under the aegis of the 'German Roller Sports and Inline Federation' (DRIV), and then also receive a mandate from the responsible Fédération Internationale Roller Sports (FIRS) for the selection of athletes.[4] Such a selection and the associated inclusion in the so-called perspective and development squad is also more difficult than in traditional Olympic sports, given that the lack of national rankings makes the use of more or less soft criteria necessary to appoint to the first 'Skateboarding Olympia Team Germany'.

Beyond organisational peculiarities and self-created qualification criteria, however, the central question is whether and to what extent the Olympic competitions in the park and street disciplines will change the skateboard culture in the long term. In my opinion, the Olympic appearance only continues the development trend that seems to have been effective since the establishment of the X Games in the second half of the 1990s at the latest: professional and subcultural forms of skateboarding are increasingly co-existing, with fluid boundaries and close interrelationships between both of them. In addition, scene communication has often been transformed into brand communication long before the temporary participation in the Olympics (cf. Schwier, 2008), and it remains to be seen which meaningful narrative motifs of skateboarding become effective in the daily practice of local scenes after the Olympic skateboard events.

With reference to Goffman's (1959) studies on self-representation practices in everyday life, Beal & Weidman (2003) state that the public space is used by

---

4   The Fédération Internationale Roller Sports (FIRS) – that has changed its denomination to 'World Skate' (www.worldskate.org) – was selected by the IOC as the world governing body, rather than a genuine skateboard organisation. The FIRS has been selected because the IOC "considered skateboarding as a roller sport and therefore recognised the FIRS as the international governing body for skateboarding" (Batuev & Robinson, 2017, p. 390).

skateboarders both as a front stage – on which one presents one's practice to the passing audience – and as a back stage, on which actors further develop their authentic style, their self-understanding, their interpretations of the practice and their orientations, together and for one another:

"Authenticity for skateboarders is not determined by a successful front-region performance for a general audience, whereby the general audience grants authenticity to the skaters. Rather, authenticity is proven in the back region through an internalisation and public display of the norms and values of the skateboard culture, which are really recognisable only to other experienced skateboarders." (Beal & Weidman, 2003, p. 351)

In view of this, there is a lot to be said for the assumption that the Olympic Games will not only offer skateboarding a front stage paved with colourful sponsor logos, but will also be designed by the actors as a back stage on which the initiates will forget about the role of the Olympic athlete, whilst remaining true to the style and exchange knowledge that should not become public (e.g. cannabis use). A special feature of these skateboard bodies is not least that they will contain subcultural, hedonistic-expressive ideas of movement, as well as rational structures of Olympic sport. Therefore, alternative interpretations of the Olympic idea are no less likely than the self-insertion into show sport. In the run-up to and after the Tokyo 2020 Olympic Games, new – alternative and sporty – stories of skateboarding will certainly be produced that will keep skate culture moving.

CONCLUSION

From my point of view, there is a lot to be said for the assumption that skateboarding can be both a movement art that is largely influenced by the subculture, and a show sport that is aggressively commercialised. Self-empowerment and self-optimisation sometimes form two sides of the same coin. This postulates both a reciprocal effect relationship between professional skateboarding and the recalcitrant practices of local skateboarding communities, and between these scenes and the marketing complex formed by brands and media. Every push towards commercial (high-performance) sport almost automatically calls up counter-movements (e.g. DIY skate spots) and evasive movements (e.g. the renaissance of longboarding), which of course appear immediately on the radar of youth marketing, and are reflected in corresponding campaigns (e.g. Red Bull DIY). Significance-building processes that seek to separate skateboarding from the sporting context of exploitation and bring its unruly potential back to life can generally be translated step by step into marketing messages and event series. The communities of skateboarders are in some ways – voluntarily or involuntarily – key players in brand communication and commercial sport. The manifold interdependencies between the (sub)culture of skateboarding and its economy also permeate the representations of skateboarding, and skate culture at large, with its tendency towards self-mediatisation, is actively involved in these marketing processes (cf. Schwier, 2006, p. 322; Schäfer, 2015a, pp. 165-166).

At this point, it seems obvious to refer to a figure of thought in De Certeau (1984, 1990), who characterises popular culture as a practice placed between production and consumption, as an "art of being in between" (De Certeau, 1984, p. 32). Thus, skate culture is always an arena of symbolic struggles between the interests of brands and media on the one hand, and those of social actors and communities on the other one. In the course of such symbolic struggles, questions of style arise continuously, and between "urban rebellion and neoliberal self-design" (cf. Schweer, 2014, p. 167), new attitudes, forms of action and subcultural and hegemonic ways of staging emerge. From this point of view, the art of being in between in skateboarding consists of skilfully manoeuvring between unruly movement practice, corporate branding, and the Olympic spirit. This art is ephemeral, brittle and probably only comes into its own in the commonly experienced everyday practice of skateboarding.

REFERENCES

Atencio, M., Beal, B. & Wilson, C. (2009). Distinction of risk: Urban skateboarding, street habitus, and the construction of hierarchical gender relations. *Qualitative Research in Sport and Exercise* 1, 1, 3-20.

Atencio, M. & Beal, B. (2016). The 'legitimate' skateboarder. Politics of private-public skateboarding spaces. In Lombard, K.-J. (Ed.), *Skateboarding: Subcultures, Sites and Shifts* (pp. 108-120). New York: Routledge.

Atencio, M., Beal, B., McClain, Z. & Wright, E. (2016). 'No One Wants to Mess with an Angry Mom'. Females' Negotiation of Power Technologies Within a Local Skateboarding Culture. In Thorpe, H. & Olive, R. (Ed.), *Women in Action Sport* (pp. 175-190). London: Palgrave Macmillan.

Atencio, M., Beal, B., Wright, E. & McClain, Z. (2018). *Moving Boarders. Skateboarding and the Changing Landscape of Urban Youth Sports*. Fayetteville: The University of Arkansas Press.

Batuev, M. & Robinson, L. (2017). How skateboarding made it to the Olympics. *International Journal of Sport Management and Marketing* 17, 381-402.

Beal, B. & Weidman, L. (2003). Authenticity in the Skateboarding World. In Rinehart, R. E. & Sydnor, S. (Eds.), *To the Extreme. Alternative Sports, Inside and Out* (pp. 337-352). Albany: SUNY.

Bernett, H. (1984). Die 'Versportlichung' des Spiels – dargestellt am Exempel der Entwicklung des Faustballspiels. *Sportwissenschaft* 14, 2, 141-165.

Bindel, T. (2008). *Soziale Regulierung in informellen Sportgruppen*. Hamburg: Czwalina.

Bock, K. (2017). *Kommunikative Konstruktion von Szenekultur. Skateboarding als Sinnstiftung und Orientierung im Zeitalter der Digitalisierung*. Weinheim, Basel: Beltz Juventa.

Borden, I. (2016). Southbank Skateboarding, London, and urban culture: the Undercroft, Hungerford Bridge, and House of Vans. In Lombard, K.-J. (Ed.), *Skateboarding: Subcultures, Sites and Shifts* (pp. 91-107). New York: Routledge.

Borden, I. (2018). Another Pavement, Another Beach. Skateboarding and the Performative Critique of Architecture. In Butz, K. & Peters, C. (Eds.), *Skateboard Studies* (pp. 246-266). London: Koenig Books.

Bouchet, P., Hillairet, D. & Bodet, G. (2013). *Sport Brands*. New York: Routledge.

Brixey, W. (2012). *Skateboarding vs. the Olympics: A brief History*. http://www.jenkemmag.com/home/2012/09/04/skateboarding-vs-the-olympics-a-brief-history.

Butz, K. (2012). *Grinding California. Culture and Corporeality in American Skate Punk*. Bielefeld: transcript.

Butz, K. & Peters, C. (Eds.) (2018). *Skateboard Studies*. London: Koenig Books.

Cantin-Brault, A. (2015). The Reification of Skateboarding. *International Journal of Science Culture and Sport* 3, 1, 54-66.

Chiu, C. (2009). Contestation and Conformity: Street and Park Skateboarding in New York City Public Space. *Space and Culture* 12, 1, 25-42.

Deinet, U. & Reutlinger, C. (2004). Einführung. In Deinet, U. & Reutlinger, C. (Eds.), *'Aneignung' als Bildungskonzept der Sozialpädagogik* (pp. 7-15). Wiesbaden: Springer VS.

Derecik, A. (2015). Sozialräumliche Aneignung von Räumen durch Jugendliche. In Erhorn, J. & Schwier, J. (Eds.), *Die Eroberung urbaner Bewegungsräume* (pp. 13-29). Bielefeld: transcript.

De Certeau, M. (1984). *The Practice of Everyday Life*. Berkely: University of California Press.

De Certeau, M. (1990). *L'invention du quotidien, I. Arts de faire*. Paris: Gallimard.

Eichler, R. & Peters, C. (2012). Skateboarding als globalisiertes Körper-Raum-Spiel. In Kähler, R. & Ziemainz, J. (Eds.), *Sporträume neu denken und entwickeln* (pp. 151-158). Hamburg: Czwalina.

Gumbrecht, H.-U. (2017). Ethische Grenzen der Faszination. Warum Sportereignisse ihre Zuschauer fesseln. *Pop. Kultur und Kritik* 11, 124-143.

Goffman, E. (1959). *The Presentation of Self in Everyday Life.* New York: Anchor Books.

Hitzler, R. & Niederbacher, A. (2010). *Leben in Szenen. Formen juveniler Vergemeinschaftung heute.* Wiesbaden: VS Verlag.

Honea, J. C. (2013). Beyond the Alternative vs. Mainstream Dichotomy: Olympic BMX and the Future of Action Sports. *The Journal of Popular Culture* 46, 6, 1253-1275.

IOC (2016). IOC Approves Five New Sports for Olympic Games Tokyo 2020. https://www.olympic.org/news/ioc-approves-five-new-sports-for-olympic-games-tokyo-2020.

Lombard, K.-J. (Ed.) (2016a). *Skateboarding: Subcultures, Sites and Shifts.* New York: Routledge.

Lombard, K.-J. (2016b). Trucks, tricks, and technologies of government: analyzing the productive encounter between governance and resistance in skateboarding. In Lombard, K.-J. (Ed.), *Skateboarding: Subcultures, Sites and Shifts* (pp. 169-181). New York: Routledge.

Lorr, M. J. (2016). Skateboarding as a technology of the collective. In Lombard, K.-J. (Ed.), *Skateboarding: Subcultures, Sites and Shifts* (pp. 139-151). New York: Routledge.

Löw, M. (2001). *Raumsoziologie.* Frankfurt am Main: Suhrkamp.

Peters, C. (2011). Skating the City – Feldforschung auf der Kölner Domplatte. In Bindel, T. (Ed.), *Feldforschung und ethnographische Zugänge in der Sportpädagogik* (pp. 144-156). Aachen: Shaker.

Peters, C. (2016). *Skateboarding – Ethnographie einer urbanen Praxis.* Münster: Waxmann.

Peters, C. (2018). 'Reclaim Your City!' Skateboarding and Do-It-Yourself Urbanism. In Butz, K. & Peters, C. (Eds.), *Skateboard Studies* (pp. 200-216). London: Koenig Books.

Rinehart, R. E. (2004). Sport as Constructed Audience: A Case Study of ESPN's The Extreme Games. In Rowe, D. (Ed.), *Critical readings: Sport, Culture and the Media* (pp. 313-327). Maidenhead: Open University Press.

Schäfer, E. V. (2015a). Sport mit den Mitteln des Pop. Skateboardvideos: Bewegungslernen, Vergemeinschaftung und Jugendmarketing. *Sport und Gesellschaft – Sport and Society* 12, 2, 149-170.

Schäfer, E. V. (2015b). Raum schaffen und Stadt machen: Body Spaces und Sportmobiliar in der Skateboard-Praktik. In Kähler, R. (Ed.), *Städtische Spielräume für Sport, Spiel und Bewegung* (pp. 69-78). Hamburg: Czwalina.

Schäfer, E. V. & Alkemeyer, T. (2018). Skateboarding und die Pop-Werdung des Sportsubjekts. In Busche, H., Heinze, T, Hillebrandt, F. & Schäfer, F. (Eds.), *Kultur – Interdisziplinäre Zugänge* (pp. 107-126). Wiesbaden: Spinger VS.

Schweer, S. (2014). *Skateboarding. Zwischen urbaner Rebellion und neoliberalem Selbstentwurf.* Bielefeld: transcript.

Schwier, J. (1998). *Spiele des Körpers. Jugendsport zwischen Cyberspace und Streetstyle.* Hamburg: Czwalina.

Schwier, J. (2006). Repräsentationen des Trendsports. Jugendliche Bewegungskulturen, Medien und Marketing. In Gugutzer, R. (Ed.), *body turn, Perspektiven der Soziologie des Körpers und des Sports* (pp. 321-340). Bielefeld: transcript.

Schwier, J. (2008). Inszenierungen widerspenstiger Körperlichkeit. Zur Selbstmediatisierung jugendlicher Sportszenen. *Zeitschrift für Soziologie der Erziehung und Sozialisation* 28, 3, 271-282.

Schwier, J. (2016). Die Sportshow. Zur Eventisierung von Bewegungs- und Sportkulturen. In Dust, M., Lohmann, I. & Steffens, G. (Eds.), *Jahrbuch für Pädagogik 2016. Events und Edutainment* (pp. 107-117). Frankfurt am Main, Berlin, Bern, Bruxelles, New York, Oxford, Wien: Peter Lang.

Schwier, J. & Erhorn, J. (2015). Trendsport. In Schmidt, W. (Ed.), *Dritter Deutscher Kinder- und Jugendsportbericht* (pp. 179-200). Schorndorf: Hofmann.

Schwier, J. & Kilberth, V. (Eds.) (2018). *Skateboarding zwischen Subkultur und Olympia. Eine jugendliche Bewegungskultur im Spannungsfeld von Kommerzialisierung und Versportlichung.* Bielefeld: transcript.

Stern, M. (2010). *Stil-Kulturen. Performative Konstellationen von Technik, Spiel und Risiko in neuen Sportpraktiken.* Bielefeld: transcript.

Stern, M. (2011). Stil-Kulturen im Trendsport. In Bindel, T. (Ed.), *Feldforschung und ethnographische Zugänge in der Sportpädagogik* (pp. 133-143). Aachen: Shaker.

Stratford, E. (2002). On the edge: A tale of skaters and urban governance. *Social & Cultural Geography* 3, 2, 193-206.

Tappe, S. (2011). Eröffnung des sozialen Raums durch das Skateboard. In Bindel, T. (Ed.), *Feldforschung und ethnographische Zugänge in der Sportpädagogik* (pp. 231-244). Aachen: Shaker.

Vivoni, F. (2018). City of Social Control. Skateboarding and the Regulation of Public Space. In Butz, K. & Peters, C. (Eds.), *Skateboard Studies* (pp. 110-127). London: Koenig Books.

Woolley, H. & Johns, R. (2001). Skateboarding: The City as a Playground. *Journal of Urban Design* 6, 2, 211-230.

From Stairs to Podium

Skateboarding and the Olympics:
Stages in a 50-Year Debate

Eckehart Velten Schäfer

INTRODUCTORY REMARKS

Since the inclusion of skateboarding into the Summer Olympic Games has been announced, the practice has received increased attention – and there is a certain degree of astonishment in European and German media: *Bayerischer Rundfunk, for* example, contrasts its "style" and "freedom" with the "rules" of the Olympics (Pietschmann, 2016). "Can this really go well?" asks *Frankfurter Allgemeine Zeitung* (Eder, 2015). Also, *Die Zeit* contemplates the contradictions between Olympia and a practice that is all about "lifestyle" instead of "sports" (Hartmann, 2014), stating that resistance against "commercialisation" and a "style culture sell-out of coolness" is wide-spread within the skateboarding world.

But what does this commonplace actually refer to? Is skateboarding really so categorically different from classical sports? Does this apply to its entire history which will soon span six decades? The rhetorical question hints to the thesis of this essay: Having undergone several fundamental transformations since the first skateboards were sold in American toy shops in the late 1950s, the practice oscillates between straightforward anti-sports and much more sports-compatible cultural formats. Against this background, its inclusion in the Olympic is less astonishing. Indeed, Olympic skateboarding was a matter of debate within the practice on several occasions before the 2016 announcement – in 1964, 1976, 1984 and 2007.

This essay aims to outline the extent to which and the historical moments or phases when skateboarding is closer or further from the classic sport of which the IOC games are the top event. Firstly, this requires a set of instruments to reconstruct the transformations within its history. This is what Elizabeth Shove, Mika Pantzar and Matt Watson offer in their model of "dynamics of social practice" (Shove, Pantzar & Watson, 2012). They define social practices as active integrations of three elements, namely *competences*, *material* and *meanings*. Secondly, this purpose requires a scheme of criteria to distinguish between 'close to sports' and 'distanced from sports' formats of skateboarding. In the German sociology of sports, such a scheme is offered by Günter Gebauer, Thomas Alkemeyer, Bernhard Boschert, Uwe Flick and Robert Schmidt (Gebauer et al. 2004) who – alongside Jürgen Schwier (1998; 2000) systematised and promoted the sociological debate on new versions of culture of human motion merging around the turn of the millennium.

Following Shove et al., the following briefly examines what exactly is meant by "competences", "material" and "meaning" with regards to skateboarding – and, based on that, develops a scheme to differentiate 'sports-related' and 'sports-remote' forms of skateboarding (Chapter 1). Against this background, sections 2, 3, and 4 will discuss what constellations of competences, material, and meaning fostered the abovementioned Olympic aspirations in skateboarding culture – and why these aspirations faded. Finally, the results of this are summarized and an outlook is given on how they can be discussed in a broader societal-theoretical view (section 5).

CLASSIC SPORTS AND NEW PLAY

So what are the "elements" of skateboarding? By "competences", Shove et al. (2012, p. 14) mean "skill, know-how, and technique" (p. 23), i.e. different forms of knowledge ranging from implicit, embodied, tacit knowledge – know-how – to more reflected modes of knowing. "Materials" are "things, technologies, tangible physical entities and the stuff of which objects are made", as well as "infrastructures, tools, hardware and the body itself" (ibid.). As "meanings", Shove et al. (2012) address various forms of motivations and perceptions that are explicitly and implicitly connected with participation in the practice – everything motivating its participants and making the practice socially recognisable. *Explicit* meanings therefore include "symbolic meanings, ideas and aspirations", thus the "social and symbolic significance of participation at any one moment", i.e. the socially regulated representation of a practice. *Implicit* meaning is what Theodore Schatzki (1996, p. 89) names "teleoaffective structures", i.e. involuntary mental activities, emotions and motivations – in short, the *longings* that define a practice and are embodied in its participants.

Regarding sportive practices like skateboarding, however, it seems advisable to partially re-arrange this scheme – which is actually meant to be an analytical strategy but not a substantial classification. Firstly, of course, the term "competences" refers to the actual bodily movements that constitute the practice, as well as the dynamic history of skateboarding tricks. But, secondly, the dimension of implicit meaning – those teleoaffective structures – cannot even analytically be separated from the realm of "competence" as these embodied longings substantially inform its bodily practice and constitute the practice as a meaningful entity. "Materials" are all the artefacts and infrastructures that are used by skateboarders and inform their daily doings – ranging from the cut of the boards and the chemicals used for production of wheels to protective equipment and, most notably, video technology, which plays a significant role in the history of the practice (cf. Schäfer, 2015a). However, the following focuses on the materiality of the various terrains used by skateboarders, i.e. the built artefacts that are the material substrate of those competences. Finally, when implicit meaning is attached to the "competences", *explicit* – and, of course, formative interpretations of the practice both in niche and mainstream media, skateboard graphics etc. remain to be analyzed as "meanings".

Regarding this latter dimension it is quite obvious how sports-related and anti-sports incarnations of skateboarding can be identified. At certain points in its history, the practice is represented both in niche and mainstream media as a 'subculture'; in other phases, however, it is widely regarded as a more or less legitimate sport. But how can these two poles be reconstructed with regards to the materials of the practice – its terrains? In their model-like distinction of so-called *New Play* from classic organized and competitive sport[1], Gebauer et al. depart from the mid-19th century. During this time a relatively autonomous "space of sport" emerged as a social entity – and this topological differentiation also manifested itself topographically. Popular "pre-forms of sport" did not yet constitute a "separate social space" and did not set themselves apart from everyday life in terms of space and time. Modern sport as it emerged in the mid-19th century, however, is based on spatial segregation. While "urban street play" suffered a

---

1   Gebauer et al. (2004) use triathlon and inline hockey on a public square to set New Play apart from sports such as indoor handball but also mention skateboarding. Other texts stemming from this context of discussion deal with free climbing, paragliding and snowboarding (cf. Stern, 2010) as well as skateboarding (cf. Schmidt, 2002; Alkemeyer & Schmidt, 2003).

major decline due to the "economic use of the road network", its "halls and sta-
diums detached bodily movements from their everyday functional contexts to
stylize them into isolated, self-purpose sportive forms of movement" – whereby
"participants and spectators were sharply separated" (Gebauer et al., 2004, p.
28).

Present-day "Inline-Skaters, BMXers, Skateboarders, Streetballers" (ibid., p.
25) and the like, however, tend to undo this "Domestication" of sports. They perform their "arts of movement" in pedestrian zones, on market squares, in front of
representative buildings and on the "asphalt surfaces of abandoned industrial
plants". Such places have to be "conquered, marked as spaces of play", which
includes a practical confrontation with their functions, discourses, "mythologies
and material resistance[s]" (ibid., p. 26).

Furthermore, according to Gebauer et al. the physical and sensual horizons of
the very movements of such practices refer to something rather different from
the code of victory and defeat that is constitutive for traditional sports. While
"the use of the body in traditional sport is primarily instrumental and directed
towards a result", the movements of New Play are "progression-oriented, experimental and fluid" (ibid., p. 119). They do not aim at a countable, objectified
and therefore comparable result, but first and foremost at the sensual experience
of their execution: In "movements like gliding and turning, through high speeds,
feelings of detachment from the normal, of euphoric intemperance" (ibid.) are
evoked and aspired – and these "inner" experiences translate into a socially recognizable aesthetic of moving. Although such movements also require a lot of
trying and learning, these practices are not divided between 'serious' competition on the one hand and 'training', in the sense of science-like perfection of the
practice's movements, on the other. Thus, New Play is not *disciplinarily* formatted, but appeals to *expressivity*. In these practices of "presentational and insce-
nating sportivity" (Schmidt, 2002, p. 31) which can also be referred to as "low
sports" in contrast to "high sports" (cf. Schäfer & Alkemeyer, 2018, p. 81f), meters, seconds or scores are not distinctive but the capacity to perform the 'spirit'
of the practice in an 'authentic' way. These practices are – as Gebauer's et al.
volume is titled – all about experienceable as well as recognizable ways to move
"loyalty to the style".

In this concept, style means far more than the "artistic score" known from,
for example, sports like figure skating or ski jumping. These scores are based on
a clearly defined catalogue of criteria – examining the posture of the legs while
performing a *Rittberger*, judging the accuracy of a *Telemark* landing of a ski

jump[2]. In New Play, however, "style capacity" is "not linked to standardisation and objectified benchmarking" (Stern, 2010, p. 153). In New Play, the informal, hard-to-verbalize, but always recognisable stylishness actually replaces formal structures like clubs and associations that organize traditional sports. It is a medium of creating communities, connecting participants in transnational cultures of style resembling fan scenes within pop music.

A WELL-'MEASURABLE SPORT' (1964/1976)

According to Gebauer et al, practices such as skateboarding escape the formalized logics of sports in that their very movements undermine traditional sport's mode of objectified comparison. This is echoed in the above-mentioned journalistic accounts of the contrast between "styles" and "rules". From this perspective, at first glance it may seem quite astonishing that in skateboarding discussions about an inclusion into the Olympics are not a recent phenomenon. They are, in fact, almost as old as the practice itself. This question arises as early as 1965, in the editorial of the first issue of *Quarterly Skateboarder*. Quite in contrast to what has just been summarized, this article states that skateboarding intrinsically leans towards competition (cf. Brooke, 2005, p. 33).

Contrary to popular knowledge, in the 1960s and 1970s skateboarding by no means is just the proverbial 'surfing on land'. In that period, there are basically two modes of riding a skateboard: firstly the 'discipline' of figure skateboarding (named freestyle, somewhat misleading according to today's understanding) and racing, i.e. slalom and downhill. In this period, skateboarding processes and emulates movements from a wide spectrum of sources. Slalom, skateboarding's supreme discipline in the sixties and early to mid-seventies is closely related to skiing. In figure skating movements of a gymnastic[3] or ice- and roller-skating

---

2   In ski jumping, for example, according to Stern (2010, p. 169), the 'artistic score' and the objectified achivement tend to converge as what is measured as 'good posture' within the jump generally also helps maximizing the jumping distance.

3   For example exercises such as the so-called *L-Sit*, in which the riders support themselves with their hands on the slowly rolling board until a right angle is formed between the upper and lower body – in p-bars gymnastics this is called an *L-Hold* – or hand- and even headstands on the slowly rolling board.

provenance are combined with 'tricks' from 1960s surfing[4]. The above-mentioned editorial of *Quarterly SkateBoarder* places the practice between skiing and surfing: "It's similar in many ways to surfing and to skiing, not only in maneuvers and techniques [...]". Compared to surfing (now also an Olympic discipline), in this article skateboarding is portrayed as the

"[...] more 'measurable' sport [...] and therefore lends itself more to competition: In the slalom there is no question on who the winner is [...]. Flatland [...] performance will be a matter of judgement but at least the asphalt isn't moving – everyone gets an equal opportunity." (Brooke, 2005, p. 33)

Remarkably, this sport-oriented mode of riding corresponds to a tendency towards the organisational forms of sport. Referring to the mid 1970s, Porter (2014, Pos. 101) observes "a real drive to establish and legitimize skateboarding as a sport with defined rules, associations, and competitions". This also is true for the Federal Republic of Germany: organized competitive skateboarding takes off in 1976 with "Bavarian Championships" organized by "Skateboard-Club Tegernseer" (cf. Stauder 1977, p. 115). Shortly after that, an event called "First National Munich Skateboarding Championships" is staged in the Bavarian capital and attracts "some thousand spectators" (ibid.). At that point in history, Munich emerges as the centre of Skateboarding in West Germany, giving home to – short lived – organizations like "Dachverband Deutscher Skatebordfahrer" (DDS) and "Europäische Skateboard Assoziation" (ESA). After the demise of those organizations, "Deutscher Rollsportbund" (DRB) takes over as skateboarding's governing body in West Germany in 1978 (cf. Seewaldt, 1990, p. 25).

The fact that, at this time, the practice develops such structures is rooted in the terrains it uses – which hardly correspond to the characteristics given by Gebauer et al.. Figure skating not only takes place in public places like parking lots but – at least in the Federal Republic and Western Europe – also school sports halls (cf. Torbet, 1977, p. 46). Even more so, the racing disciplines demand closed-off 'slopes' and thus either facilities that are functionally separated from social life – which sometimes even provide lifts similar to skiing resorts (cf. Tietz, 1989, p. 690) – or legal entities that can obtain the closure of a suitable side road on weekends. This drive towards an association-shaped spatialization of the practice is constituted not only in the locations of these slopes, but also in their

---

4 For example exercises like the so-called *nose wheelie:* placing both feet on nose of the board so that the rear axle can be lifted while driving. This emulates the *hang ten* in surfing.

surfaces: skateboard textbooks of the 1970s spread internationally largely congruent guidelines regulating the setting of slalom courses down to the detail. These courses – and with them the movements of the riders – are standardized to an even greater extent than in the Ski World Cup, for example, where they differ from slope to slope and run to run (cf. Torbet, 1976, p. 114f).

Under these circumstances, Olympic ambitions even intensify after 1965. As early as the mid-1970s, US mass media circulate rumours about a possible inclusion of skateboarding into the schedule of the 1980 summer games (cf. Yochim, 2010, p. 48).

ONE BREATH OF OLYMPIC AIR (1984)

It could be argued that this "sixties paradigm of skateboarding" (Peralta, 2001, 00:49:12) is irrelevant for the practice's later developments. In fact, in the later 1970s, initially parallel to this paradigm of racing and figure skateboarding, a transformation of the practice emerges that makes this 'prehistoric' phase forgotten in retrospect. The result of this transformation is – now in fact recurring to the manoeuvres of surfing which had become much more dynamic than in the 1960s but, notably, soon reaching far beyond surfing's repertoire – a thoroughly new style of skateboarding that quickly becomes dominant. To this new and emerging style of skateboarding – dubbed as the *Dogtown* Style[5] – all the above mentioned characteristics of New Play in fact fully apply.

It's especially in the steep walls of the 'found' dried out swimming pools that are so often mythologized in the skateboarding world where skateboarders start to make up totally new modes of bodily movement in a newly discovered, vertical space of play[6]. A repetitive 'swinging up' in opposite walls allows playing on and over their edges since about 1976. The names given to these new skateboarding manoeuvres hint to the fundamental change the practice is subjected to. This new generation of skateboarding tricks is process-oriented rather than result-oriented. For example, the term *grind*, describing the sliding of the

---

5   The name refers to an underprivileged district of Santa Monica in Greater L.A. known as Dogtown at the time in youth slang, where this style of skateboarding originally emerged.

6   In the later 1970s, especially in the US, there were also purpose-built structures that emulated these backyard pools. However, these skateparks had to be closed until around 1980 with very few exceptions due to insurance law problems (cf. Borden, 2001, p. 175; Brooke, 2005, p. 66).

axles on the edge, is not only onomatopoeic, but also represents an *attitude* that, in the skateboarding jargon, is often referred to as *aggressive skateboarding* (cf. Brooke, 2005, p. 57). Moreover, the transition to this new style of 'vert' skateboarding is characterized by a very close relation to both the symbolics and motorics of a certain style of (un-)popular music, namely the punk/hardcore scheme. Only from now on, skateboarding can be related to as a 'subculture'; partially leaving the realms of sports, it becomes a part of pop culture (cf. Schäfer & Alkemeyer, 2018) Butz (2012) reconstructs in detail the bodily and mental *modus operandi* of 'skate punk' which is represented by the fact that in vertical skateboarding there is a manoeuvre called *Rock 'n' Roll* and another one called *Pogo:* just like in the sphere of music and dance the latter can be described as a radicalization of the first.

This way of riding a skateboard is no longer about the objectifiable perfection of predefined movements but about the creation of new ones. Centered on aesthetics rather than scores it brings about a totally new understanding of 'performance' in sports. Now, a 'good' skateboarding performance is not defined by, for example, speed (as it was in slalom or downhill skateboarding) but by an 'authentic' bodily/mental display of punk rock ethos. So, now, skateboarding in its very movements *intrinsically* distances itself from what traditionally is called a 'sport'. However, as early as in the first half of the 1980s, the pendulum starts swinging back. The savage bodily experiments that characterized vertical skateboarding's invention are differentiated into four trick families, namely *Liptricks*[7], *Airs*[8], *Handplants* or *Inverts*[9] and *Footplants*[10]. A new catalogue of standard manoeuvres arises, offering 'hard' criteria for judging a skateboard run: Are manoeuvres from all families shown, the easier or the more difficult ones? Is the rider capable of performing the difficult ones 'wall to wall'? Ex-skateboarding professional Tommy Guerrero, for example, obviously has such a re-sportified form of skateboarding in mind when, looking back on the late 1980s, he calls vertical skateboarding "pretty compulsory":

---

7   Manoeuvres in which axes or the bottom of the board play with the edge (lip), for example tricks like *grinds* and *rock 'n' rolls* mentioned above.

8   Manoeuvres in which the riders jump over the edge and then land again in the 'wall'.

9   Manoeuvres in which the riders hold the board by their feet with one hand while the free hand rests on the edge in a head position; not to be confused with the static handstand in older figure skating, which can also be practiced without a skateboard.

10 Manoeuvres in which a foot is taken off the board at the edge to push off.

"There was pretty much the same bag of tricks that everybody drew from, though some could do them longer, faster, higher, or more stylishly than others [...]. 'Do a standard trick here and then this trick or that trick'." (Howell & Greeven, 2005, p. 29)

A mode of skateboarding allowing criteria like "longer", "faster" and "higher" clearly resembles traditional sports – even though, at this time, the speed of a grind or the altitude of an air are estimated rather than actually measured in skateboarding competitions. At the same time, the criterion of "style" tends to swing back towards an "artistic score" comparable to ice skating or gymnastics, although the basic mode of presentation and staging never completely recedes.

The fact that in just a few years the wild experiments in Dogtown's pools are transformed into a more or less standardized, measurable sporting activity is rooted, again, in the surfaces and localities of skateboarding's terrains. Vertical skateboarding moves from 'found' swimming pools to *half-pipes,* the surfaces of which are modelled on the 'found' pools walls but optimized for skateboarding[11]. This shift in surface and locality makes a significant difference for the practice: those swimming pools are extremely steep, irregularly modelled and crossed by dysfunctional elements such as drainage shafts, ladders etc. – so that a *line* that even leads into vertical space with enough momentum must first be worked out. This material resistance of the surface fosters an experimental and improvisational way of riding. In addition, runs in found pools can hardly be compared supra-locally because the walls and the shape of these pools differ considerably in detail: one and the same manoeuvre might be quite easy to perform in one pool but rather difficult in another. In a halfpipe, to the contrary, the path to the vertical does not have to be sought. On the less steep, uniform transitions of these ramps, riders fully can concentrate fully on manoeuvring at or above the edge. In addition, half pipes all over the world are very similar, a fact that promotes the standardization of skateboarding's body techniques – while it is obvious that the appropriation of swimming pools cultivates another set of 'virtues' than the legitimate use of functional architecture. The half pipes of the late-1980s are thus exactly the opposite of what Gebauer et al. describe as the typical location of New Play. They are enclosed sports facilities functionally separated from everyday life. While in Germany they are mostly provided by

---

11 More precisely, the half-pipe is a combination of architectural elements from those swimming pools and *fullpipes* – pipe elements that in many places in California and Arizona in the 1970s were waiting to be sunk into the ground as part of major water management projects and thus offered themselves as vertical skateboarding terrain (cf. Schäfer, 2015b, p. 70).

traditional sports or youth culture clubs, in the USA they often stand on private property – or are maintained by associations such as even the arch-conservative *Association of Christian Young Men* (YMCA).

Vertical skateboarding's transformation from a 'subcultural' practice to a more or less conventional sport is mirrored and promoted in the representations of the practice. Roughly speaking, *Thrasher,* founded in the early 1980s, propagates a 'subcultural' version, while somewhat younger *Transworld Skateboarding Magazine* aims at branding the practice 'clean' and sport-oriented (cf. Beal, 2013, p. 20f). In the US, the *National Skateboarding Association* (NSA) – which became a major force in the practice in the mid-1980s and organises a competition series, some of which is broadcast on television, and even creates a permanent ranking – is decisively interested and involved in this mainstreaming. In Germany, Deutscher Rollsportbund (DRB) – later renamed *Deutscher Rollsport- und Inlineverband* (DRIV) – remains important as an organizing body in competitive skateboarding.

In this setting, skateboarding once again develops into a quite popular spectator sport, at least in the US. So it's not surprising that, again, the Olympics become an issue of concern within the practice. This time already, this 'discussion' gets very concrete: A group of skateboarders, including halfpipe star Tony Hawk, shows their skills as part of the closing ceremony of the 1984 Summer Games on a halfpipe-like facility set up in the Olympic Stadium of Los Angeles.

FROM ESPN TO IOC (2007/2016)

The Californian organizers certainly intended this performance as a preview of an Olympic inclusion of the practice. But, nevertheless, it was actually soon forgotten. This is firstly due to the concept of sport within the Olympic system at the time. In German-speaking countries, older skateboarders still remember the not quite wrong but very derogatory TV commentary denouncing skateboarding as some kind of a funfair "show" but never a serious sport. But there is also an endogenous reason: five or six years after this first breath of Olympic air, the form of skateboarding shown at the Olympic stadium hardly exists any more. On the basis of the *ollie*, i.e. jumping from the horizontal by 'kicking' the skateboard's tail, street skateboarding became the dominant style of riding around 1990. Now, skateboarders let the board swirl under their feet in a variety of ways, jump up or over smaller or larger obstacles in the street, grind and slide[12]

---

12 With the so-called boardslide the bottom of the board slides over an obstacle.

curbs, park benches, planters or stair railings instead of the edges of vertical walls – using all the types terrains that Gebauer actually et al. have in mind in their model cited above.

Particularly in the emerging phase of street skateboarding (until about 1995), its movements – which now go with hiphop instead of punk/hardcore – again elude the model of sport basally. At first, a small-scale, hyper-technical and experimental style of riding prevails, which is completely geared to the creation of new movements and motion variants. From a participant view, Hälbich (2008, p. 63) describes the "goal" of this as creating "increasingly difficult manoeuvres with often barely comprehensible kickflip[13] variations", while "speed and style faded into the background". Some of these highly complex movements certainly even occur by chance. Others, according to Hälbich, are tried until they can be recorded on video as an "evidence" – and are then "never done again" (ibid.).

Under these circumstances, clubs and associations are now losing their influence because they are no longer needed to operate special-purpose skateboarding facilities. However, such a mode of movement per se is far from the logic of sports because it hardly can be objectified: one local crew may specialize in skating curbs, another in stairs – which one skates 'better'? Now, the variety of terrains and thus of movements formally explodes – a process that goes hand in hand with a once again widespread anti-sport and anti-competition attitude within this new generation of street skateboarders, proclaiming an 'artistic' skateboarding subject. *Thrasher* meets this mood and its practical background in 1992, publishing a manifest-style piece titled "Contests suck":

"How is it possible to judge something that comes from the soul? Where can you find qualified and unbiased observers to tabulate an art form? How can you process a large amount of skaters in a limited amount of space so they can best demonstrate their creative talents?" (N.N., 1992, p. 38)

Already the use of street spaces habitualizes an "anti-discipline" that German anthropologist Horst Ehni (1998, p. 119) describes very aptly. For some years, street skateboarding proves to be so resistant to the spatio-temporal regulation requirements of competitions that it becomes quite difficult to carry them out at all. Time and again, attempts to format street skateboarding in a competitive manner end up in sheer chaos. Sometimes there are even violent clashes between

---

13 A kickflip is an ollie in which the board is swirled around its longitudinal axis under the feet during the jump. These manoeuvers often are combined with varials, i.e. turns around the transverse axis.

stewards and skaters who are not prepared to use the course in an 'ordered' way, i.e. individually or in certain groups (cf. Schweer, 2014, p. 122; Schäfer, 2000). In an often-quoted essay, Beal (1995) interprets a relevant situation as "social restistance". These anti-disciplinary attitudes are reinforced, especially in the US, by the fact that at the same time as street skateboarding, urban policies of *zero tolerance's* become hegemonic and deviant use of space is criminalized in consequence (cf. Lüdemann & Ohlemacher, 2002, p. 143ff; Chiu, 2009, p. 35).

Moreover, the initially hyper-technical movements of emergent early-1990s street skateboarding are not suitable for a broader audience. This concern also drives the major economic players on the skateboard scene to join forces in 1995 and form the IASC (*International Association of Skateboard Companies*). A major goal of this organization clearly is to make the practice more accessible to mainstream viewers. This concern becomes very clear in the protocol of a preparatory meeting in 1994:

"[...] Right now the general public can't understand skateboarding. It's too technical and too inconsistent. [...] Right now skating does not look fun. [...] We must encourage some change. Modern street skating is rad but we must add to it [...]" (IASC, 1994)[14]

In fact, this longing within the skateboard industry should be fulfilled. In the later 1990s, a further, slowly progressing transformation of the practice begins, leading skateboarding out of the niche of a hard-to-understand 'nerd' culture into which the practice had manoeuvred itself around 1990. Instead, according to Hälbich (2008, p. 63), more and more "clear, safe movements" on skateboards seen on the streets. The focus on the above mentioned hyper-technical kickflip manoeuvres fades in favor of a more diverse style of skateboarding also accentuating manoeuvre groups such as *wheelies* or *manuals*[15], grinds and slides, whereby it remains characteristic for street skating that these elements often are combined when tackling one street obstacle. No later than around the millennium this slow but steady transformation of skateboarding's body techniques results in yet another trend of sportification of the practice, even if this by no

---

14 This protocol has been available for years on the Internet at www.dansworld. com/meeting-html. The author tried to verify its authenticity by mails to persons named as participants, but there were no answers. However, since the document is already cited in Borden (cf. 2001, p. 26), it seems justified to use it subject to a certain reservation.

15 Riding on only one axle or two wheels.

means encompasses all participants and, at the same time, provokes creativity oriented 'counter-styles', as examined by Veith Kilberth in this volume.

Again, this pendulum swing back toward the realm of sports is massively influenced by a change of skateboarding's terrains. Similar to the development in vertical skateboarding shown above, this repeated transformation is accompanied by the return of a majority of riders from obstacles 'found' in the streets to special purpose functional architectures. The stairs, railings, curbs etc. on which street skateboarding unfolded in the late 1980s and early 1990s now are emulated – in increasing quality – in halls or on special skateboarding parks[16]. After 2000, the "largest share" of skateboarding hours takes place there (Fiehl, 2005, p. 3). In the course of this spatial containment, re-legitimization and also regulation of the practice, its 'subcultural', anti-disciplinary imprints erode one again. In addition, these purpose-built architectures based on street architectures also lead to a certain standardization of manoeuvres, even if these courses are less similar from place to place than, say, half-pipes.

This redevelopment of skateboarding is driven by major commercial players establishing new kinds of sports events around skateboarding and skateboard culture. The most influential format might be the *X Games,* staged and televised since 1995 by the American sports television network ESPN. This format intervenes deeply in the practice, also and foremost with regards to its bodily movements. In the assumed interest of a mass audience, first the half-pipe is revived as a discipline. Later the *mega ramps* emerge – huge structures resembling ski jumping – allowing extreme and exaggerated versions of vertical skateboarding manoeuvres and, thus, establishing new modes of bodily movements within the practice. So-called 'park' skating, also updating moves from the vertical phase on an installation reminiscent of a lunar landscape, will be the second discipline shown at the Tokyo 2020 summer Olympics. However, this format of skateboarding developed in events other than the *X Games* (cf. Kilberth again in this volume).

In this new, highly competitive segment of the practice, the core requirements of sports – objectification and comparability of movements – are largely imposed by new judging technologies. For example, *Street League Skateboarding* uses evaluation software that displays the 'score' in real time. This suggests agonal strategies to the competitors which are relatively new in skateboarding in

---

16 In the US, new legal regulations play an important role here, which in the late 1990s relieve the operators of such facilities of the above-mentioned liability problems that led to the closure of most skateboard facilities around 1980 (cf. Howell, 2008, p. 491; Borden, 2001, p. 175).

this form: skaters can now "calculate whether they want to do a simple but safe trick that earns them fewer points or a risky but highly remunerated trick" (Schweer, 2014, p. 118). Such objectification and hierarchization of skateboard manoeuvres also influence the everyday practice of skateboarders who do not participate in such events.

To sum it up, after 2000 the 'Olympic question' gets on the agenda yet once again. Under the impression of the *X Games* – which meanwhile tend to be a real competitor to the IOC games, not only in the US but also in several Latin American and Asian countries, especially among young audiences – IOC now shows itself to be very open for skateboarding and similar sporting activities. Olympic skateboarding – which had been heralded somewhat hastily in 2007 by the press, only to be announced in 2016 – is due to the skateboard industry, which opposed the then-planned inclusion under the aegis of the word cycling association UCI (cf. Beal, 2013, p. 36). But at that time, skateboarding, at least in a growing segment, was ready to be part of the Olympics since a decade at least.

BETWEEN SUBCULTURE AND SPORTS CULTURE

This very brief and surely partly overdrawn sketch of historical styles of moving on a skateboard, of skateboarding's terrains and self-interpretations shows that the practice's inclusion in the Olympics is by far less surprising than often assumed. Three times in its history, skateboarding has shaped sports-related forms – but at the same time always has produced variants that intrinsically elude classical sport. Its inclusion into the Olympics seems particularly logical regarding its terrains: two consecutive times the practice has 'read' the potential of found (sub-) urban objects and infrastructures for skateboard play to develop artefacts that have long been Olympic. With the *half-pipe* and the *rails of slopestyle,* skateboarding has already created the basis for quite a handful of Olympic disciplines, albeit so far at the Winter Games. So why should the original be missing?

With regards to scientific writing about practices of New Play, skateboarding's pendulum movement between 'subculture' and 'sports culture' reconstructed here shows that these practices of New Play must not be too categorically and statically separated from the field of conventional sport. The 'pure' form of New Play that, for example, Gebauer et al. (2004) construct is applicable for skateboarding only in two quite short historical moments, namely in emergent vertical skateboarding between the late 1970s and early 1980s and in the invention phase of street skateboarding between, roughly speaking, 1990 and

1995. So the findings that Gebauer et al. published in their booklet about "Treue zum Stil" ("Loyalty to Style") has undeniably been of great use as an instrument for the investigation of practices of New Play to this day, but this model cannot be treated as an overall characterization.

It may be more 'interesting' for social scientists to focus on those moments and elements in which such a practice differs fundamentally from traditional sport, but, then, the subject is not thoroughly investigated. Even hockey on inline skates, which Gebauer et al. still regard as a reference practice for the New Play, has long since been transformed into a 'proper' sport whether as "inline hockey" (using a puck) or as "skater hockey" (using a ball). As soon as a practice ceases to be a mere *sports trend* and develops into a somewhat unfortunate so-called *trend sport,* science has to take a closer look when it really wants to explore the object of investigation and not only to find a suitable example for the explication of sociological narratives.

At the same time, sports sociology – if it assumes that there are forces in the field of sport that do not only apply to this field alone (cf. Bourdieu, 1992, p. 196-197) and that this social field (precisely because it is relatively autonomous) can be viewed as a showcase of the social – must always also pursue the question of how physical-sensuous practices of sport and the general formation of social order relate to one another. In the case of skateboarding, the status of the practice should be discussed within the broader process of social change affecting 'Western' societies in the later 20th century, which is commonly described as transition from 'industrial' to 'post-industrial' society, from 'fordism' to 'post-fordism', or from 'modernity' to 'post-modernity'.

In this respect, Reckwitz' (2010, p. 75) model of bourgeois subjectivation offers itself as a starting point. He conceives modernity as a sequence of three subject orders (Subjektordnungen) – "bourgeois modernity", "organized modernity" and "postmodernity". In a field of power between "material culture" and "aesthetic movements", a sequence of "dominant subject cultures" (Subjektkulturen) emerges, whereby the "morally sovereign general subject" of bourgeois modernity is followed by the "post-bourgeois employee subject" of organized modernity and the "consumerist creative subject" of postmodernism. In this model, the "aesthetic movements" – Romanticism of the 19th century, avant-garde of the early 20th century, and the *counterculture* of the later 20th century – can be read as catalysts for those transformations by challenging and delegitimizing the respective older order, while at the same time contributing to the consolidation of a new hegemonic status quo.

It is now very obvious how to add skateboarding to this scheme. In its 'pure' forms it functions as a sportive performance of those *counter cultures* or subcultures: it delegitimizes Organized Modernism, which – like 'its' sport – follows a "code of the socio-technical" (Reckwitz, 2010, p. 338) which "fundamentally gradualizes and quantifies achievements [...]" (ibid., p. 357) by embodying a code of creativity and aestheticization and creating subjective – 'felt' not measured – horizons of achievement. In its sports-related phases, on the other hand, the practice compromises to create *new* modes of gradualization and quantification. In these phases, it can be, then, understood as a sportive performance of those processes of acculturation in which once anti-systemic elements help to establish a new, here postmodern, hegemonic subject order. In this respect, more detailed studies on skateboarding can also be carried out with a view to a question that remains somewhat unclearly answered in Reckwitz's large draft: which features of that historic *counter culture* in which frameworks actually turn out to be order-conforming or even order-establishing with regard to the postmodern subjectivity – and which features remain 'disturbing factors' that under certain circumstances can lead to fractures in a postmodern hegemony?

REFERENCES

Alkemeyer, T. & Schmidt, R. (2003). Habitus und Selbst. Zur Irritation der körperlichen Hexis in der populären Kultur. In Alkemeyer, T., Boschert, B., Schmidt, R. & Gebauer, G. (Eds.), *Aufs Spiel gesetzte Körper. Aufführungen des Sozialen in Sport und populärer Kultur* (p. 77-102). Konstanz: UVK.

Beal, B. (1995). Disqualifying the official. An exploration of social resistance through the subculture of skateboarding. *Sociology of Sport Journal* 12, 3, 252-267.

Beal, B. (2013). *Skateboarding. The Ultimate Guide*. Santa Barbara/Denver/Oxford: Greenwood.

Borden, I. (2001). *Skateboarding, Space and the City. Architecture and the Body*. Oxford/New York: Berg.

Bourdieu, P. (1992). Programm für eine Soziologie des Sports. In Bourdieu, P. (Ed.), *Rede und Antwort* (p. 193-207). Frankfurt (Main): Suhrkamp.

Brooke, M. (2005). *The Concrete Wave. The History of Skateboarding*. Toronto: Warwick Publishing.

Butz, K. (2012). *Grinding California. Culture and Corporeality in American Skate Punk*. Bielefeld: transcript.

Chiu, C. (2009). Contestation and Conformity: Street and Park Skateboarding in New York City Public Space. *Space and Culture*, Vol. 12, 1, 25-42.

Eder, M. (2015). 'Skateboarding braucht Olympia nicht'. (Interview mit Titus Dittmann), *Faz.net*, 06.10.2015.

Ehni, H. (1998). Den Skatern auf der Spur. In Schwier, J. (Ed.), *Jugend – Sport – Kultur: Zeichen und Codes jugendlicher Sportszenen* (p. 109-123). Hamburg: Cwzalina.

Fiehl, A. (2005). Vorwort, *Boardstein* 06/2005, 3-4.

Gebauer, G., Alkemeyer, T., Boschert, B., Flick, U. & Schmidt, R. (2004). *Treue zum Stil. Die aufgeführte Gesellschaft*. Bielefeld: transcript.

Hälbich, F. (2008). *Die Geschichte des Skateboardings. Von den Anfängen bis heute*. Hamburg: Diplomica.

Hartmann, R. (2014). Der Ausverkauf der Coolness. *Zeit Online*, 19.08.2014.

Howell, A. & Greeven, A. (2005). *Art, Skateboarding & Life*. New York: Ginkgo Press.

Howell, O. (2008). Skatepark as Neoliberal Playground. Urban Governance, recreation Space, and the Cultivation of Personal Responsibility. *Space and Culture* 11, 4, 475-496.

IASC (1994). Gentlemen's agreement. http://www.dansworld.com/meeting-html.

Lüdemann, C. & Ohlemacher, T. (2002). *Soziologie der Kriminalität. Theoretische und empirische Perspektiven*. Weinheim, München: Beltz.

N. N. (1992). Contests Suck. *Thrasher*, 04/1992, 38-43.

Peralta, S. (2001). *Dogtown and Z-Boys*. Sony Pictures Classics (DVD).

Pietschmann, N. (2016) Wie Olympia wieder hip werden will. *Br.de*, 02.06. 2016.

Porter, N. (2014). *The History of Women in Skateboarding*. Kindle Edition.

Reckwitz, A. (2010). *Das hybride Subjekt. Eine Theorie der Subjektkulturen von der bürgerlichen Moderne zur Postmoderne*. Weilerswist: Velbrück.

Schäfer, V. (2000). Skater stören nicht. *Jungle World online*, 19.07.2000.

Schäfer, E. V. (2015a). Sport mit den Mitteln des Pop. Skateboard-Videos: Bewegungslernen, Vergemeinschaftung und Jugendmarketing. *Sport und Gesellschaft* 12, 149-170.

Schäfer, E. V. (2015b). Raum schaffen und Stadt machen: Body Spaces und Sportmobiliar in der Skateboard-Praktik. In Kähler, R. S. (Ed.), *Städtische Freiräume für Sport, Spiel und Bewegung* (p. 69-78). Hamburg: Czwalina.

Schäfer, E. V. & Alkemeyer, T. (2018). Skateboarding und die Pop-Werdung des Sportsubjekts. In Busche, H., Heinze, T., Hillebrandt, F. & Schäfer, F. (Eds.), *Kultur – interdisziplinäre Zugänge* (p. 81-100). Wiesbaden: Springer.

Schatzki, T. R. (1996). *Social Practices. A Wittgensteinian Approach to Human Activity and the Social*. Cambridge: Cambridge University Press.

Schmidt, R. (2002). *Pop – Sport – Kultur. Praxisformen körperlicher Aufführungen*. Konstanz: UVK.

Schweer, S. (2014). *Skateboarding. Zwischen urbaner Rebellion und neoliberalem Selbstentwurf*. Bielefeld: transcript.

Schwier, J. (1998). Stile und Codes bewegungsorientierter Jugendkulturen. In Schwier, J. (Ed.), *Jugend – Sport – Kultur: Zeichen und Codes jugendlicher Sportszenen* (p. 9-30). Hamburg: Czwalina.

Schwier, J. (2000). *Sport als populäre Kultur. Sport, Medien und Cultural Studies*. Hamburg: Czwalina.

Seewaldt, C. (1990). *Alles über Skateboarding*. Münster: Monster Verlag.

Shove, E., Pantzar, M. & Watson, M. (2012). *The Dynamics of Social Practice. Everyday Life and how it Changes*. London: Sage.

Stauder, H. (1977). *Skateboard Fahren. Für Anfänger und Fortgeschrittene*. München: Nymphenburger.

Stern, M. (2010). *Stil-Kulturen. Performative Konstellationen von Technik, Spiel und Risiko in neuen Sportpraktiken*. Bielefeld: transcript.

Tietz, H. (1989). Planung und Ausbau von Skateboard-Anlagen. *Neue Landschaft* 34, 690-697.

Torbet, L. (1976). *Skateboard. Technik, Kniffs, Tricks und Figuren*. München: Heyne.

Yochim, E. C. (2010). *Skate Life. Re-Imagining White Masculinity*. Ann Arbor: University of Michigan Press.

The Olympic Skateboarding Terrain between Subculture and Sportisation

Veith Kilberth

AREAS OF CONFLICT BETWEEN SUBCULTURE AND SPORTISATION

The current debate surrounding skateboarding's 2020 debut as an Olympic discipline reveals new opportunities for skateboarding, but also polarised responses to the processes of adaptation and conformity inherent to institutionalised sports. Ultimately, this adds pressure to the very habitus of skateboarding, as it has to be reconfigured at a fundamental level. How exactly do these transformative forces interact within skateboarding? And how has skateboarding dealt with this underlying conflict between subculture and sportisation in the past, especially when it comes to giving shape to its future?

This chapter responds to these questions via literature research, incorporating the most recent academic publications on skateboarding (Atencio & Beal, 2016; Atencio et al., 2018; Bock, 2017; Borden, 2019; Cantin-Brault, 2015; Dupont, 2014; Peters, 2016; Schäfer, 2017; Schweer, 2014 and Snyder, 2017). Highly relevant insights stem from Eckhard Velten Schäfer's (2017) dissertation, which aims to achieve the reconstruction of a 'true history' of skateboarding based on a practicological-genealogical approach. I consider my own background as source material as well. As a former professional skateboarder and with a degree in Sports Science, I have been working in the skateboard industry for more than twelve years. Transferring my insights into scientific analysis is further supported by my co-ownership of both a skateboard marketing agency and a skatepark planning agency.

The underlying tension between skateboarding's subcultural roots and the process of sportisation can be further highlighted by exploring the ongoing configuration of the skatepark terrain. The inclusion of skateboarding in the Olympic Games coincides with the definition of two official competitive events: Street and Park. Both events take place on specifically defined terrains, which in the past have undergone crucial transformations. They are the outcome of historical developments, allowing for a genealogical reconstruction and interpretation of these spaces.

Following this approach, my analysis investigates both Olympic disciplines of skateboarding by outlining the terrains and their predisposed performative movement patterns on a meta-level, while reconsidering their historical development. In so doing, I propose the constitutional traits behind skateboarding in a structural analogy to Bourdieu's concept of habitus, through which I explain the history of skateboarding. Based on these findings, my analysis will discuss the current state of affairs and potential future scenarios for skateboarding at the intersection between sportisation and cultural authenticity.

OLYMPIC TERRAIN

This analysis is based on the assumption that both Olympic skateboard disciplines – Street and Park – are in terms of their presentation and embodiment either adapted from or entirely based on existing unofficial world championship formats, such as X Games, Street League Skateboarding Nike SB World Tour and Vans Park Series (cf. Schäfer, 2017, p. 126). A logical reason for the inclusion of Street and Park in the Olympic Games is that these disciplines are ideal representations of the fragmented world of skateboard terrain, which can be divided into the two main categories – street skating und transition skating.[1] It is also a logical conclusion because street accounts for an estimated 80 percent of active skateboarders, making it the most important discipline (cf. Atencio & Beal, 2016, p. 110; Schäfer, 2017, p. 20). As I argue below, the so-called half-pipe, the former leading terrain for transition, would be better constituted as a competitive structure, but has played only a marginal role among active riders outside of the competitive arena for years at end.

In order to form a connection between the delineation of skateboard terrains and their usage styles, this analysis will draw on the definition of games as ar-

---

1   Transition or *tranny skating* is the umbrella term for all skateboard ramps, obstacles, and terrains that feature rounded forms of all sizes (cf. Borden, 2019, p. 209).

ticulated by Roger Caillois (1982). This definition is especially suited to analyse the structural movements and motives of participants in *new sports practices* and style cultures, which have emerged in the late 1990s as alternatives to traditional competitive sports. Recent works have defined new forms of movements, including skateboarding, using the typology of games according to Caillois, whilst positioning it as part of a 'sociology derived from play' (cf. Gebauer et al., 2004; Le Breton, 1995; Schäfer, 2017; Stern, 2010)

The model defines four game categories and two play styles labelled with the following Greek monikers:

- *Alea* – ludic situations that depend on pure chance, like lottery, casino roulette and dice-rolling games.
- *Mimicry* – Games of masquerade and dress-up such as carnivals related to concepts of illusion, imitation and pretence.
- *Ilinx* – Activities where there is risk of life and vertigo. Tightrope, bungee jump and other extreme sports are some examples.
- *Agon* – Competitions marked by physical prowess and tests of endurance, for instance in traditional competitive sports.

These four forms of games, which may overlap at times, also fall into two antagonistic play styles: *Paidia* refers to wild, improvised play, while *Ludus* resembles regulated, structured play. *Paida* and *Ludus* represent opposite parts of a spectrum between free creativity and rule-bound complexity. In what follows, I will apply these categorisations to skateboarding and its terrains.

The Park Terrain

Diachronically, this analysis will start with the discipline Park, the older one of the two skateboarding terrains. The Park terrain consists of a combination of shapes and forms from the transition skating. These are organic, round and conic shapes, mostly consisting of rounded bowl-shaped ramps. On an overall area of around 600 to 1000 square meters and at heights ranging from 1.6-3.8 meters from top to bottom, these bowl-shaped obstacles are arranged in connected sections that form a coherent course. These courses are created anew for every competitive event, focusing on individualised and creative course designs. As far as the origins of these shapes are concerned, the ramps and elements in a Park course represent the entire historical development of transition skateboarding and its origins in backyard pools.

The individual obstacles in a Park course are arranged in such a fashion that they allow skaters to connect tricks from one area to the other, thereby offering opportunities for performing so-called transfer moves. The intersections between obstacles form connections in loosely standardised constellations known as hips, spines, channels etc. The edges of the bowl-shaped ramps also give space to creative play, as they feature elevations and interruptions called channels, extensions, escalators, tomb stones, and love seats. The edges are equipped with rounded metal pipes, and partially feature pool copings.[2]

Park Terrain Movement Patterns

Overall, the compact and versatile Park terrain is designed to offer riders opportunities to unlock a maximum number of different paths (lines) at high speeds across the entire course. Skating at such a high speed, paired with options for combinations and transfers as well as the fast-paced intervals of tricks and the diversity of ramp elements, demand a high level of improvisation from Park skaters. Due to the relatively short time for preparation and the curved ride-up for each next move, Park skateboarding puts an emphasis on the creative use of the course as well as a diverse vocabulary of movement patterns and the capacity to maintain flow. The official website of the Vans Park Series sees the patterns of movement inherent to Park terrain as they are informed by, "speed, style, flow, amplitude and creativity" (Vansparkseries.com, 2017).

Translated into practice, these criteria amount to a combination of high speeds with overall aesthetic expression (style), optimal fluidity of motion (flow), maximum use of available terrain (amplitude), and a diverse use of all obstacles (creativity). In other words, as opposed to placing an emphasis on the athletic progression of single manoeuvres, the Park terrain favours a pattern of motion in which flow, aesthetic expression, playful creativity and the diverse use of the terrain are the focus.

Another important aspect is the practice of Park skating without protective gear. Due to the fact that the terrain only features very few vertical sections and also consists of elements at lower height, the Park discipline – at least in the Men's event – tends to be performed without any protection.[3] This marks a significant departure from its predecessor in transition skateboarding, namely skat-

---

2   This term refers to a rounded concrete edge similar to California-style outdoor swimming pools.

3   It will be interesting to see whether protective gear will be mandatory at the Olympic Games.

ing halfpipes. After all, protective gear and pads are staples of regulated sports, rendering skateboarding as a predictable and plannable practice (cf. Butz, 2012, p. 71; Borden, 2019, p. 209; Schäfer, 2017, p. 109). The combination of high-speed riding with a great number of improvised manoeuvres – especially performed on concrete surfaces, as opposed to wood – increases the risk of physical injury. Skateboarding without the use of protective gear is more than a symbolic statement showcasing an acceptance of risks. It also directly translates into the physical consequences that are impacting the body when a skateboarder falls or must abort a manoeuvre. It is to be expected that this practice will, in the medium to long term, lead to heightened incidences of injuries, as well as a shorter lifespan of professional careers in park skateboarding compared to the halfpipe terrain.[4]

The relevance of risk-taking and riding 'on the edge', which has been observed by Peters in his ethnographic study of street skateboarders on Cologne's Domplatte plaza (cf. Peters, 2016, p. 204) and has also been noted in other stylistic practices such as paragliding, free climbing and snowboarding by Stern (2010) – is also evident as a fundamental trait of skateboarding in this short genealogy of the transition terrain. Compared to halfpipe skateboarding as the previously dominant and most established form of vert skating, the Park discipline encourages its own type of transition rider:

"They're like tranny guys and maybe skate the Pool Party, but they can't win the Pool Party, that's for vert skaters nowadays. It's for guys with pads flying 8-feet and spinning. So we were trying to find and establish a platform for skaters like Curren Caples or Grant Taylor, what we called park terrain." (Schwinghammer, 2016)

This is how Vans' marketing manager, Justin Regan, describes the type of rider addressed by the Park discipline. Along these lines, Park riders are a type of skateboarder that can be classified as transition skaters, but they are not merely reduced to vertical riding in the way of traditional halfpipe or pool skaters. The two pro skateboarders mentioned here, Curren Caples and Grant Taylor, represent this new type of ATV-rider, an acronym for *all terrain vehicle*. ATV-riders excel on all types of skateboard terrains, including street. This broader, more generalised ability, compared to the specialised riding styles of previous eras, is ideal for the new style of Park riding; a style of riding that favours playful as-

---

4   This is indicated by the rising number of injuries, for instance at events such as the Vans Park Series, which are often interrupted by harsh falls and injury-related eliminations of skateboarders.

pects of Paidia and can be classified in the Ilinx category with elements of Alea. At the same time, the structure of the type of rider also determines the structure of the Park terrain.

In summary, the Park terrain can be described as a playful enterprise, strongly marked by qualities of Paidia in Caillois' model of games, which mainly takes place in the Ilinx category, and, as demonstrated, is marked by elements of Alea and Mimicry.[5]

Reconstruction of the Park Terrain

As a discipline, Park represents a reconfiguration of the transition terrain as a new interpretation of vertical skateboarding. This becomes clear by reconstructing the historical evolution of halfpipe skateboarding, previously the pinnacle or *ultimate form* of skateboarding (cf. Mokulys & Nawrocki, 1991; Schäfer, 2015, p. 154), which allows for delineating the motion patterns of vertical skateboarding.

During the skateboarding boom of the mid-1970s, purpose-built pools – as the second generation of skatepark terrain – were integrated in an increasing number of commercial skateparks. From the perspective of US companies, the immense surge in skateboarding's popularity rendered these parks as "one of the 70's most profitable business opportunities" (Borden, 2001, p. 58). Skateparks were commercialised into full-service operations catering to all aspects of skateboarding, including products such as hardware and protective equipment sold on-site via retail. Naturally, these private investments in skateparks contributed significantly to the increase in participation, as well as the evolution of riding techniques from a sports perspective. But after a few years, around 1978, many of these commercial skateparks were forced to file for bankruptcy, up to a point where almost all skateparks in the US closed around 1980. The predominant reason seemed to be the so-called Liability Crisis, during which disproportionate insurance fees for the high-risk practice of skateboarding drove park operators into insolvency (cf. Atencio et al., 2018, p. 16; Brook, 1999, p. 45; Schäfer, 2017, p. 158).

But upon closer inspection, this crisis appears as more of a symptom than a cause of skateboarding's great bust at the end of the 1970s. From my perspective, it is more likely that the massive drop in skateboarding's mass popularity in

---

5   The Agon category only comes into play in the competitive format, when skateboarders use the terrain within a pre-defined time limit, while their run is being scored by judges in comparison with other competitors.

the late 70s is the main reason of the downfall of skateparks, as hinted at by Borden (2001, p. 174; 2019, p. 134). From the perspective of skatepark operators, it means that sharply rising insurance rates had already been preceded by declining numbers in paying customers, which made their economic situation difficult, if not downright unsustainable.

Blümlein and Vogel (2018, p. 464) propose that the decreasing popularity of skateboarding in the late 1970s could have been a direct consequence of the sportisation taking place within the skatepark terrain:

"Perhaps the rapid progression of riding technique at skateparks had raised the bar too high, and many newcomers found skateboarding too difficult as to warrant continued interest [...] Park skating garnered a negative reputation for being 'elitist' – not to mention expensive because of park fees and required equipment." (Blümlein & Vogel, 2018, p. 464)

Factors such as the increasingly difficult level of manoeuvres, the construction of demanding skateboard facilities, the social segmentation through entrance and membership fees, the formation of elite rider groups in these years as well as the lacking diversity of the pool riding practice in its early stages, could well have presented barriers prohibiting access to a broad number of would-be skateboarders.

Skateboarding in the United States vanished almost entirely in the early 1980s, as well as in Germany (cf. Brook, 1999, p. 45; Schäfer, 2017, p. 158). In order to secure options to skate on vertical terrains, the remaining skateboarders were forced to return to found spaces or craft their own structures for skateboarding. "Skateboarders were now underground, die-hard, hardcore and – whether they liked it or not – totally DIY!" (Reinhardt, 2016, p. 15) Born out of necessity, skateboarders crafted their own DIY or do-it-yourself ramps. Many riders from the core scene constructed their own simplified versions of vertical terrain, mostly in backyards, out of wood: The so-called halfpipe was a simplified, modified structure at a width of ca. two to five meters with rounded transitions featuring far less vertical wall than a pool, while being connected by a flat bottom.

During a short experimentation period, halfpipes evolved into standardised sports structures, originally developed and designed by the core skateboarding scene. Besides perfecting the halfpipe, riders also developed a differentiated repertoire of halfpipe manoeuvres, or tricks. Much of skate trick evolution happened during exclusive gatherings of the core scene, mostly in private backyards shielded from the public eye (cf. ibid., p. 15). Compared to pool skating, halfpipes supported a focus on single tricks, thanks to the linear and repetitive back-and-forth motion into the vertical section, their optimised geometry, and longer set-up time before the next trick due to their longer flat bottom (cf. Borden, 2001, p. 102). This heightened focus on individual tricks, executed on informally standardised terrain, directly resulted in a rapid progression of trick difficulty and a heightened pace of athletic differentiation by individual performance. Fuelled by a massive influx of halfpipes in public spaces together with a large degree of commercialisation and spectacularisation, halfpipe skateboarding emerged as the highest level of skateboard performance until the late 1980s. In the waning years of the 1980s, halfpipe riding – and skateboarding as a whole – reached a new peak and the industry experienced another boom period (cf. Beal, 2013, p. 24). From a competitive perspective, halfpipe skateboarding offered a large degree of standardised structures, thereby making the terrain widely interchangeable and the riders' skills easily comparable. This coincided with the rise of an elite class of vertical skateboarders, who dominated at competitions and gained fame beyond the skateboarding scene through connections to the music and lifestyle market (cf. ibid., p. 24).

In light of the increasing sportisation, regulation and predictability of the halfpipe format, some parts of the skateboard scene began trending towards street skateboarding around 1990. This shift was supported by a rapid evolution of riding skills, including improvements regarding the ollie manoeuvre – the controlled lift-off with the skateboard under the rider's feet. The ollie opened up seamless connections between riding on flat ground and launching on top of objects, thereby making the city accessible for skateboarding on several levels (cf. Schäfer, 2017, pp. 160-161). During this phase of growth, street skateboarding appeared as an experimental, playful-creative, and most of all non-conformist athletic practice – thereby diametrically opposed to the symbolism and expressions of halfpipe skating. Within a relatively short time-span, street skateboarding took the crown as the most prominent skateboarding discipline (cf. ibid., p. 160). Participation in halfpipe skateboarding flatlined almost entirely, together with the construction of new halfpipes (cf. ibid., p. 166). In skateparks built throughout the late 1980s, the transition terrain increasingly featured in modified and diverse shapes such as significantly smaller ramps (cf. Borden, 2001, p. 81). This era also marked the rise of miniramps, miniature versions of halfpipes (cf. Borden, 2019, p. 191), which were also called fun ramps in the context of halfpipe skating's continued decline. Miniramps offered a focus on fun and so-called lip tricks on the edge of the ramp, making them significantly easier to perform tricks on compared to full-fledged halfpipes. Also, there was a significant reduced need to use safety equipment (cf. Borden, 2001, p. 82).

The start of the Xtreme Games competition series – now known as the X Games – in 1995 led to a second wave of halfpipe skating, as a competition format tailored towards television audiences. In 1999, the halfpipe era reached its athletic peak when, during a live broadcast, pro rider Tony Hawk landed the world's first 900° aerial in front of a major audience (cf. Striler, 2011, p. 43). Around the turn of the century, a new breed of competition series emerged using terrain that already matched the characteristics of the Park discipline, for instance the Marseille Bowl Riders contest in France in 1999. But it would take until the year 2008 for Park skating to be included in the X Games as the Super Park event. Ever since, the Park competition scene has grown around the world and is now mainly represented by the Vans Park Series as its official world championship. As a result, Park riding has now taken the place of halfpipe skating and represents, as a future Olympic event, the most important type of vertical skateboarding.

This short reconstruction of the vertical terrain affords some interesting insights. First of all, it can be stated that the emerging vertical skateboarding of the late 1970s was strongly characterised by Ilinix and partially Alea in the mode of Paidia. The adaptation and imitation of movement patterns from surfing also brought in a significant element of Mimicry, especially in the early days of pool skating (cf. Schäfer, 2017, p. 98). Only with the standardisation of the halfpipe terrain in the 1980s, vertical skateboarding evolved into a ludic-agonal sport. And with the emergence of Park as a creative and diverse terrain in the early 2000s, the practice of vertical riding returned to its original mode of play. This fundamental difference also suggests that the more formalised halfpipe riding would be structurally far more suited as an athletic competition discipline, making it the more logical alternative for the International Olympic Committee.

One particular difference between halfpipe and Park riding needs mentioning. The design of Park terrain inspired by Paidia and Ilinx is laid out in a way that limits the level of difficulty of tricks – especially vertical tricks – because of the terrain itself. We can conclude that in the Park discipline, the riders' existing repertoire of tricks is applied to a creative terrain. On the contrary, the halfpipe terrain applies the potential trick repertoire to a standardised terrain to differentiate the level of difficulty. Thereby, the de-standardisation of the terrain is the prerequisite for the level of athletic trick progression. The agonal tendency is hereby countered by the design of the terrain, with its structures informed by Paidia and traits such as creativity and unpredictability.

Viewed from the perspective of sportisation, the example of halfpipe skateboarding also illustrates that a successful television format for a skateboard competition does not necessarily reflect the terrain preferred by the majority of the scene. Stronger yet, it can even thrive without larger participation.[6] This can create a kind of time lag, where the skateboard scene has already developed new practices that proliferate outside or far ahead of commercial exploitation (cf. Mountain, 2019, 20:30).

The Street Terrain

As a discipline, Street recreates urban space and other skateable objects found in the built environment. These objects are placed on a Street course – an even, mostly rectangular surface covering 500 to 1,000 square meters. This area usually exhibits a linear structure, arranging the angular objects – as opposed to the round structures of Park terrain – on several levels from 0.3-2 meters in height. The individual obstacles and sections are arranged in a way that encourages riders to traverse them in sequence. The far ends of Street courses are for the most part equipped with transition elements to allow riders to build speed. The distances between Street elements (including ledges, rails, downrails, stairs, and ramps, as well as landing spots in between) allow for two things. First, providing riders with enough space to build speed between tricks by *pushing* with their feet. Second, to allow enough time to prepare for the next trick. In terms of their dimensions, Street elements represent a synthesis between 'megafied recreations' of street furniture and true-to-size, authentic obstacles. Many modern courses feature a large, spectacular stair set with handrails and staircase banisters (*Hubba ledges*) in a prominent location on the Street course, known as the *Big Section*. Street courses are predominantly built out of concrete and are decorated with colourful contrasts, greenery and other street-oriented details. Street courses for the international Street League competition series are designed and constructed anew for each new event. The positioning of obstacles on the rectangular area almost always follows a linear structure with significant space for run-up and landing between objects.

---

6   Another example for the discrepancy between skateboarding as a spectacular competition format and the number of participants is the *Mega Ramp* event. Initially pioneered by pro skateboarder Danny Way and funded by his sponsors, this new mode of transition skating was developed into a mass-marketable TV format by a US broadcasting network.

Street Terrain Movement Patterns

The motion patterns inherent to street skateboarding are fundamentally characterized by riding on even, smooth surfaces. On a horizontal level, riders access obstacles by levitating into the air via the impulsive propulsion manoeuvre known as the *ollie* (e.g. the basic technique for almost every street manoeuvre), while traversing back and forth across the linear course. In between objects on the course, riders frequently propel themselves forward by pushing with one foot in order to increase their speed. This marks a fundamentally different transfer of energy and exertion of force than the acceleration via dynamically shifting the riders' centre of gravity (*pumping*) that characterises Park skating.

Reconstruction of the Street Terrain

Even though street skateboarding did emerge in the mid-80s, it would not rise to full prominence and gain a major breakthrough until the early 1990s (cf. Schäfer, 2017, p. 160). Compared to transition skateboarding, street skating represented a distinctively new iteration of the entire practice. A mode of skateboarding that didn't exist by the grace of purpose-built structures but was accessible across the world, in any place, and for all participants (cf. Borden, 2001, p. 182). As a consequence, the formative years of street skateboarding mostly utilised found terrains in the urban realm. The emergent motion patterns of street skating were very much experimental, creative, and marked by playfulness. In the early 1990s, translating this new type of street skating into a formal competitive format for larger audiences proved challenging (cf. Schäfer, 2017, p. 116). The main barriers to creating a competitive format were the precise, experimental and highly technical motion patterns of this new form of skateboarding, as well as the outspoken opposition of its participants after an era of commercialisation. In that sense, street skaters saw themselves as "somewhat of a counter movement against the 1980s skateboarding establishment" (Reinhardt, 2016, p. 20), and proved widely uncooperative. The skateboarding scene at large, with street skating as its new main focus, made conscious efforts to insulate itself from any attempts at regulation and even the slightest degree of sportisation (cf. Schäfer, 2017, p. 246; Borden, 2019, p. 24; Beal, 2013, p. 27).

It would take until the mid-1990s for the practice to undergo transformation once again. In 1995, the Extreme Games – now the X Games – presented a spectator-friendly version of street skateboarding with Street as an official event (cf. Schäfer, 2017, p. 77). On a compact course, a number of exaggerated obstacles were arranged to showcase the spectacular – or extreme – aspect of street skating. The success of the X Games and the transformation of the practice led to a new boom of skateboarding in the late 1990s. The previously self-contained motion pattern practices of micro-street-skateboarding on small elements were gradually opened and supplemented by bigger tricks. At the end of the 1990s, the practice of street skateboarding trended towards megafication (cf. ibid., pp. 77-78). Pushing the physical boundaries of the practice in terms of the dimensions of stairs, gaps, handrails and other obstacles became the new focus. This test of physical prowess also happened on found terrain, that is, on the streets. But right around 1998, the Liability Crisis in California gave way to less rigid legislation, once again encouraging the operation of skateparks. This time, public facilities were the predominant type of newly constructed skateparks (cf. Beal, 2013, p. 33; Borden, 2019, p. 86).

In response to the increasing number of participants in street skateboarding, as well as the increasing appropriation of public spaces by street skaters (cf. Whitley, 2009, p. 10), a new generation of outdoor and indoor skateparks emerged across the world.

A new era of skatepark construction dawned in 2005 with the opening of the world's first Skate Plaza in Kettering, Ohio (cf. Borden, 2019, pp. 210-211). This outdoor facility was designed to resemble public plazas in American cities that had been home to skateboarders as found terrain during street skateboarding's formative years. True to style, the Skate Plaza implemented high-end materials, smooth surfaces, benches and other natural – meaning angular – objects catering to the needs of street skaters. This premium version of skateparks, which creator Rob Dyrdek dubbed as a real alternative to street skating on public urban plazas (cf. Atencio & Beal, 2016, p. 110), would prove to be the model for the Street courses in the Street League competition series, and ultimately, the Olympic Street skateboarding terrain in some modified shape or form (cf. Schäfer, 2017, p. 126).

In summary, the Plaza or Street League terrain, with its linear arrangement of elements on a course, marks a strong focus on single tricks. Despite the fact that street courses are freshly designed and erected for each new event, the individual street skateboarding obstacles – such as curbs, ledges, rails, banks and handrails – offer a high degree of standardisation and thereby follow a ludic-agonal tendency. Ilinx remains a fundamental element in all of skateboarding, as the simple gliding on wheels across smooth concrete surfaces can induce somewhat of a rush. This sensation also factors into risky moves in street skateboarding, such as launching from gaps and sliding across the edges of obstacles. And while Ilinx is a fundamental aspect of street skating, it manifests less strongly than in Park skating.

At first sight, the Street terrain seems anything but similar to halfpipes. But upon closer inspection, significant parallels appear: the combination of a focus on single tricks together with the standardised nature of riding surfaces/courses is a major shared aspect of both Street and halfpipe riding. Much like skateboarding's previous main discipline, the Street terrain is marked by a strong ludic-agonal tendency. The Street terrain also focuses on pushing the athletic progression of the practice. It values the level of trick difficulty and makes the practice increasingly measureable, objective and comparable – all of which make it a perfect candidate for the logic behind sportisation.

Approached from a historical perspective, this also poses the question as to how much longer the athletic differentiation in street skateboarding will be able to continue. In light of the developments of halfpipe skateboarding, the logical consequence would be that a intense period of sportisation would be followed by a countermovement, ultimately leading to the downfall of the discipline in its current shape and form.[7] Traditionally, these patterns of development have always led to the progression of the entire practice.

THE STREET COUNTERMOVEMENT

The unofficial precursor of the Olympic skateboarding terrain, the Street League Skateboarding competition series, faces a growing number of critics within the skate scene. In what follows, this phenomenon will be examined as a countermovement,[8] which reveals further constitutive traits of skateboarding through its oppositional stance. As stated above, the preferred terrain within the actual skate scene can develop ahead of – or in opposition to – its competitive terrain. This is especially visible in the countermovement against sportisation, which has been thriving in the skate scene outside of the competitive context since around 2012.

---

7   Four additional factors need to be considered in this comparison to halfpipe skateboarding. First, due to the replication of actual city furniture, street skateboarding features increasing elements of mimicry. Second, the standardisation of street objects progresses in a far subtler manner; courses appear far more diverse thanks to their unique decorations. Third, participants engage in street skating without safety gear, further heightening its risk factor. And finally, the motion patterns on the street course as outlined here closely mirror those of actual street skating, especially in a plaza setting.

8   This is exactly the noticeable movement within skateboarding that Sebastian Schweer (2014) labels in this book as *heterodox skateboarding* or *heterodox skate style*.

In this context, it is not coincidental that the Street League competition format was established globally in 2010 and has been a stronger driver of skateboarding's sportisation – even stronger than the X Games – ever since (cf. Schweer, 2014, p. 123; Cantin-Brault, 2015, p. 63; Schäfer, 2017, p. 126). Cantin-Brault also identifies professional skateparks and large-scale competitions such as Street League as the two main factors behind the ongoing standardisation of skateboarding. In his line of argument, the resulting objectification, quantification and comparability of skateboarding render it as a replaceable commodity that loses its true identity in the process (cf. ibid., 2015, pp. 54-66).

In its performative expressions, the countermovement aims to elude the logical progression inherent to sportisation. The fundamentally different interpretation and forms of sense-making of street skateboarding manifest themselves in the most minute details of the practice: through a distinct set of protagonists, brands, fashions, spaces, manoeuvres, skateboards, videos, etc. (also cf. Schweer in this book). Most of the time, these particular characteristics can only be singled out and understood by adept followers of skateboarding. In terms of terrain, the countermovement finds its spatial equivalent in the currently resurging DIY-practice (cf. Peters, 2016, p. 293; Schäfer, 2017, p. 210). This terrain revolves around self-made skateboard artefacts. These 'urban interventions' appropriate public spaces by modifying existing street spots with the help of concrete, plaster and other aids. The DIY-movement also uses these tactics to unlock previously unskateable terrain as spots. These constructions, oftentimes laboriously created by a handful of riders working in unison, typically face an uncertain lifespan, as their very existence surpasses the boundaries of legality, leaving removal by the authorities as a constant threat. But this transient nature and the illegal dimension of DIY-projects also constitute a considerable part of their attraction to protagonists (cf. Peters, 2016, p. 162)[9]. At the same time, the DIY-craze is far from a novel phenomenon but harkens back to a practice from skateboarding's formative years. This practice can also be characterised as heterotopia[10] (cf. Schweer, 2014, pp. 51-64), or the "desire of the core scene for exclusive community building, a return to the traditional values of skateboard culture" (Peters, 2016, p. 155). In an exaggerated sense, these imperfect, self-styled DIY-artworks constitute an alternative plan to the pre-fabricated, artificial genteel sceneries of Street

---

9   Viewed from the perspective of Alea, the aspects of chance and luck not only factor into riding the terrain, but also the physical fate of the terrain itself.

10   Schweer (2014, pp. 51-64) refers to Foucault's concept of *Heterotopia* to DIY-skate spots. In short, these are 'other spaces' functioning according to their own rules.

League courses. In their concrete form, DIY unmistakably represents aspects of community, creativity, non-conformity, sovereignty and authenticity.

Not only the physical terrain, but all constellations of this countermovement are informed by playful-creative modes of expression, a re-cultivation of time-honoured practices, and a strong emphasis on aesthetics and authenticity in the mode of Paidia. At the same time, the movement is not to be mistaken for a mere retro version of skateboarding simply focused on performing old school tricks. In actuality, it represents more of a conglomerate of old and new riding techniques, pieced together in the tradition of sampling, thereby creating new modes of expression.[11] Far removed from the competitive arena, these practices are documented and broadcast in elaborate photo and film productions. The alternative mode of expression in these media is enhanced via stylistic tools and is distributed via international media outlets to the global scene. These specific special interest media are the most important sources of information to the skateboarding community, and the main gateways for new information (cf. Bock, 2017, pp. 37-40 and p. 181).

Currently regarded as the movement's main protagonist, Swedish professional skateboarder, artist and entrepreneur Pontus Alv has already labelled this countermovement as the underground in a 2014 magazine interview. In the interview, he cynically says thanks to the large brands for creating a clear concept of the enemy, against which like-minded skateboarders can unite:

"Thank you, Monster Energy Drink, thank you Street League, and thank you all for that. It only makes the underground grow stronger. A lot of people are converting the other way, it's a present for all of us." (Michna, 2014)

Pontus Alv had already outlined his own vision of skateboarding in the 2005 skateboarding video 'The Strongest of the Strange', marked by his signature bold aesthetics. The prominent display of DIY-skate spots in the video can be interpreted as a critique against the standardisation of skateboarding and a wake-up call to skaters to reclaim their sovereignty. Created in Malmö, Sweden, this video had a game-changing effect on the global skate scene due to its inter-

---

11 Ironically, the attempt to escape commercialisation by adopting certain practices often results in the creation of new trends. Taking into account a certain time lag, these initiatives and trends have proven to become reclaimed and oftentimes proliferated by commercial forces, illustrated by examples such as 'Red Bull DIY' (cf. Peters, 2016, p. 165).

medial proliferation (cf. Peters, 2016, p. 156; Reinhardt, 2016, p. 35; Schäfer, 2017, pp. 172-173).

Seen from the outside, it needs to be pointed out that skateboarders have consciously chosen to stand out from the 'norm' by opting for a specialised athletic activity that does not correspond to traditional organised sports and normality (cf. Atencio et al., 2018, p. 217; Colberg, 2010, p. 24; Yochim, 2010, p. 89). If we now assume that this need for differentiation is deeply embedded into the identity of skateboarding, it can also be concluded that the desire to stand out from the norm will continue to proliferate and differentiate within the skateboarding community. Placed in highly idealistic terms, this means the following. Fuelled by an idealistic impulse, the countermovement sets out to rebel against the lamentable sportisation and standardisation of skateboarding. Its participants divert the focus away from athletic skills in the sense of trick difficulty, only to find confirmation within the aesthetic expressions of self-made skateboard artefacts (DIY), supplemented by the elevation of older skateboard manoeuvres (old school tricks) and their execution (style) in an expressionistic, communal fashion style that once again visibly marks skateboarders as 'special' from the outside. Overall, it is a movement which, according to Reckwitz (2017), seems to strive for the singular, the authentic and the unique. It reaches these goals by looking back to the past to reclaim and valorise unique characteristics from skateboarding history. Following Reckwitz (2017) and perfectly compatible with his theory of modernity, we can speak of a movement that rejects the rationalisation (of sportisation) in favour of a culturalisation of 'authentic skateboarding'.[12]

SYNOPSIS OF THE OLYMPIC TERRAIN AND SPORTISATION

Summarising the reconstruction of the Olympic terrain in relation to the process of sportisation, we can identify a pattern and a certain kind of dispositive constellation of obstacles, which largely create the dynamic of athletic differentiation. On the one hand, it becomes clear that the perpetual sportisation results from the fundamental development pattern (cf. Schäfer, 2017, p. 166) of initially 'found' skateboard terrain in the urban realm (empty backyard swimming pools, skateable city furniture, etc.). This is then transformed into compact competition

---

12 To qualify this argument, it needs to be said it is difficult to scientifically prove the existence of such a countermovement, as well as to measure its scope in relation to the overall dimension of sportisation and its geographical distribution in the skateboarding scene. This would require a different methodology and extensive data collection.

courses in a controlled environment, thus allowing for the standardisation, permanent availability (in skateparks) or presentation in a competitive format. On the other hand, sportisation also significantly results from the constellation of obstacles in space, which allow for a focus on the complexity of individual manoeuvres (tricks). Following Schäfer (ibid., p. 166 and p. 176), it needs to be pointed out that the ludic-agonal quality of the practice not only results from the standardisation of the terrain – for instance in skateparks – but also the constellation of individual elements (street obstacles and rounded Park elements) in such a way that they allows for the repetitive practice of individual tricks in separate sections. No other constellation has single-handedly been a larger contributor to sportisation than the standardisation of elements and the seamless access to these micro-spaces for the constant repetition of manoeuvres.

THE SKATEBOARDING HABITUS

When it comes to the most significant landmarks and reorientations of skateboarding, there seems to be a force at work that cannot be explained in rational or economic terms. It is a force that seems to follow a different, 'sociocultural logic' within the skate scene. My thesis builds upon the assumption that the reason for the wave-like patterns in skateboarding's popularity (cf. Brooke, 1999) emerge from a deeper structural quality. This deeply rooted quality informs the entire skateboarding practice at all times and throughout all reconfigurations. I would like to call this phenomenon the habitus of skateboarding, which I will explain in following. Much like Bourdieu's initial concept of habitus to explain social behaviour, it can be applied to the transformative processes within skateboarding. For this purpose, the concept of habitus will be applied, not on the level of subjects, but as a structural analogy (cf. Bourdieu, 1984).

First, a short explanation of the concept. Originally stemming from philosophy, the term habitus was expanded by Pierre Bourdieu and Nobert Elias, who introduced it to the terminology of sociology in the 1960s. Habitus serves as an explanatory model for social behaviour and is increasingly being used in an interdisciplinary manner. In a social context, habitus consists of everything that defines a human being in itself. It structures all actions while facilitating and prohibiting certain patterns of behaviour. "The habitus is a structure, determined by the history of a person." (Hasselbusch, 2014, p. 44) Habitus takes effect from the inside-out on human behaviour, whilst behaviour has an effect from the outside-in. Habitus is created by a person's experiences and can be modified throughout

one's lifespan; childhood and adolescence have proven to be especially formative periods (cf. Bourdieu, 1993, p. 113 and p. 120; Hradil, 2001, p. 90).
When applying the concept of habitus to skateboarding, I replace the individual human in this framework by the movement practice of skateboarding.
Similar to how the origin of human beings as social entities during childhood
and adolescence continues to determine the rest of their development, the practice of skateboarding is equally strongly influenced by its origins.[13] The practice
is constantly brought into relation with and is confronted by its past. Everything
that the subcultural iteration of skateboarding can aspire to be, is already structurally pre-defined, because "the habitus is like a living system: flexible and
highly adaptable, but at the same maintaining the identity of the subject" (Krais
& Gebauer, 2017). This description can be universally applied to skateboarding,
as the practice is constantly subject to dynamic processes of change, such as
sportisation, and is being portrayed in different lights, all the while maintaining
its own subcultural, non-conformist identity. The habitus is the reason

"[…] why an agent's whole set of practices […] are both systematic, inasmuch as they are
the product of the application of identical […] schemes, and systematically distinct from
the practices constituting another life-style" (Bourdieu, 1984, p. 166).

Applied to skateboarding, this statement could be interpreted as follows. The
habitus of skateboarding is the reason that the whole set of practices of the manifestations of motion patterns in Street, Park, etc. are the result of applications of
identical development patterns. All of these patterns simultaneously exhibit a
systematic character. This differentiates them systematically from other movement practices. This exact pattern becomes apparent in the dynamic process,
meaning that in the subcultural framework, skateboarding creates practices that
partially become reclaimed by commercialisation, but ultimately manage to
break free in order to unlock new playing fields. Consequently, this exhibits the
same stereotypic development cycle that continues to differentiate skateboarding

---

13 For clarification, it needs to be stated that skateboarding first emerged in the 1950s
    (Borden, 2019, p. 3; Hälbich, 2008; Schäfer, 2017, p. 56). But it took until the mid-
    1970s for surfing as the 'core sport' to infuse skateboarding with its 'aggressive riding
    style' by providing a fundamental 'stylistic element' for the riding practice, which has
    remained a defining force on a subcultural level until today and amounts to much of
    its uniqueness (cf. Peters, 2016, p. 299; Schäfer, 2017, p. 234). Vertical skateboarding
    also took until the 1970s to develop and presents the starting point for this reconstruc-
    tion of the terrain.

from other sports. The same systematic nature becomes evident in the following quote: "The habitus is not only a structuring structure, which organizes practices and the perception of practices, but also a structured structure" (Bourdieu, 1984, p. 166).

Applied to skateboarding, this statement implies that the habitus not only determines the structure of skateboarding but is also determined by its historical development. If we consider skateboarding's subcultural roots to be its origins, embedded into the structure, and the process of sportisation as an adaptive feat of skateboarding, then the historical analysis of the practice reveals the following. As soon as skateboarding veers too far into the realm of 'sports', the skate scene begins to reconfigure at a certain point in order to pursue other directions that elude sportisation in their symbolism. This 'inner corrective force' of the skate scene can be interpreted as a structural characteristic of the habitus, which continues to exert significant influence on the behaviours of the scene as a structural force. The importance of this nonconformist and subcultural quality can hardly be overstated, then, as it occurred in the formative years of both major categories – transition and street skating.

CONCLUSION

In the debate on the sportisation versus culturalisation of skateboarding – somewhere between sports and art – we also need to keep in mind that athletic progression has always been an existential aspect of skateboarding as a movement practice. However, in the competitive format and terrain as a ludic-agonal expression, this tends to increasingly conflict with other constitutive characteristics of skateboarding's habitus, namely: self-determination, non-conformity, unpredictability, risk, creativity, authenticity, diversity and community.

The analysis has demonstrated that the competitive terrain tends to be largely rooted within the skate scene, but this doesn't necessarily represent the authentic participation by the scene. Following this state of affairs, it would be plausible that the increasing sportisation of skateboarding because of the Olympic Games would lead to a split into two spheres: a world of economised, spectacularised competitions and a world of culturalisation. But separating the skateboard community into two opposite camps – the *competition skaters* and the *agents of the countermovement* – according to this logic would be an act of oversimplification. Keeping the concept of habitus in mind, it is important to note that almost all of the elite competitors on the Street League Skateboarding circuit take it upon themselves to head out on self-directed missions to create authentic videos filmed in the streets – outside of their appearances at major contests.[14] These for-ays into the urban realm serve to produce "manifestos of self" (cf. Schäfer 2015, p. 149). These displays of skateboarding on original terrain and the associated symbolic meaning (subcultural, non-conformist and creative) form a sociocul-tural connection to the core of the scene.[15] According to Schwier (2016), this self-medialisation can serve to earn a sense of belonging as well as "expanding one's sub-cultural capital" (ibid. p. 115).[16] This type of capital is composed al-most solely of documented manoeuvres performed in 'real' street spaces (cf. Dupont, 2014, p. 565). Video documentations in authentic settings (street: found spaces; transition: found spaces and expressive skatepark terrains) generally hold the highest relevance when it comes to building acceptance and reputation within the skate scene:

"While skaters who do well in skate contests will likely be well compensated, their contest winnings must be supplemented by video parts in order to ensure their reputation. Skate-boarding contests are about performing the tricks you know you can land; for a video part skaters push themselves to do the most creative, most challenging tricks they can imag-ine." (Snyder, 2017, p. 171)

It is thus the video footage accumulated into subcultural capital – not competi-tion rankings – that defines the status of a rider within the scene and thereby de-

---

14 The use of 'found' spaces for skateboarding still triggers frequent conflicts with the law due to noise complaints, vandalism, trespassing and overall traffic endangerment (cf. Wouter, 2014, p. 55). These illegal exploits coincide with a criminalisation of skateboarding, which can also be seen as nonconformist behaviour and is, in part, celebrated by the scene as rebellious and aggressive behaviour and tends to be consid-ered accordingly by outside observers.

15 It needs to be noted that the production of moving images on skateboarding is not en-tirely free of branded imagery. Its contents can also exhibit a ludic-agonal tendency in the sense of a 'trophy hunt for stair count records' (cf. Schäfer, 2017, p. 211) that would resonate with many 'competition skateboarder'.

16 In accordance with Bourdieu's field theory (cf. Fuchs-Heinritz & König, 2014), au-thor Sarah Thornton (1995) has proven that subcultural music scenes are far from be-ing non-hierarchical, but in fact are marked by hierarchies structured informally by 'subcultural capital'. The adaptation of this kind of capital along Bourdieu's theory to subcultural communities was also verified by Julia Reinecke (2012) for the street art scene, which stands in close connection to the skateboarding scene (cf. ibid., p. 131).

termines the market value of individual skateboarders from the perspective of prospective sponsors (cf. Peters, 2016, p. 239; Snyder, 2017, p. 171).[17]

The habitus of skateboarding thereby offers an explanation for the fact that self-medialisation is also a constant currency among riders participating in large-scale competitions – despite the generous economic incentives for participating in these events (prize money and marketing for athlete sponsorships).

The sociocultural ties to found spaces, as presented in this analysis, come with far-reaching consequences. What is implied is that every single ambitious street skateboarder must, at one point, leave the boundaries of the skatepark and head out into public space to amass the necessary subcultural capital. In that light, skateparks would serve as more than a mere "segregation of skateboard riding" (Peters, 2016, p. 153) or a form of "taming" (Cantin-Brault, 2015, p. 57) (street) skateboarding or training grounds for competition skating. They also serve as incubators for the targeted preparation for authentic street skating (cf. Vivoni, 2018, p. 125). As the sportisation of skateboarding commences, this socioculturally rooted aspect – deeply embedded into skateboarding's very structure – serves as an implied protective mechanism for the scene. It serves to protect skateboarding from a complete assimilation with the performance sports logic inherent to eventisation and sportisation. As a converse argument, an 'inflation' – or 'devaluation' – of authentic documentations of skateboarding (in photos and videos) as its main cultural currency would have a devastating effect on the identity – especially in terms of self-determination – of the practice.

OUTLOOK

As my terrain analysis has exemplified through the countermovement and the behaviour among competition skaters, the skateboard scene is finding manifold ways for dealing with the processes of sportisation and commercialisation. These strategies include the emergence of a new type of rider, whose aim lies in building a generalised skillset as opposed to advancing the difficulty of tricks in one discipline. The Park terrain, as an antagonist to the standardisation of skateboarding, emphasises creativity and thereby limits the linear-athletic progression in order to harken back to the predispositioned movement patterns of its forma-

---

17 I have arrived at this assessment based on my five years experience as a sponsored professional skateboarder and my 14 years working experience in marketing, which includes the scouting, recommendation, selection and coaching of sponsored skateboarders for endemic skateboard brands and those outside the skateboard industry.

tive years. Park skaters, who prefer riding without the use of protective gear and thereby accept a high degree of risk-taking, are proving their talent for improvisation. These riders risk their physical health to a large degree just to escape the mandates of sportisation and predictability. Other pro skateboarders choose to supplement their contest participation by documenting their tricks on handrails and stairs in the built environment to signal their authenticity and connectedness to the scene. Meanwhile, we note a countermovement within the scene that, in response to the pressures of sportisation, is cultivating time-honoured practices and thereby continues to draw more and more followers.

As it appears, no practice within the skate scene is immune to the effects of commercialisation (cf. Schweer, 2014, p. 169; Schwier, 2016, p. 114). From the perspective of brands, both the capitalist exploitation logic of sportisation as well as the distinct positioning in the oppositional countermovement could prove interesting opportunities for marketing. In cases where brand name manufacturers invest budgets into supporting – or enabling – scene efforts and initiatives against sportisation, the forces of commercialisation could even work against the process of sportisation and potentially unlock alternative brand positions. Contrary to wide-spread arguments, it is therefore important to understand that the often negative connotations of the commercialisation of skateboarding are not by default an identity-changing factor. It must rather be understood as an enhancer of certain aspects. The central question, then, remains: will the skate scene be able to use these economic incentives without incurring an enduring asymmetry at the expense of its habitus?

In conclusion, a likely future for professional skateboarders is twofold. First, there are opportunities for the protagonist of sportisation, who enters competitions as an object of commercialisation to secure economic incentives in their own interest, while simultaneously acting as a subject of the skate scene by accumulating subcultural capital via self-stylisation in the media. Second, one could speak of the protagonist of 'culturalisation', who initiates self-directed (sub)cultural projects, oftentimes financed by sponsor funds, and thereby indirectly acts as an object of commercialisation and medium for brand messages.[18] By following these patterns of action delineated in this argument, the skateboarders as protagonists of commercialisation are still able to maintain their 'true identity' both in an athletic and cultural sense.

This scenario of 'both at the same time' instead of 'either or' is also in line with the paradigmatic course of action established by Reckwitz for the new mid-

---

18 This type of sponsoring follows the principle of a relationship between artists and patrons.

dle class of later modernity (cf. 2017, p. 301). The skateboarders described here embody, at least partially, the singular lifestyle as a 'symbiosis between romanticism and bourgeoisie' (ibid., p. 305). Here, there is the combination of the romantic ideal of self-realisation (skateboarding as an artistic movement practice and subcultural practice) and bourgeoisie value perceptions (skateboarding as a professional sport and career path), in which skateboarders also weigh factors such as income and financial security.

But as a fair warning, we need to state that such a prognosis must be taken with caution due to the fundamental dynamics and unpredictability inherent to skateboarding.

With regards to skateboarding's terrains, one of the main themes for future research would be the ways in which the design of public skateparks could be negotiated at the tense intersection between Olympic sports funding and the scene's sociocultural interests. As an additional line of research, the sportisation of skateboarding could be scientifically explored in the context of intermediality.

REFERENCES

Atencio, M. & Beal, B. (2016). The 'legitimate' skateboarder. Politics of privatepublic skateboarding spaces. In: Lombard, K.-J. (Ed.), *Skateboarding: Subcultures, Sites and Shifts* (pp. 108-120). New York: Routledge.

Atencio, M., Beal, B., Wright, E. M. & McClain, Z. (2018). *Moving Boarders: Skateboarding and the Changing Landscape of Urban Youth Sports*. Fayetteville: The University of Arkansas Press.

Beal, B. (2013). *Skateboarding: The Ultimate Guide*. Santa Barbara, California: Greenwood.

Beaver, D. T. (2012). By the Skaters, for the Skaters. The DIY Ethos of the Roller Derby Revival. *Journal of Sports and Social Issues* 36, 1, 25-47.

Blümlein, J. & Vogel, D. (2018). *Skateboarding is not a Fashion: The Illustrated History of Skateboard Apparal 1950s to 1984*. Berkeley, CA: Gingko Press.

Bock, K. (2017). *Kommunikative Konstruktion von Szenekultur. Skateboarding als Sinnstiftung und Orientierung im Zeitalter der Digitalisierung*. Weinheim, Basel: Beltz Juventa.

Borden, I. (2001). *Skateboarding, Space and the City*. Oxford: Berg Publishers.

Borden, I. (2019). *Skateboarding and the City – a Complete History*. London: Bloomsbury.

Bourdieu, P. (1984). *Distinction: A Social Critique of the Judgement of Taste*. Abingdon, Oxford: Routledge.

Bourdieu, P. (1993). *Sozialer Sinn. Kritik der theoretischen Vernunft*. Frankfurt am Main: Suhrkamp.

Brooke, M. (1999). *The Concrete Wave*. Los Angeles, Toronto: Warwick.

Butz, K. (2012). *Grinding California. Culture and Corporeality in American Skate Punk*. Bielefeld: transcript.

Caillois, R. (1982). *Die Spiele und die Menschen. Maske und Rausch*. Frankfurt am Main, Wien, Berlin: Ullstein.

Cantin-Brault, A. (2015). The Reification of Skateboarding. *International Journal of Science Culture and Sport* 3, 1, 54-66.

Colberg, T. J. (2010). *The Skateboarding Art*. Washington: Lulu Press.

Dupont, T. (2014). From Core to Consumer. The Informal Hierarchy of the Skateboard Scene. *Journal of Contemporary Ethnography*, 43, 5, 556-581.

Fuchs-Heinritz, W. & König, A. (2014). *Pierre Bourdieu: Eine Einführung*. Konstanz: utb.

Gebauer, G., Alkemeyer, T., Boschert, B., Flick, U. & Schmidt, R. (2004). *Treue zum Stil. Die aufgeführte Gesellschaft*. Bielefeld: transcript.

Hasselbusch, I. (2014). *Norbert Elias und Pierre Bourdieu im Vergleich. Eine Untersuchung zu Theorieentwicklung, Begrifflichkeit und Rezeption*. Pädagogische Hochschule Karlsruhe: Manuskript.

Hälbich, F. (2008). *Die Geschichte des Skateboardings*. Hamburg: Diplomica Verlag.

Hradil, S. (2001). *Soziale Ungleichheit in Deutschland*. Wiesbaden: VS Verlag.

Krais, B. & Gebauer, B. (2017). *Habitus*. Bielefeld: transcript.

Le Breton, D. (1995). *Lust am Risiko. Von Bungee-jumping, U-Bahn-surfen und anderen Arten, das Schicksal herauszufordern*. Frankfurt am Main: dipa-Verlag.

Michna, I. (2014). The Pontus Alv Interview. (http://www.jenkemmag.com/home/2014/02/17/pontus-alv-interview/; accessed on October 21, 2017).

Mokulys, G. & Nawrocki, T. (1991). *Halfpipe Skateboard Book*. Münster: Monster Verlag.

Mountain, L. (2019). Lance Mountain – The Nine Club With Chris Roberts – Episode 127. (https://www.youtube.com/watch?v=lPG1xvG-flA; accessed on Janurary 29, 2019).

Reckwitz, A. (2017). *Die Gesellschaft der Singularitäten: Zum Strukturwandel der Moderne*. Berlin: Suhrkamp.

Reinecke, J. (2012). *Street-Art. Eine Subkultur zwischen Kunst und Kommerz*. Bielefeld: transcript.

Reinhardt, G. (2016). Eine gefühlte Geschichte von Skateboarding. In: Raben 001. *Projektdokumentation 2013-2016* (pp. 1-41). Kassel: Howls from the Margin.

Peters, C. (2016). *Skateboarding – Ethnographie einer urbanen Praxis*. Münster: Waxmann.

Schäfer, V. (2015). Sport mit den Mitteln des Pop. Skateboard-Videos: Bewegungslernen, Vergemeinschaftung und Jugendmarketing. *Sport und Gesellschaft – Sport and Society* 12, 2, 149-170.

Schäfer, V. (2017). *Dogtown und X-Games – Körper, Räume, Zeichen: Zur wirklichen Geschichte des Skateboardfahrens*. Carl von Ossietzky Universität Oldenburg. Unpublished disseration.

Schweer, S. (2014). *Skateboarding. Zwischen urbaner Rebellion und neoliberalem Selbstentwurf*. Bielefeld: transcript.

Schwier, J. (2016). Die Sportshow. Zur Eventisierung von Bewegungs- und Sportkulturen. In Dust, M., Lohmann, I. & Steffens, G. (Red.), *Jahrbuch für Pädagogik 2016. Events und Edutainment* (pp. 107-117). Frankfurt/Main, Berlin, Bern, Bruxelles, New York, Oxford, Wien: Peter Lang.

Schwinghammer, S. (2016). Justin Regan about the Olympics. There are a lot of speculations about what skateboarding in the Olympics will be like. (http://www.soloskatemag.com/justin-regan-about-the-olympics; accessed on October 18, 2017).

Stern, M. (2010). *Stil-Kulturen – Performative Konstellationen von Technik, Spiel und Risiko in neuen Sportpraktiken*. Bielefeld: transcript.

Striler, A. R. (2011). *X Play Nation of Action Sports Game Changers*. San Diego: Striler Publishing.

Snyder, G. J. (2017). *Skateboarding LA. Inside professional street skateboarding*. New York: New York University Press.

Thornton, S. (1995). *Club Cultures – Music, Media and Subcultural Capital*. Cambridge: Polity Press.

Vansparkseries.com. (2017). Vans Park Series FAQs. (http://www.vanspark series.com/about; accessed on October 18, 2017).

Vivoni, F. (2018). City of Social Control. Skateboarding and the Regulation of Public Space. In Butz, K. & Peters, C. (Eds.), *Skateboard Studies* (pp. 110-127). London: Koenig Books.

Whitley, P. (2009). *Public Skatepark Development Guide*. Portland: Skaters for Public Skateparks, International Association of Skateboard Companies, and Tony Hawk Foundation.

Wouter, M. (2014). *Stadträume: Skateräume. Handlungsempfehlungen zum Umgang mit Skateboarding in der Stadtplanung.* TU Dortmund. Master's Thesis.

Yochim, E. C. (2010). *Skate Life. Re-Imagining White Masculinity.* Ann Arbor: University of Michigan Press.

Skatepark Worlds

Constructing Communities and Building Lives

Iain Borden

Over the last two decades, a veritable skatepark renaissance has been underway. Fuelled by the popularity of street-skating, the X Games, Tony Hawk's Pro Skater video game (Activision, 1999), new legislation reducing liability claims, a slew of magazines and the emergent internet, skateboarding was on rise. By 2000, over 180 skateparks of various sizes, complexity and ownership had already opened across the US, while expert constructors like Airspeed, California Skateparks, Dreamland, Grindline, PTR/Placed To Ride, Purkiss Rose, SITE, Team Pain and Wormhoudt were also appearing.[1]

Today, similar expertise exists globally, from Convic in Australia, to Canvas, Freestyle, Gravity, Maverick and Wheelscape in the UK, or Constructo and The Edge in France, Vertical in Switzerland, Mystic in the Czech Republic, G Ramps and Lndskt in Germany and Spectrum and New Line in Canada. The results can be impressive. "To say that Oregon's Newberg and Lincoln City skateparks are masterpieces is not an exaggeration", asserts Jocko Weyland (2002, p. 318).

"These works put their builders in league with artists like Richard Serra, Robert Smithson and James Turrell: the parks are beautiful environments, awesome to look at and, on some level, superior to sculpture because they combine aestheticism with athletic functionalism." (Weyland, 2002, p. 318)

---

1   Sections of this chapter are also contained in Borden, I. (2019). *Skateboarding and the City: A Complete History*. London: Bloomsbury.

Yet skateparks offer far more than fantastical forms and exciting riding surfaces. In particular, different users, whether from constructing, operating, riding or just hanging out at skateparks. But this very distinction can lead to occasional disquiet, particularly with non-skaters, some of whom exhibit what Taylor and Khan (2016) call a "moral teenaphobic panic" over young people socialising together, and so perceive skateparks as having negative impacts through injuries, noise, graffiti and disorder (cf. Woolley & Johns, 2001). Even liberal-minded champions of vernacular landscapes like Jackson (1984, pp. 130-132) have voiced concerns. "Noisy, deliberately artificial in its man-made topography, used by a boisterous and undisciplined public, and dedicated to violent expenditure of energy", worried Jackson, for whom the skatepark "repudiates and makes a mockery of everything the word *park* has stood for" (ibid., p. 130).

Given the unfortunate prevalence of such misguided opinions, skateparks are unsurprisingly often located in marginal sites, placed out-of-town next to the recycling bins, car park or other low-quality site. Yet concrete skateparks actually produce similarly low levels of noise as playgrounds, one Australian study found no correlation with graffiti incidence, and still other New Zealand and UK studies have actually identified reductions in crime after skatepark construction; at the UK's Dorchester, elderly residents and police alike noted the huge community benefits of their centrally-located skatepark, including a forty-five per cent fall in antisocial behaviour (cf. Taylor & Marais, 2011; McFadyen & Longhurst, 2014; BBC, 2014). In short, skateparks typically offer distinct social, cultural, health and even economic advantages, often stretching far beyond the act of skateboarding.

In this chapter I explore these aspects of skateboard culture, showing how skateparks themselves can create new forms of community, and also how social enterprises can use skateboarding and skateparks to enable social change at challenging locations worldwide.

CONSTRUCTING COMMUNITIES

Some claim that the unstructured nature of skateboarding (in contrast to the rules, training and supervision of regular sports) leads to antisocial violence, public nuisance, vandalism and substance abuse: "If you let the skaters", opined one Seattle objector, "you are just opening our neighborhood to pushers, pimps, paedophiles, and prostitutes" (Carr, 2012, p. 71). Yet such outbursts are typically based on false perceptions rather than actual evidence. Indeed, to the contrary, and as numerous studies demonstrate, skateparks help build adolescents' autonomy, social skills, self-confidence, friendships and peer-group status. Encouraging skaters to learn about cooperation, design, negotiation and aiding others, plus gaining a sense of ownership, belonging and responsibility, are key features of skateparks (cf. Bradley, 2010; Carr, 2012; Jones & Graves, 2000; Goldberg & Shooter, 2007).

Problems do of course arise, for, as Daniel Turner and John Carr have shown, like any public space skateparks are areas of negotiation, where 'noise, low-level mischief, and reproduction of patriarchy are often inseparable from developing community, the building of self-esteem, and the creation of positive life paths'. Very occasionally, conflicts are irresolvable, as when skaters who repeatedly transgress skatepark rules (typically ranging from helmet-wearing, session times and entrance fees to bans on smoking, alcohol and abuse) are excluded or simply boycott the facility. In such instances, skateparks may lose some of the very people they were most intended to reach (cf. Turner, 2013a, pp. 189-210 and 211-214; Carr, 2012, p. 72).

Community Scenes

Nonetheless, positive qualities are substantial, and indeed skateparks readily answer Putnam's plea for less of the "civic broccoli" which is "good for you but unappealing" and more "ingenious combinations of values and fun" (Putnam, 2000, p. 406). For example, Sendra (2015, pp. 820-836), following the philosopher Gilles Deleuze, argues that less-regulated and free-access skateparks like London's Stockwell operate as urban "unbound points", offering zones of creativity and resistance. In more practical terms, as the Montreal-based study by Dumas & Laforest (2009) shows, skateparks not only lead to fewer injuries than street-skating or indeed mainstream sports, but also provide "opportunity structures" for enhancing skaters' social, psychological and physical well-being; another Canadian research project concluded that skateparks were more than just places to skate, being realms where riders were "welcomed, accepted and encouraged" (Shannon & Werner, 2008, pp. 39-58). Similarly British skateparks in rural and deprived locations help build social capital, as places where "teenagers actively contribute to shaping their communities" (Weller, 2006, pp. 557-574). Local skaters often back up these academic assertions, as with Kevin and Hollywood, two Michigan skaters interviewed by Robert Petrone. "For some of these kids it's a second home", explained Kevin of his local Franklin skatepark. "This is my way to get away from everything, from my home stress, work stress. I come up here every night. Meet up with my friends and skateboard a little." Or as Hollywood simply stated, "if I didn't have this skate park, I'd be in jail" (Petrone, 2008, p. 94).

Clearly then, as Dumas & Laforest (2009) state, skateparks can be "favourable spaces for attracting youth to safe and active lifestyles", and many local authorities worldwide have wisely concurred; for example, Queensland, Australia, considers a skatepark to be "a hub for community life" and "a catalyst for healthy community life in which young and old socialize, have fun, develop new skills, make new friends, hang out and much more" (ibid., pp. 19-34; Bradley, 2010, p. 290).

These beneficial effects are in part due to the act of skateboarding itself, and partly due to social groupings, but also due to changes in recent skatepark design. In 2000 Jones & Graves (2000, p. 290) criticised six 1990s Oregon skateparks as being "inside the bowl" designs rather than community spaces. Similarly, Chiu (2009, pp. 38-39) noted criticisms of New York's Hudson River skatepark for being "like a cage" and a "forced environment" with strict opening hours, plus, when compared to street-skatespots, less authenticity. But by around 2010, skateparks were becoming less dangerous and more welcoming of skaters of different ages, genders and backgrounds. Besides their more varied riding terrains, skateparks now also often include water fountains, lighting, seating, tables, barbecue and hang-out areas, while artful landscaping, avant-garde architecture and interior design, skate shops, cafés and even Wi-Fi are increasingly common. Integration within larger urban design and landscape projects can also occur. Chicago's substantial 2,000 m2 Burnham skatepark nestles alongside a nature prairie, bird sanctuaries, water trail, bicycle paths, playground, marina and beach house, while New Zealand's Marine Parade skatepark in Napier is accompanied by a splash park and concert venue, so creating "a public space that belongs to all of Napier and beyond" (Vivioni, 2010, pp. 55-60; www.chicagoparkdistrict.com; www.napier.govt.nz).

The best skateparks, then, are far more than just isolated and exclusive terrains accessible only by courageous males. For example, although undoubtedly some women have felt excluded from skateparks, this is not always the case; one Vancouver skatepark explored by Kelly, Pomerantz & Currie (2008) has offered a marginal space for its Park Gang riders to enact political expression, first challenging and then gaining respect from male counterparts, while also developing alternative female identities. Similar qualities were also evident in 2010s Ontario, where newcomers frequented skateparks in order to gradually enter the skate scene, while community-oriented skateparks in public parks, and which attract a wide range of rider abilities and ages, can prove more attractive to female skaters (cf. Harris, 2011, pp. 117-132; Carr, 2016).

Many skateparks worldwide today work hard at fostering this kind of atmosphere, using female-only and age-specific sessions along with numerous jams, Halloween evenings, graffiti and DJ workshops, school-related projects and other events to encourage accessibility and sense of belonging. "It's not just a skatepark", explains the manager of Dundee's Factory Skatepark, "it's a twenty-first century community facility" (Turner, 2013b, p. 1254). Other places, such as the DIY Parasite skatepark in New Orleans, reflect transgressive behaviour through their semi-illegal construction but also, through their collaborative nature, encourage positive social behaviour and individual development (cf. Edwards, 2015, p. 45).

Age variety is another significant feature of many current skateparks, and besides the most commonplace teenagers, skaters under ten-years-old are also prevalent (typically accompanied by parents), and sometimes receive lessons. Much older skaters are also frequently drawn to skateparks; a 2015 survey by the Skaters Over 50 Facebook group showed that sixty-two per cent of these riders preferred skatepark and transition skate terrains, compared to just twenty-two per cent for street and sixteen per cent for freestyle, slalom and downhill (cf. www.facebook.com/groups/skatersover50/permalink/756733984435970/).

For example, the $2.8 million 6,000 m2 Denver skatepark is situated near the city's downtown, offering early morning and flood-lit evening sessions to cater for working-age skaters. "It turns out we had a huge unmet need for skating", acknowledged Parks & Recreation officer Leslie Roper, "and we're very happy with the result" (Harnik & Gentles, 2009, pp. 34-38).

Neoliberal Training and Hybrid Economies

Over the last decade, one common strain at skateparks has been the development of stewardship programmes, where young adults learn to procure, operate, monitor and maintain their facilities, as well as to teach learner riders. Apart from the obvious benefits in maintaining terrain and encouraging new riders, those involved gain a sense of pride, achievement and civic responsibility, and so become active and respected community members. According to Peter Whitley (2009) of the Tony Hawk Foundation, the process of petitioning for a skatepark, for example, often builds substantial civic engagement, during which "skateboarders go from getting tickets and having their boards confiscated to being on a first-name basis with city council members" (Edwards, 2015). Once a skatepark is constructed, even deeper community ties can be formed; at the tough working-class Franklin skatepark in Michigan, studied by Petrone (2008,

p. 98 and 118), skaters self-police graffiti, weed-smoking, litter and loud music, and even organise counter-vandalism measures.

As Daniel Turner (2013b; 2017), Ocean Howell (2008, p. 476) and others highlight, through this kind of 'civilizing process' urban managers use skateparks to nurture certain character traits in youngsters, principally "personal responsibility, self-sufficiency, and entrepreneurialism", all of these being qualities which equate directly with neoliberal values (cf. Beal et al., 2017). As such, skateparks can also be part of a larger process, in which the relationship between citizens and the state changes from one of 'entitlement' to 'contractualism' – skaters get skateparks not because they deserve them, but because they earn them through appropriate social behaviour and contributions (cf. Howell, 2008, p. 475).

Issues of commerce and consumption can also be at play, as with the heavy marketing benefits readily discernible at Berlin's Nike SB Shelter and London's House of Vans (2014). Occupying 2,500 m2 of Victorian railway arches, House of Vans integrates free-access skateboarding (bowl and street course) alongside art, music and film facilities (cf. Borden, 2016). Operating as a continuous advertisement for its billion-dollar backer, the nuanced design (by Tim Greatorex, Pete Hellicar and Marc Churchill) and the wide programme of activities are far more generous than the kind of corporate annexation of skateboarding of which some international brands have been accused. It is also a step beyond the kind of corporate sponsorship (Mountain Dew, Pepsi etc.) which, according to Tony Hawk (2015), supports professionals yet still remains outside of core skate values.

House of Vans, then, marks a shift away from the outright opposition between, on the one hand, the 'authentic' realms of street-level, spontaneous and unfunded actions and, on the other hand, the 'inauthentic' world of spectacularized, controlled and commercial projects. Instead, House of Vans is what Lessig (2008) has termed a 'hybrid' economy, operating simultaneously as a commercial economy for financial gain and as a sharing economy for collaborative and collective benefit. In short, House of Vans shows how some skateparks might combine profit, media and control with credibility, performance and disorder.

Tourism and Regeneration

Beyond Vans-style marketing, wider skatepark ambitions may also include tourism and even urban regeneration. "Skateparks are no longer seen as a grudging way to deal with the so-called problem of skateboarders", explains Kyle Duvall "Instead, cities have begun to see them as assets, even showpieces" (Duvall,

2016). Hence alongside neighbourhood facilities, some cities appreciate how skateparks appeal at wider regional, national or even international levels, and so nest within wider planning goals.

One of the first cities to understand this possibility was Louisville, Kentucky, whose Extreme Park (2002) was partly aimed at attracting new visitors. Costing $2 million, the Metro Government's 3,700 m2 Wormhoudt-designed skatepark boasted a street course, vert-ramp, several bowls, full-pipe and flood-lit 24/7 opening. The booster intention was successful, and, explained Mayor David Armstrong, Louisville's reputation changed from "a sleepy little southern town" to "an exciting, youthful extreme town". A $2.2 million reconfiguration (2015) replaced some of the original features with a new bowl, street course, flow-bowl and full-pipe with dramatic upper perforations. Similarly, the SITE-designed 6,200 m2 Black Pearl skatepark (2005) in the Cayman Islands was constructed both for locals and to boost tourism; Tony Hawk has described it as a "monstrous" ridable landscape that takes over a week to explore (cf. Hawk & Hawk, 2010, pp. 134-136; see also www.sitedesigngroup.com).

Also with an eye on tourism is Denmark's $5.5 million indoor-outdoor 'Streetdome' in Haderslev, designed by Rune Glifberg, Ebbe Lykke and CEBRA architects. Constructed by Grindline, the 4,500 m2 facility contains a grass-domed weather-proof arena, as well as provision for kayaking, music, parkour and climbing. This "cultural and experiential powerhouse" acts as a "facilitator" where "urban sport, street culture and youthful souls all meet together" (www. streetdome.dk). A similar multi-arts programme drives Spain's Factoria Joven ('youth factory') in Merida, where in 2011 architects SelgasCano combined skateboarding, climbing and cycling functions, along with provisions for computing, dance, theatre, video and graffiti, all located amid brightly-coloured architecture (cf. Katz, 2011).

As these kinds of project suggest, skateboarding can generate significant revenues and attract new facilities to its host venues. For example, spectacular events like the X Games may not necessarily aid local skaters, but Los Angeles nonetheless benefitted to the tune of $50 million for its 2010 X Games, while, for hosting the final round of the Vans Park Series in 2016, Malmö successfully negotiated for Vans to provide the permanent Kroksbäck skatepark, which also acts as a social space for low-income housing residents (cf. Bradley, 2013; Wright, 2016). And on an even larger scale, and perhaps unique in skateboarding history is the world's first multi-storey concrete skatepark, an 'urban sports centre' funded by the Roger de Haan Charitable Trust and in 2018 under construction in Folkestone, UK. Unlike typical out-of-town sites, this skatepark sits within a masterplan to transform a run-down yet central area into a sustainable creative quarter, and so will help to both encourage youth to stay in Folkestone and to attract new residents. The skatepark – designed by Guy Hollaway Architects and Maverick, with some advisory input from myself – is appropriately ambitious, intersecting innovative architectural design, three storeys of fluid ridable surfaces and substantial community facilities.[2] Here, skateboarding, design artistry, community engagement and urban regeneration are all at play.

BUILDING LIVES

Skateboarding's sharing culture, as explored by Paul O'Connor (2016), has an intrinsic rhythm of inclusivity. This ranges from a simple gesture like catching a skater's wayward board, to passing on equipment to impoverished riders, and, as we shall see, acts of charity and benevolence. In addition, skateboarding offers a 'prefigurative' politics which, in its practices and ethos, embodies the world its wishes to create. This is a significant extension to my previous emphasis on skateboarding's critique of capitalism, namely that, alongside skateboarding as a performative critique of capitalism's values and tenets, so skateboarding culture suggests participation and inclusion as ways to live in the world (cf. Borden, 2001, pp. 173-260). This prefigurative politics, stresses O'Connor (2016, p. 41), is therefore not focused solely on appropriating urban space, but also contains a 'transformative edge' which seeks to preserve "the values, attitudes, and knowledge" (ibid., p. 41) of skateboarding.

How then might this occur? Skateboarding, it has been frequently argued, can potentially challenge barriers of class, race, age and gender (cf. Borden, 2019, Chapter 3). Its qualities of friendship, sharing and independence, as well as its non-hierarchical organisation, opposition to rules, cynicism towards commercial exploitation, and embracing of both failure and achievement, all impart skateboarding with a different attitude to urban living than one of anonymised, self-centred society. But if this is skateboarding's internal logic, how might it move outside of itself, and so influence or aid others?

Skateboarders have often sought to raise funds for charities and special causes. Thousands of such acts have been undertaken, and to cite but a few, Jack Smith has crossed the USA several times to generate funds for medical charities, David Cornthwaite's 3,621 mile expedition from Perth to Brisbane during 2006 and 2007 generated £20,000, in 1994 'TransWorld' launched Board AID to fo-

---

2 See the article 'Guy Hollaway Plans to Put Folkestone on the Map' in the Magazine *Dezeen* (15. May 2015), www.dezeen.com.

cus on teenagers with AIDS, and in 2005 the 'Lords of Dogtown Art Collection' exhibition supported Boarding for Breast Cancer (cf. O'Connor, 2016, p. 37).

Beyond these substantial acts of fund-raising, yet another benefit of skateboarding rests in its relationship to education, learning and wider social enterprise, and it is these areas that we now turn.

Education and Learning

As Petrone's study of Michigan skateparks demonstrates, learning to skate is simultaneously collaborative and individualised, anti-competitive and aspirational, and trans-generational and embodied, and so is often apprentice-like in its procedures. It is also dependent on the skater actually wishing to participate and on a range of teaching modes. In particular, skaters can be both mentors and learners, thus allowing every participant to make original contributions to communities (cf. Petrone, 2008, pp. 167-168 und pp. 227-235). This suggests that skateboarding's mode of learning is inherently flexible and open, consequently extending opportunities for assimilation, acquisition and understanding, and clearly these attributes also have the potential to be highly relevant for education (cf. O'Connor, 2016).

How might this work in practice? Sometimes, as Russ Howell (2008) and Ben Wixon (2009) have both argued, this can mean skateboard riding itself being directly inserted into school curricula (cf. Gillogly, 1976). Indeed, Maine's Gould Academy and Malmö's Bryggeriet Gymnasium both boast indoor skateparks which 'blur the boundaries between school and leisure', with Bryggeriet even extending across its curriculum the formative assessment educational approach of Dylan William and the equivalent skateboarding ethos of constantly checking one's own development (cf. www.bryggeriet.org).

Nor is this just about a few schools. In the 2010s, New Zealand's OnBoard Skate has promoted skateboarding within schools' physical education programmes, while the 'New PE' – including skateboarding, snowboarding and land paddling – has been actively promoted across North America. In the USA, the Skate Pass company's system has been developed to stimulate not only child health but personal expression, cooperation and friendship, and its curriculum development and teacher training, backed by ready-made packages of skateboards and safety equipment, have consequently been taken up across the US, as well as in Canada, Germany, Singapore and the Dominican Republic. In a more competitive vein, US organisations like the National Scholastic Skateboarding League (founded 2010) and the National High School Skateboard Association (founded 2008) facilitate inter-school skateboard contests with scheduled fixtures and league tables (cf. Loewe, 2008).

Many of these initiatives have particularly connected with hard-to-reach kids, with those suffering from obesity and with those many children who dislike the combative, stressful and regulated nature of traditional school sports such as football, tennis, gymnastics and athletics. For example, in 2004, pro skater Stevie Williams and his father Steven Lassiter set up Philadelphia's Educate to Skate Foundation, with the express aim of running after-school programmes for at-risk youth. The impact of these kinds of project on participants can be immediate and significant; as one father commented of his kids after a Skateboarding Australia session in Brisbane, "because their bodies are all excited, they're really positive about their homework. I've seen my boys just gain so much confidence" (Stewart, 2013; cf. Willing & Shearer, 2016).

Since the mid-2000s, CreateaSkate, a non-profit initiative set up by skateboard manufacturer Paul Schmitt, has offered a different kind of school programme, this time focusing on skateboard decks and encouraging pupils to deploy their mathematics, science, language, design and engineering skills. Similar thematics lie behind other projects, such as the Action Science programme of science, technology, engineering and mathematics offered by Bill Robertson (aka Dr Skateboard), the Skatepark Mathematics Extravaganza (2014) which engaged Texan high school students in real world explorations of data-gathering, physics, geometry and algebra, a Brazilian-Portuguese project using the ollie move to teach Newton's laws of physics, and the UK's FAR Academy syllabus for designing and building decks (cf. Robertson, 2014; Dias, Carvalho & Vianna, 2016; www.thefaracademy.co.uk). For the humanities, Georgina Badoni (2009) has shown how the classroom-based study of skateboards designed by Native Americans can yield unique insights into historical events, personal stories, cultural beliefs and traditions, while the Colonialism Board Company uses skateboards enhanced with historical documents to educate Canadians about their country's colonialist past (cf. Baica, 2015). Entrepreneurialism too can be addressed; at Toronto's Oasis Skateboard Factory, students work on developing skate brands and managing a design business (cf. Dart, 2015).

Finally, university-level education is another active territory for exploring skateboarding and its related cultural and social dimensions. Alongside the research and teaching undertaken by academics worldwide, there are now a handful of intensive offerings. Zachary Sanford offers a course on action sports management at the University of Dayton, Ohio, covering themes such as authenticity, criminality, the X Games, the Olympics and representations of athletes, and Neftalie Williams runs a programme on skateboarding business and culture at the University of Southern California. A few academic departments also have concentrations of PhD researchers focused on skateboarding-related studies, including those at University College London's Bartlett School of Architecture and Waikato University's Sport and Leisure Studies.

Social Enterprise

Skaters often articulate how skateboarding has saved them from a life of drugs, gangs and crime. "All the people I know like, they all fucking in jail", remarked London rider Karim Bakthouai. "I didn't want that, I ain't about that, I'd rather be skating" (Borden, 2016, p. 94). And as White (2015, pp. 80-103) reports, skateboarding shields black and ethnic Bronx riders from police harassment, provides an affirmative community and helps skaters avoid gang membership. Beyond the actual riding of skateboards, providing skateparks is another way to engage with at-risk members of society, while even more can be done via those social enterprises which deploy skateboarding to engage with youth, the disempowered and the disadvantaged.

Perhaps the most successful and well known of skateboarding social enterprises is Skateistan. Oliver Percovich, the Australian skater who in 2008 founded Skateistan in Kabul, Afghanistan, and is now its executive director, explains how, after many decades of civil war and fluctuating ruling powers, the children who make up seventy per cent of the Afghanistan Muslim population have only roadsides in which to play. Girls are banned from riding bicycles or flying kites, but they are allowed to skateboard, and so Skateistan teaches girls and boys alike to ride alongside an arts-based curriculum ranging from world cultures, human rights and environmental studies to nutrition, hygiene and storytelling.[3]

The aim here is to break the cycles of violence, desperation and poverty to which Kabul youth are commonly accustomed, and instead to build confidence and other skills.

"When it comes down to it, kids just want to be kids", explains Percovich. "Skateboarding provides that because it's fun and challenging. It lets them forget their problems for a

---

3 See Fitzpatrick, J. (Ed.) (2012), Skateistan: the Tale of Skateboarding in Afghanistan. Kabul: Skateistan; Skateistan – To Live and Skate Kabul, (dir. Orlando Von Einsiedel, 2011); Skateistan – Four Wheels and a Board in Kabul, (dir. Kai Sehr, 2010); Afghanistan's Girl Skaters – Kabul 2012, www.vimeo.com/46337060; Skateboarding in Afghanistan, Orlando Percovich, TEDxSydney', (2014), www.youtube.com/watch?v =HnYN2yDqZew; and www.skateistan.org.

moment. Once kids are hooked on skateboarding, so much more is possible. Skateboarding itself teaches important life skills, like creativity and problem solving." (Borden, 2015)

Through this approach, and aided by key workers such as Max Henninger, Shams Razi, Sharna Nolan and many others, Skateistan's achievements have been considerable, even when measured simply in terms of skateboarding. By 2012, some 500 Afghan kids were skaters, of which forty per cent were female; a year later, it reached 850 youth weekly with between forty and fifty per cent female participation in all activities. Skaters like Noorzai Ibrahimi and Merza reached an advanced level, joining the DC Shoes Europe pro team on a visit to the United Arab Emirates, while disabled skaters like Mohammad Bilal Mirbat Zai also won competitions. Two skateparks, one in Kabul and another in Mazar-e-Sharif, were built.

Skateistan's most significant achievements, however, lie beyond skateboarding itself. Keen to avoid charges of cultural imperialism and imposing western skateboarding on Kabul children, Skateistan provides wider knowledge and social skills; as O'Connor notes, change at Skateistan ultimately comes not from skateboarding per se but from the bodies of the riders, such that "skateboarding is in multiple ways a vehicle for transformation but not the driving force" (O'Connor, 2016, p. 38). In short, at Skateistan skateboarding is the method, and not the destination.

In this context, Skateistan's 'Skate and Create', 'Back to School' and 'Youth Leadership' programmes variously teach the kids about health and nutrition, operate workshops on arts, computing and environmental issues, and hold sessions on Dari language, mathematics and Qur'anic study, as well as helping children to build confidence, courage, self-esteem and trust. Working, learning and playing with each other, the kids develop friendships across Pashtun, Hazara, Tajik and Uzbek ethnicities, as well as recognising gender-based equality; one of the first things the boys learn is that the girls have equal rights to skate.

"Even in the most desolate of situations", notes Lukas Feireiss, "skateboarding, as a performative instrument for transformation, teaches the children of Skateistan not to accept the city and therefore society as it is, but to create their own city, their own spaces and their own futures. In its essence, the power of skateboarding in Afghanistan is about what it symbolizes: the freedom of movement and the empowerment of the individual beyond all restrictions and conventions." (Fitzpatrick, 2012, p. 191)

Or as the fourteen-year-old Afghan girl Negina simply states, "skateboarding lets me feel like I'm flying" (Fitzpatrick, 2012, p. 275). These achievements are substantial and profound, helping to do no less than, according to Skateistan volunteer Sophie Friedel, 'build peace', and in 2013 Skateistan was included in 'The Global Journal's' list of one hundred top NGOs (cf. Friedel, 2015, p. 59). Many professionals have visited and supported Skateistan, including Cairo Foster, Tony Hawk, Louisa Menke, Kenny Reed and Jamie Thomas, while Black Box, Fallen, IOU Ramps, Route One, Skateroom, Spitfire, Theeve, TSG and Zero are among the skate companies to have provided support, as have Architecture for Humanity, the Canadian, Danish, Finnish, German, Norwegian, Swiss and US governments, the Kabul municipality and the Afghan National Olympic Committee. As a result of this kind of worldwide backing, by 2015 Skateistan was able to spread its operations beyond Kabul, setting up facilities in northern Afghanistan, Vietnam, Cambodia and Johannesburg.

Numerous other social enterprises are also using skateboarding for community aims. Holly Thorpe (2016) has identified how skateboarding and other alternative sports have helped form "therapeutic landscapes" in post-disaster zones caused by war, earthquakes and hurricanes, and so allow youth to redefine physical and emotional disaster geographies and rebuild social networks and connections. Since 2008 Board Rescue has provided equipment to low-income kids and at-risk youth in the US, showing children how exercise, determination, practice and commitment can lead to positive results. During the 2010s, large numbers of other community-oriented projects – like Stoked Mentoring in the USA, Cuba Skate in Cuba, Ethiopia Skate and Megabiskate in Ethiopia, Janwaar Castle in Madhya Pradesh, India, Skate-aid, SkateQilya and SkatePal in Palestine, 7Hills skatepark in Amman, Jordan, Engineers Without Boarders and Outlangish in Cape Town, Latraac in Athens, Skate Style in Cambodia, Bedouins in Tunisia and the international chapters of Skate for Change – have all deployed skateboarding to counter deep-rooted issues like alcohol and drug abuse, unemployment, poverty, violence, religious intolerance, ethnic and gender prejudices, and access to education. Amid abandoned properties in Detroit, for example, the Ride-It Sculpture Park (2012) uses art and greenspace to form a youth-oriented skatepark and community hub, while, as 'I Am Thalente' (a film by Natalie Johns, 2015) shows, South Africa's Indigo Skate Camp project has enriched the lives of Thalente Biyela and other local Durban kids (cf. www.youtube.com/watch?v= ADtErLjggH8).

Even more projects are also active. A.Skate (www.askate.org) provides skate lessons for those with autism and raises awareness about this condition, thus addressing related problems with self-esteem, anxiety, truancy, depression and suicide. Also in the US, the All Nations Skate Project, Stronghold Society and Wounded Knee 4-Directions skateparks have addressed violence, drugs, alcohol and suicide among Native youth; some support has come here from Jeff Ament of rock band Pearl Jam, who has also helped fund several skateparks in less-privileged neighbourhoods (cf. Ament, 2015; Nieratko, 2015; Weaver, 2016 see also www.strongholdsociety.org).[4] Canada's The Forks skatepark in Winnipeg runs skate camps plus film and photography workshops for under-privileged youth, and is co-located with the world's first Human Rights Museum (cf. Daniello, 2007). In all these projects, skateboarding is part of an answer to complex social conditions, where both the act of skateboarding itself, and the avenues it opens up, are of equal value.

Complementary to many of these initiatives is the Tony Hawk Foundation, which supports disadvantaged communities and at-risk children through skatepark provision. Started in 2001 by Hawk and his sponsors, the Foundation supports public skateparks and related projects, partly by giving design and construction advice, and partly by supplying funding. By 2017, the foundation had helped 569 US skateparks to the tune of over $5.5 million, provided over 900 skateparks worldwide with technical assistance, donated $100,000 to Skateistan and reached over 5.4 million skaters per year. As with Skateistan and other community initiatives, the benefits often go far beyond skateboarding itself. "A skatepark project can teach young people a lifelong lesson in the power of perseverance", explains Hawk & Hawk (2010, p. 155). "Kids discover they can accomplish something by working within the system rather than beating their heads against it. They learn how to communicate in a way that will encourage adults to listen, and they go from feeling alienated to empowered" (ibid., p. 164).

REFERENCES

Ament, J. (2015). Jim Murphy. *Juice Magazine*, 22, 1, 88-97.
Badoni, G. (2009). *Native American Art and Visual Culture Education through Skateboards*. MA dissertation: University of Arizona.
Baica, D. (2015). Saskatchewan Skateboard Company Teaches Riders About Colonial History. *CTV News* (22 August 2015), www.ctvnews.ca.
BBC (2014). Street Patrol UK. www.youtube.com/watch?v=BZlkjWEtaU8.
Beal, B., Atencio, M., Wright, M. & McClain, Z. (2017). Skateboarding, Community and Urban Politics: Shifting Practices and Challenges. *International Journal of Sport Policy and Politics*, 9, 1, 11-23.

---

4   See e.g. 'Skate life an an Indian Reservation Skate or Die' (www.youtube.com/watch?v=SYRINJZZqWU).

Borden, I. (2001). *Skateboarding, Space and the City*. Oxford: Berg Publishers.

Borden, I. (2015). The New Skate City: How Skateboarders Are Joining the Urban Mainstream. *The Guardian*, 'Cities' section, www.gu.com/p/46yh7/stw.

Borden, I. (2016). Southbank Skateboarding, London, and Urban Culture: the Undercroft, Hungerford Bridge, and House of Vans. In: Lombard, K.-J. (Ed.), *Skateboarding: Subcultures, Sites and Shifts* (pp. 91-107). Abingdon: Routledge.

Borden, I. (2019). *Skateboarding and the City – a Complete History*. London: Bloomsbury.

Bradley, G. L. (2010). Skate Parks as a Context for Adolescent Development. *Journal of Adolescent Research*, 25, 2, 288-323.

Bradley, B. (2013). Detroit Vying for X Games. *Next City* (28 May 2013), www.nextcity.org.

Carr, J. (2012). Activist Research and City Politics: Ethical Lessons from Youth-Based Public Scholarship. *Action Research*, 10, 1, 61-78.

Carr, J. (2016). Skateboarding in Dude Space: the Roles of Space and Sport in Constructing Gender among Adult Skateboarders. *Sociology of Sport Journal*, 34, 1, 25-34.

Chiu, C. (2009). Contestation and Conformity: Street and Park Skateboarding in New York City Public Space. *Space and Culture*, 12, 1, 25-42.

Daniello, F. (2007). The Plaza at the Forks, Winnipeg. *Concrete Skateboarding*, 3, 53-63.

Dart, C. (2015). Toronto's Most Unlikely High School is a Skateboard Factory. *Yahoo Canada News* (4 May 2015), www.ca.news.yahoo.com.

Dias, M. A., Carvalho, P. S. & Vianna, D. M. (2016). Using Image Modelling to Teach Newton's Laws with the Ollie Trick. *Physics Education*, 51, 4, 1-6.

Dumas, A. & Laforest, S. (2009). Skateparks as a Health-Resource. *Leisure Studies*, 28, 1, 19-34.

Duvall, K. (2016). What is the Future of Skateparks?, *Ride* (24 August 2016), www.theridechannel.com.

Edwards, A. (2015). *Swamp Suburbia and Rebellion against a Culture of Crime: the Birth of Black Skateboarding in the Big Easy*. MSc Urban Studies dissertation: University of New Orleans. https://scholarworks.uno.edu/td/1968.

Fitzpatrick, J. (Ed.) (2012). *Skateistan: the Tale of Skateboarding in Afghanistan*. Kabul: Skateistan.

Friedel, S. (2015). *The Art of Living Sideways*. Berlin: Springer Verlag.

Gillogly, B. (1976). Russ Howell. *SkateBoarder*, 2, 4, 44.

Goldenberg, M. & Shooter, W. (2007). Skateboard Park Participation: a Means-End Analysis. *Journal of Youth Development*, 4, 4, 1-12.

Harnik, H. & Gentles, C. (2009). Coming to a City near You. *Parks & Recreation*, May, 34-38.

Harris, G. (2011). *The Belonging Paradox: the Belonging Experience of Committed Uncertain Members*. PhD thesis: Queen's University Kingston.

Hawk, T. (2015). Who You Callin' a Sell Out? *The Berrics* (23 January 2015), www.theberrics.com.

Hawk, T. & Hawk, P. (2010). *How Did I Get Here? The Ascent of an Unlikely CEO*. Hoboken: Wiley.

Howell, O. (2008). Skatepark as Neoliberal Playground: Urban Governance, Recreation Space, and the Cultivation of Personal Responsibility. *Space and Culture* 11, 4, 475-496.

Jackson, J. B. (1984). *Discovering the Vernacular Landscape*. New Haven: Yale University Press.

Jones, S. & Graves, A. (2000). Power Plays in Public Space: Skateboard Parks as Battlegrounds, Gifts, and Expressions of Self. *Landscape Journal*, 19, 1-2, 136-48.

Katz, M. (2011). Factoria Joven Skate Park. *Design Milk* (28 October 2011), www.design-milk.com.

Kelly, D. M., Pomerantz, S. & Currie, D. H. (2008). "You Can Break So Many More Rules": the Identity Work and Play of Becoming Skater Girls. In: Giardina, M. & Donnelly, M. (Eds.), *Youth Culture and Sport*, (pp. 113-125). Abingdon: Routledge.

Lessig, L. (2008). *Remix*. New York: Penguin Press.

Loewe, T. (2008). Skateboarding Kickflips into PE. *USA Today* (24 June 2008), www.usatoday.com.

McFadyen, J. & Longhurst, G. (2014). *Parks for Sport and Recreation*. Hamilton City Council: research report. https://issuu.com/parksandleisure/docs/pla183_issuu.

Nieratko, C. (2015). Pearl Jam's Bassist Has Personally Funded More Than a Dozen Skateboard Parks. *Vice* (24 August 2015), www.vice.com.

O'Connor, P. (2016). Skateboard Philanthropy: Inclusion and Prefigurative Politics. In: Lombard, K.-J. (Ed.), *Skateboarding: Subcultures, Sites and Shifts*, (pp. 30-46). Abingdon: Routledge.

Petrone, R. (2008). *Shreddin' It Up: Re-Thinking "Youth" through the Logics of Learning and Literacy in a Skateboarding Community*. PhD thesis: Michigan State University.

Putnam, R. D. (2000). *Bowling Alone*. New York: Simon & Schuster.

Robertson, W. H. (2014). *Action Science*. Thousand Oaks: Corwin.

Rodgers, B. (2016). Park Projects turn Skateboarders from Rebellion to Advocacy. *Seminole County News*, (21 January 2016), www.orlandosenti nel.com.

Sendra, P. (2015). Rethinking urban public space: assemblage thinking and the uses of disorder. *City*, 19, 6, 820-836.

Shannon, C. S. & Werner, T. L. (2008). The Opening of a Municipal Skate Park. *Journal of Park and Recreation Administration*, 26, 3, 39-58.

Stewart, K. (2013). Affirmative Action. A Skateboard Documentary. www.you tube.com/watch?v=7CJaTJ12wpY.

Taylor, M. & Khan, U. (2011). Skate-Park Builds, Teenaphobia and the Adolescent Need for Hang-out Spaces. *Journal of Urban Design*, 16, 4, 489-510.

Taylor, M. & Marais, I. (2011). Not in My Back Schoolyard. *Australian Planner*, 48, 2, 84-95.

Thorpe, H. (2016). 'Look at What We Can Do with All the Broken Stuff!' Youth agency and sporting creativity in sites of war, conflict and disaster. *Qualitative Research in Sport, Exercise and Health*, 8, 5, 554-570.

Turner, D. (2013a). *The Civilised Skateboarder: a Figurational Analysis of the Provision of Adventure Recreation Facilities*. PhD thesis: Glasgow Caledonian University.

Turner, D. (2013b). The Civilized Skateboarder and the Sports Funding Hegemony: a Case Study of Alternative Sport. *Sport in Society*, 16, 10, 1248-1262.

Turner, D. (2017). Performing Citizenship: Skateboarding and the Formalisation of Informal Spaces. In: Turner, D. & Carnicelli, S. (Eds.), *Lifestyle Sports and Public Policy* (pp. 13-26). Abingdon: Routledge.

Vivioni, F. (2010). *Contesting Public Space: Skateboarding, Urban Development, and the Politics of Play*. PhD thesis: University of Illinois at Urbana-Champaign.

Weaver, H. S. (2016). Where Wounded Knee Meets Wounded Knees. Skate parks and Native American youth. *AlterNative*, 12, 5, 513-26.

Weller, S. (2006). Skateboarding Alone? Making Social Capital Discourse Relevant to Teenagers' Lives. *Journal of Youth Studies*, 9, 5, 557-74.

Weyland, J. (2002). *The Answer Is Never: a Skateboarder's History of the World*. London: Century.

White, K. (2015). *"We Out Here": Skateboarding, Segregation and Resistance in the Bronx*. MA Dissertation: Fordham University. https://fordham.bepress. com/dissertations/AAI1584734.

Whitley, P. (2009). *Public Skatepark Development Guide*. Portland: Skaters for Public Skateparks, International Association of Skateboard Companies, and Tony Hawk Foundation.

Willing, I. & Shearer, S. (2016). Skateboarding Activism: Exploring Diverse Voices and Community Support. In: Lombard, K.-J. (Ed.), *Skateboarding: Subcultures, Sites and Shifts* (pp. 44-56). Abingdon: Routledge.

Wixon, B. (2009). *Skateboarding: Instruction, Programming and Park Design.* Champaign: Human Kinetics.

Woolley, H. & Johns, R. (2001). Skateboarding: the City as a Playground. *Journal of Urban Design*, 6, 2, 211-230.

Wright, P. (2016). Is Malmö the Most Skateboarding-Friendly City in the World?, *Huck* (24 August 2016), www.huckmagazine.com.

Can You Sell Out if You've Never Been in?

The Olympics and Creating Spaces for
Gender Inclusion in Skateboarding

Becky Beal & Kristin Ebeling

> "We are already used to not having anything. So, aside from our own love of skating and the community we've built, there's really nothing to lose at this point for anyone. Even the most hard-core street skater on the girl's side is ready for the Olympics."
> *Elite woman skater, in Wheaton & Thorpe, 2018, p. 332*

Since the 1990s there has been talk of including skateboarding in the Olympics. The discussion around Olympic inclusion was initially framed as problematic by many skaters because it could entail a loss of control by the skateboarder-owned or originated companies (from here on referred to as 'core' industry). Simultaneously, these 'outside' entities including multi-national corporations would have growing influence which some worried would further erode the traditional culture of skateboarding pushing it closer to the norms and structures of more mainstream sport (a process often referred to as 'sportification'). The argument culminated with the fear that skateboarding would become regulated and lose its more artistic and DIY grassroots vibe. The standard retort was to 'keep it real' and not to 'sell out' to mainstream interests. This concern over the power shift and changing structure is legitimate. Sportification is happening and is represented in standardization and increased regulated competition with such things as skate camps, curriculum for skateboarding in school physical education, and the proliferating types of amateur and professional competitions. And, the IOC and corporations such as Nike and Adidas have brought more global attention and extended the number of stakeholders in skateboarding. The Olympic inclusion of skateboarding can be seen as the epitome of sportification. And although it's true that the Games represent when an activity becomes a 'sport' it would be hard to say that skateboarding wasn't that already for many years. It's been the norm for the last decade for skaters to have their own personal trainers, represent sponsors like Red Bull, and compete to earn notoriety in skateboarding, in events such as Tampa Am, Vert Attack, and Vans Park Series. Therefore, we contend that the core skate industry elite gets upset when the sportification doesn't center them, not at sportification itself.

On the other hand, women have found this sportification to have positive effects, especially with providing them with professional opportunities, many of which they never imagined before (cf. Wheaton & Thorpe, 2018). The Olympics have a very significant impact on women's opportunities. The IOC currently requires sports to demonstrate gender equity and not just in the numbers of women competitors but also support staff and members of governing bodies at the national and international levels. This expectation of gender inclusion, in turn, puts pressure on national and regional competitions to include women as the IOC regulates the equity guidelines for qualifying competitions. It is reasonable to see why many, especially women, have supported this movement.

Skateboarding has a history of marginalizing girls and women and, thus, the Olympics play a crucial means for their inclusion. In this chapter we identify different mechanisms or processes of social inclusion and social exclusion and examine how those processes have played out in skateboarding. Donnelly and Coakley (2002) capture the essence of social inclusion:

"Processes of exclusion and inclusion always involve power relations. The situations in which these processes occur are organized around norms and traditions that influence or determine who is welcome and who is not." (Donnelly & Coakley, 2002, p. 327)

We will identify different arrangements of power including more formalized in the political and economic capital of the IOC and major skateboarding corporations to the informal networks of skate crews and their codes of authenticity. This chapter, then, provides an overview of the different ways girls and women have been excluded and the work many people have done to create more welcoming and inclusive skate spaces.

POWER DYNAMICS IN SKATEBOARDING: A BRIEF OVERVIEW

Organizational Power, Gender, and the Olympics

Becoming a sanctioned Olympic sport is a process of negotiation among the most powerful governing bodies of those sports. Control over the future of a sport is always central to those discussions and the IOC's regulations frame the negotiation process. For example, the IOC requires that sports must be affiliated with an international governing body that is not industry based (cf. Batuev & Robinson, 2017). This was problematic for skateboarding because it has a long history of supporting informal networks and, thus, did not direct concerted efforts on developing an international organizing body. Additionally, the one centralized organization that was created to promote skateboarding was affiliated with the commercial industry, The International Association of Skateboard Companies. Yet, when talks of Olympic inclusion became serious, the industry leaders created the International Skateboarding Federation (ISF) in 2002 in order to fight for control of skateboarding as it became more 'sportified'. Other international governing bodies, especially the Fédération Internationale de Roller Sports (FIRS), were positioning to be the IOC recognized body. Tony Hawk noted in 2011, "The ISF was the skateboard industry being proactive and preparing for the Olympic opportunity [...] I think it is a good thing that the skateboarding industry was organized enough to protect itself" (from Batuev & Robinson, 2017, p. 10). Initially the IOC recognized FIRS as the legitimate governing body primarily based on its history of regulatory legitimacy. Whereas ISF was seen as having cultural legitimacy. Thus, the IOC asked FIRS and ISF to work together (ibid.). The final compromise was a merger of IFS and FIRS to create World Skate which is now sanctioned to organize Olympic 2020 Skateboarding competitions. The key point here is that the elite in the skateboarding industry organized to maintain significant control while it becomes increasingly mainstream. For example, Gary Ream is the Former president of ISF, also the owner of Woodward Camps (which is an elite training facility for 'action sports'), and he is currently working at World Skate as the chair of the World Skateboarding Commission.

To maintain some control of the skateboarding the industry elite, primarily white men, had to compromise with the IOC. Ironically, the IOC (also dominated by white men, see Wheaton & Thorpe, 2018) required the inclusion of women. This, in turn, opens doors for some women to benefit financially, but doesn't guarantee that women will be embraced by the historically 'core' industry or their 'fellow' skaters. In the background of these negotiations between core skate industry and the IOC, women and their allies have been navigating the male dominated skate scene and creating inclusive skate spaces for decades. We contend that the increased opportunity structures for women (as represented by the Olympics) are necessary, but that it does not automatically equate to the full inclusion of women's voices, concerns, or interests. Therefore, we address and explain how the codes of authenticity have been crucial in marginalizing girls' and women's voices and full participation in the skateboarding scene.

Informal Power, Gender, and Codes of 'Authenticity'

As documented by previous research, the debates around 'authentic' ways of being a skateboarder illustrate power dynamics within skateboarding (Atencio, Beal, & Wilson, 2009; Beal & Weidman, 2003; Bäckström, 2013; Donnelly, 2006; McKay, 2016; Porter, 2003, Ranikkoa et al., 2016; Wheaton & Beal, 2003). The notion of authenticity as embodied by risk-taking, creative, and mostly white cisgendered boys and men was fostered through the industry in the 1980s and reinforced throughout much of its history since (Beal, 2013; Beal & Wilson, 2004; Chivers-Yochim, 2010; Dupont, 2014; Rinehart, 2005). In turn, this version of authenticity has served to marginalize other groups of people, especially women, trans, or queer identified people. Because gender has been conflated with codes of authenticity it becomes embedded in this argument of 'keeping it real' or 'selling out'. In fact, whether intentional or not, we contend that the inclusion of girls and women gets associated with sportification and thus, 'selling out', which re-centers historical cisgender male privilege.

Below we will provide an overview of the key concepts and strategies of inclusion. We follow that by explaining how these are played out in skateboarding. In particular, we pay attention to informal gatekeeping as it has been significant historical barrier for women in both skateboarding's communities and industry. Then we highlight the work of people developing gender inclusive spaces. And, finally, we will ponder whether and in what ways the inclusion of skateboarding into the Olympics will impact gender dynamics at the daily and grassroots levels of skateboarding.

GENDER INCLUSION IN SPORT

Social inclusion has been an important topic of research for those in the field of sport and physical activity (e.g., Bailey, 2005; Collins, 2004; Collison et al.,

2017; Donnelly & Coakley, 2002; Frisby, 2011; Spaaij, Magee & Jeanes, 2014). These researchers point out that providing resources (e.g., social and economic capital) is vital so that people have enriched and equitable opportunity structures. Additionally, establishing democratic processes that enable all participants to have their voice heard and valued is key in creating inclusive communities. In short, people need to be given power to create 'sporting' structures and their concomitant value systems. On the flip side, exclusion happens when there are inequitable structural opportunities and when certain group's norms and values are marginalized. With respect to gender inclusion, scholars have examined how the normative structures of sport, the mediated messages/images of women athletes, and the gender composition of leadership within sport impacts inclusion. The pattern they have found is that cisgender men and masculinity structure mainstream sport (e.g., Cunningham, 2015; Elling & Knoppers, 2005; Messner, 2002; Rinehart, 2005; Thorpe & Olive, 2016; Travers & Deri, 2010). This, in turn, has the effect of marginalizing women and non-cisgender people.

Girls and women skateboarders have faced many similar obstacles for full inclusion that women in other sports have faced. Below we discuss these key factors with respect to social exclusion: the normative gender structure of skateboarding, the media representation of skaters, and leadership positions in the industry. Although we discuss each factor separately, it will become apparent that they impact each other. We especially highlight how the normative structures and the codes of legitimacy are interwoven in the traditions of skateboarding which, in turn, impact the distribution of economic resources and who is given 'legitimate' voice in shaping skateboarding.

Gendered Structure of skateboarding:
Exclusion through 'Authenticity' and Gatekeeping

A few academics have written about the history of skateboarding addressing its gender dynamics (e.g. Beal, 2013; Borden, 2019; Chivers-Yochim, 2010). Unlike many other formal sports, skateboarding had a more gender inclusive beginning, then went through a masculine entrenchment, and is now experiencing an upsurge in the diversity of participants (Atencio et al., 2018; O'Connor, 2018). Although there are many anecdotes about the origins of skateboarding, there is clear evidence about its early commercial and public phases. Its original commercial success occurred in the early 1960s and at this time was marketed as a youthful pastime. Similar to hoola hoops or frisbees, this activity was not overtly marketed as masculine. Soon neighborhood competitions and then national competitions arose in which women were included and Patti

McGee was featured on the cover of *Life Magazine* in 1965. In the mid 70s skateboarding had many different forms or styles, but most were gymnastic like or ramps and pool skating, with stylish outliers like Peggy Oki of the Dogtown and Z-Boys crew. Again, competitions and demonstrations featured both men and women. When the recession of the early 1980s hit and other informal sports were struggling to survive, industry leaders decided to distinguish skateboarding from other informal sports, so they intentionally rebranded skateboarding as an urban masculine activity. This shift is exemplified by the rise of *Thrasher Magazine* and street/urban style of skateboarding. The masculine entrenchment of the early 1980s through today can be shown by the fact that it was primarily men running the core industry and that these folks were circulating the narratives of 'authenticity' that favored risk-taking, young men who traversed urban landscapes without formal adult supervision (cf. Beal & Weidman, 2003; Borden, 2019; Wheaton & Beal, 2003). Skilled women skaters were nearly invisible in these core magazines. For example, *Thrasher Magazine*, has only three women on cover in its history (Cara Beth Burnside 1989, Jamie Reyes 1994, and Lizzie Armanto 2017). Additionally, men have been the recipients of the industry leaders' support as they have garnered the majority of branding and competition opportunities. Not surprisingly, this branding shift negatively impacted women's involvement (cf. Beal, 2013).

Within this context of skateboarding as male-centered and controlled, it is important to note how recognition and status are attained. It is this process of 'moving up' or being recognized as 'legitimate' that works as an exclusionary mechanism. Below we will describe how the informal skateboarding networks act as filters, favoring cisgender boys and men.

Importantly, status in skateboarding is not a matter of objective criteria of a predetermined outcome like a final score or time. Instead, elite status is based on creativity, skill and 'likeability' which is a subjective decision that other stakeholders make. This status construction and affirmation happens in two ways. The main process is by having your skills documented and circulated to a broad audience. This can be done with neighborhood crews posting videos of their friends skateboarding to social media, and this is where local reputations are constructed. Yet, for elite status to be conferred one generally must be sanctioned by the insiders of the industry. They are the ones who identify top skaters and circulate stories and photographic documentation of their skills, primarily through branding and advertising (having a 'signature' board is a sign of making it) or by being featured in historically 'authentic' media outlets such as *Thrasher Magazine* or a core brand's video.

Most skaters will not be professional athletes, instead the focus for them is to achieve legitimacy and status within local crews or regional networks. Importantly, the informal organization of skateboarding means that local scenes can and do vary, and that the norms and values of these local crews are developed and maintained by gatekeeping mechanisms. In his ethnographic studies of skateboarding, Tyler Dupont (2014, 2016) describes processes by which skaters are accepted and promoted. He argues that skaters must be committed to their local crew and that they provide "work" that supports their local scene. In short, they need to prioritize their crew's vitality to skateboarding's progression as opposed to overtly focusing on themselves as being competitively better than their crew members. Thus, getting along with the crew and likeability are just as important as one's skills for determining one's status. And gatekeepers or 'mentors' in these communities, predominantly men, are in position to shape the normative standards of their crews affecting who is accepted and promoted.

This process of becoming part of the skateboarding world was also described by Gregory Snyder (2017), who wrote about professional skateboarding in Los Angeles. His research echoes Dupont's in that skateboarding worlds, although informal and entrepreneurial, still have normative structures or "codes" that filter people from its center to its margins. He notes that "skating has a very strict set of rules of interaction that are always changing according to who the rule makers are" (Snyder, 2017, p. 61). Snyder explains that if skaters can be accepted by the rule makers, then those mentors will help facilitate their careers: "kids who are successful on some level at skateboarding can find a way to participate in the skateboarding industry" (ibid., p. 15). Additionally, when there are formal skate competitions the skaters are judged similarly to ice skaters or gymnasts. That is, there are a set of aesthetic and technical criteria that judges use evaluate the competitors. The judges tend to be insiders of the skate scene and their choice of criteria and assessment can be negotiated and, thus, subjective (Snyder, 2017). Fundamentally, one's social networks are essential to gaining acceptance and status as a legitimate member of the skateboarding community (ibid.; Dupont, 2014). Historically, those networks have been dominated by men. Snyder seems to gloss over any gender discrimination (or other types) when he notes:

"The rule makers' power comes not from a privileged racial, class, or ethnic position, but from their skateboarding prowess and position within the industry, combined with their likeability." (Snyder, 2017, p. 61)

Unlike Snyder, Dupont clearly acknowledges that gender impacts who is considered legitimate. In his research he found, "skaters rarely accepted women outside of their traditional supportive role" (2014). This explains why women are often valued as skaters only if they also live up to cisgender femininity. One skateboarder the first author (Beal) interviewed described her first 'sponsorship' for skateboarding. She recalled that she and three other females were taken out to dinner by the company representative and then were told they would be paid 50 dollars and get the free gear if they posed in bikinis on the beach holding their skateboards. She was extremely disappointed in how she was valued in a sexualized manner and refused the sponsorship. This 'acceptance' of women in stereotypical ways can be read as a sanction to sexually harass. Recently, some women have come forward with their stories, such as Linnea Bullion (2018) who describes her experiences as,

"Like the many times I've had my ass grabbed. Or the time someone came up to me at a contest and pinched my nipple. Or the time I gave a few skaters a ride back to their hotel and one of them presumed I only did so in order to have sex with him."

In sum, the social networks of skateboarders are underpinned by normative traditions which have privileged boys and men. Research that has focused on more recreational neighborhood crews, has also found that these same codes of authenticity are at work creating exclusionary practices by devaluing and marginalizing girls and women. (Atencio, Beal & Wilson, 2009; Bäckström, 2013; Beal, 1996; Chivers-Yochim, 2010; Dupont, 2014; Rannikkoa et al., 2016).

These networks are crucial in influencing the continuation of norms and traditions that have excluded and marginalized girls and women. Similar to most organizations, those who have been promoted had to prove their own worth or legitimacy by demonstrating skills and a commitment to the organization's ethos. Skateboarding is no different, those in positions of power in the core industry were filtered through its social networks. We don't mean to imply that all leaders in the industry have the same level of commitment to the core values. Variation in value systems does occur. Nonetheless, they do acknowledge that they must competently navigate skateboarding's core customs to be seen as legitimate (cf. Giannoulakis, 2016).

A key factor of social inclusion is to distribute resources equitably. We argue that the core networks have acted to funnel resources to men. Additionally, social inclusion requires that people share power in creating norms and values. Again, we note that women have not been given that same voice in determining core skate traditions. We now provide an overview of the resources these skateboarding networks distribute and which help to perpetuate male privilege. First, we discuss how media representations perpetuate gendered codes of authenticity.

Next, we address the lack of economic resources given to women. Essentially the pipelines for women's development are underfunded which, in turn, marginalizes them. Finally, we address the lack of formal positions of power for women in core skateboarding industry.

Gender and Media Representations: Marginalizing Girls and Women Skaters

Those who have been promoted in the industry often acquire jobs in advertsing and media where they are able to construct narratives of authenticity. Research has found that core skate media centers men who are skilled and risk-taking, poraying a 'rugged individualistic masculinity'. Concurrently, core skate media has framed women in sexualized ways or as less skilled (Atencio, Beal & Wilson, 2009; Beal & Weidman, 2003, Beal & Wilson, 2004; Chivers-Yochim, 2010; Porter, 2003; Rinehart, 2005; Wheaton & Beal, 2003). Some shifts have occurred to picture more skilled maneuvers of women, but heteronormative presentations are still favored in that representation, including long hair, tighter fitting clothes, and make-up. Several women who now work to create inclusive spaces identified sexist media representation as the driving factor, especially the common assumption that 'sex appeal' is more important than skill for women skaters (Atencio et al., 2018). Importantly, this central image has been challenged by people who have created communities that were women, trans, or queer centered, such as Unity, Skate Like a Girl, and Quell Skateboarding.

Gender and Resource Investments

To promote inclusion, resources need to be invested in opportunity structures so that people can develop skills necessary to be successful. The structural investment in women skateboarders has waned over the years. Not only have the top skate companies not sponsored women at the same rate and compensation as men, but the preeminent competitions such as X Games and Street League did not include women in their initial iterations, and then when they did, women were paid less. One of the top skateboarders of the 2000s, Lyn-Z Adams Hawkins commented,

"The opportunities are much less for women compared to men. We hardly ever get TV coverage. We struggle to even get a women's division in most competitions. X Games is the only event we have equal prize money, and there is way less support from sponsors." (Higgins, 2011)

These forms of discrimination spurred women to create an alliance to act similarly to a union to negotiate better pay (cf. Beal, 2013). Ultimately, the X Games did provide equal prize monies for men and women skateboarding in 2009, 14 years after its start.

Importantly, when organizations do invest in women, they take up skateboarding and thrive. Take the case of Skateistan, an organization dedicated to girls' empowerment through skateboarding and education. Their initial investment was in 2007 in Afghanistan and they have extended their programming to other developing countries. According to Percovich, the founder of Skateistan, in Afghanistan skateboarding is considered a 'female' sport and there are more females who skate per capita in Afghanistan than any other country (Pushing Boarders, 2018). This is what concerted effort in providing resources for the development of girl and women skaters can do. And this is why skateboarding becoming an Olympic sport is crucial. Because of the gender equity requirement from the IOC, the industry has to invest some of its resources into girls' and women's development, such as providing equity in qualifying competitions. Essentially, this is a boon for those women who aspire to be professional. It can also be seen as a boon for corporations willing to sponsor and develop women skaters which traditional sport companies, such as Nike, are doing. Thus, where core skateboarding neglected women, sportification has generated some benefits for them.

Gender and Leadership in the Core Industry

Being in a position of power to impact policy and the direction of an industry is another crucial factor of inclusion. The gender politics within the skateboarding industry is a ripe area for study, as only a few academic articles have been published directly addressing its leadership (e.g., Wheaton & Thorpe, 2018). From what we can gather, it appears that very few women have held powerful positions in the 'established' or 'core' industries. Management scholars argue that in order for women to thrive in leadership positions, that workplaces need three dimensions: "fairness for women, leveraging women's talent, and workplace support for women's values, interests, and needs" (Kossek, Su & Wu, 2017, p. 241). In particular, the notion of "leveraging talent" means that women's contributions are seen as integral to the whole enterprise and not just an addendum. The mainstream skateboarding industry has a track record of treating women's contributions as secondary. Jessie Van Roechoudt, a talented skater noted that:

"Historically, it seems that when the economy is doing well, companies start investing in building up a women's specific line and having a dedicated budget for it, but when the economy contracts, the women's programs are lines are the first to be cut. So they can re-direct that money to the guys." (cited in Pulley, 2015)

This trend can be seen by the effects of the 2007-09 recession when the top competitions such as X-Games and Dew Tour cut their women's divisions in 2010. However, the reluctance to consider women as central to the culture may be more endemic. In 2011, Vans' vice president of marketing, Doug Palladini, explained why they didn't capitalize on the buzz around Cara-Beth Burnside a prominent 1990s skater, "To females who participate in skateboarding, [Burn-side] is iconic, but that represents such a minority in skateboarding that it's diffi-cult to see how she resonates as powerfully on the brand level". He concluded that "The culture of skating is a lot less interested in being inclusive, and I think it's always been that way" (cited in Higgins, 2011). These examples indicate that the industry isn't inclined to see women's products or participation as vital to their mission.

With regard to inclusion, it is necessary that women are in positions of power to have a voice in how they are represented and in what norms and values be-come central to the skate culture. From our brief overview, it is clear that girls and women have been excluded through core skateboarding social networks. And those networks have, in turn, distributed resources primarily to men. This brings us back to the main theme of the paper, that women have felt shut out of the core community, essentially, giving them no choice to 'sell out' or not. In-stead, women skateboarders and community builders have taken up alternative methods to keep themselves and their communities afloat, including sponsorship from mainstream corporations and embracing the Olympics. We will conclude this chapter by providing examples of the proactive steps females and their allies have taken to create female centered or gender inclusive spaces.

RISE OF GENDER INCLUSIVE AND WOMEN CENTERED COMMUNITIES

As noted above, girls and women have always been skateboarding and have been dealing with implicit and explicit forms of sexism within the culture. Decades before the Olympics included skateboarding and boosted support for women, a surge of groups formed to create local and translocal women-centered communi-ties. Frustrated by the lack of infrastructural support and media coverage, these groups have focused on supporting girls and women by providing spaces to convene to practice, media outlets for their voices, and events for community building. Importantly, we find that women and their allies have created strong relationships as they work to create inclusive spaces, giving those involved a sense of being central to their crew's normative structures and value systems.

During the masculine entrenchment of the 1980s there were girl groups, but the available media technology made connecting and documentation of these groups sparse. One notable group was the 'Hags' from Los Angeles started by Sevie Bates. This was a punk rock, hard partying, skateboarding group. Many of the girls in this group did skate with Tony Alva's Z-Boys, but were not formally accepted as part of their crew or another male crew called Jax. Because of this exclusion, Bates created her crew (cf. Savage, 2017). Another pioneer from southern California was Cara Beth Burnside. She became the first woman to be featured on the cover of *Thrasher magazine* in 1989. Additionally, she had a signature shoe with Vans for a short period in the mid 1990s. A friend of hers, Patty Segovia-Krause, was frustrated at the lack of institutional support for women. To promote them, she started photographing and filming women skateboarders and snowboarders and ultimately set up the competition series, All Girl Skate Jam. The 1990s saw the rise of several groups who developed their own media (from 'zines, to videos and then ultimately social media) and skate spaces to provide support for females (cf. Beal, 2013). This encapsulates the historical trend of women breaking from relying primarily on men's networks to creating their own networks. Below we provide a few more examples. The main sources of this information come from interviews with several people who have been influential in creating inclusive spaces for women. Ebeling, the second author of this chapter, works in the skateboarding industry and was able to make those connections. From this information, we chose three cases because they represent different constraints as well as strategies for ensuring women have more opportunities and representation in skateboarding. Additionally, these stories demonstrate how the convergence of different actors, especially the grassroots movements and the Olympic inclusion, have created a current landscape that is far more embracing of non-traditional skaters such as women, queer or trans identified individuals. We begin with telling the story of the first women to be successfully promoted through the male dominated core networks, Elissa Steamer. Then we illustrate the formation and proliferation of women's networks through the fruition of the Villa Villa Cola video, *Getting Nowhere Faster*. Finally, we discuss the how these newly established women's networks have been leveraged to provide women mainstream corporate support through Lacey Baker's story.

Elissa Steamer is best known for being the first woman skateboarder to have her avatar in Tony Hawk's video game series. But her road to that monumental stage was paved through navigating the core social networks. She was raised in Florida and started skateboarding in the mid 1980s but wanted to break into the skateboarding networks so she moved to southern California when she was 19. She spent 9 years there making connections and skating with other top skaters (Beal, 2013). Key gatekeepers acknowledged her skill and helped to promote her. Some of these included Jamie Thomas and Chad Muska, professional skaters, and it was Ed Templeton, founder of the core brand Toy Machine, who included her full part in their video, *Welcome to Hell.*

It was at this moment in time, when her skating abilities caught the eye of Tony Hawk, who was casting for his video game. Tony recalls of the decision to include Elissa: "Yes it was my idea. I thought she was the best representative of female skaters at the time, as she was breaking barriers in terms of wider acceptance and destroying misconceptions about limited skill levels of women skaters" (personal communication, 2019). And with this sanctioning from Tony Hawk, Elissa was boosted from the world of skateboarding, to the larger world of videogames. And as she recalls, it actually was what helped her not get a "real job" for a very long time (personal communication 2019). This represents an iconic breakthrough for including and celebrating women's skills as skaters especially as it translated to viable economic opportunities. In turn, Elissa's core brand endorsement in *Tony Hawk's Pro Skater* impacted the next generation of women skaters. Anecdotally, Ebeling has heard many women talk about how Steamer's natural and unsexualized core skater image in this video game encouraged them to become skaters.

Although an important image of women's empowerment, Steamer was still the exception. Many others had more difficulty navigating and benefiting from the core skate networks. As noted above, many women decided to create their own skate media and spaces. A trend that took hold in the 1990s. Lisa Whitaker is an important figure in this era of women's networking. She, too, started skateboarding in the late 1980s and then became a videographer in the 90's. She worked in southern California, shooting footage of skaters some which was used by the core brand 411 video magazine (sponsored by Transworld Skateboarding). Whitaker attended the All Girls Skate Jam where she met an all women crew, Villa Villa Cola, a collective project started by twin sisters Tiffany and Nicole Morgan, which made 'zines and videos such as *Striking Fear into the Hearts of Teenage Girls.* Whitaker joined with the Villa Villa Cola crew which lead to their pivotal 2004 video, *Getting Nowhere Faster.* Importantly, the project was female based including both the production crew and the skaters. Yet, its distribution was backed by people in the core network, especially Josh Friedberg, then of 411 Video Magazine, and by core sponsors like Element and Etnies. It was premiered globally, available for purchase as a DVD at local skate shops across the world. *Getting Nowhere Faster* became the first full-length women's skateboarding video and still stands up today as a classic in women's skateboarding.

Similar to Steamer's visibility in *Tony Hawk's Pro Skater*, *Getting Nowhere Faster* was a catalyst of getting a lot of women to pick up skateboarding. Arguably, more importantly, this project strengthened women's networks and created a sense of community that didn't exist during the late nineties. The women involved in the project, all continued to skate, progress and support each other. Additionally, they have created the global media outlets The Side Project, which became Girls Skate Network. Before instagram, websites like Girls Skate Network were crucial for creating visibility and affirmation for women who skated. With this milestone of women's skateboarding set the tone for future projects, and was the groundwork for Whitaker's next influential work, board company Meow Skateboards.

Each breakthrough moment had different factors that influenced how women became included. Besides the individual skaters who pushed gendered barriers, there were supportive allies including men from the core networks. Additionally, broader economic and social factors also impact who is likely to support women. For example, Alex White who was part of the production team of *Getting Nowhere Faster* mentions that the vibrant economy played a role in getting core sponsors as those skate companies were interested in growing to try and serve this new demographic of women skaters. This desire of the core companies to grow markets in the early 2000s was illustrated by Globe Shoes starting, Gallaz, which boasted the tagline of 'footwear for females'. Although they originally focused on skateboarders, Globe ultimately shifted this to a 'lifestyle' brand, illustrating again that girls and women skaters are not central to the skateboarding core. Nonetheless, it's important here to note the pivot from the previous milestone with Elissa being in Tony Hawk's Pro Skater where there was one woman who was backed by a community of men. With the *Getting Nowhere Faster* Project, now there was a community of women coming together, and a select few men jumping on board to add their stamp of approval and support, both financial and social.

Lacey Baker represents another shift in the inclusion of women. Baker is openly queer-identified and is currently sponsored by Nike and on the US Olympic team. This is a dramatic shift from the ways in which core networks have historically filtered and promoted girls and women. We provide some background on how Baker got to this point. When Baker was 8 years old and fresh to skateboarding, Elissa Steamer was the only other woman skateboarder that was visible at the time. But, as noted above, the landscape changed with the growth of women's networks. As a teenager, Lacey would find a place in the Villa Villa Cola crew, missing out on getting a full part in their breakthrough video *Getting Nowhere Faster*, but quickly becoming an iconic figure in Girls Skate Network's blogcam videos and posts. In 2006, at age 14, Baker had a first appearance in X Games, earning bronze. Throughout the years, Baker made a name as one of the world's best, competing internationally, regularly placing at events like X Games, and filmed full video parts released by *Thrasher Magazine*. Nonetheless, Baker was still marginalized in the core networks and thus wasn't unable to fully pursue skateboarding as a professional. Lacey entered the workforce as a graphic designer, but missed skating. In 2014, Baker connected with a filmer, Tyler Smolinski, together they worked to document Baker's best skateboarding tricks. Baker noted that it is very hard to find a filmer who will fully support you as a friend and capture you authentically which was important to her as a queer-identified skater who does not conform to heteronormative standards.

Within two more years Baker's skills are in the spotlight, which lead to economic opportunities from both core and mainstream industries. Some of these included winning Street League in 2016 and 2017 and appearing in a full-length *Thrasher Magazine* part in January 2017. This exposure leads to other endorsements. Baker decided it would be wise to hire an agent to negotiate these potential sponsorships. Yulin Olliver was the agent who had considerable experience in the action sport industry including working for Street League which had partnered with Nike Skateboarding division. She was able to get Baker a contract with Nike – unprecedented for a non-feminine individual in the world of women's skateboarding. Additionally, Baker was featured in a Nike advertisement alongside NFL player and activist, Colin Kaepernick. Olliver commented on this meteoric rise of Baker, "We're breaking through the glass ceiling of even what we thought was possible when we created this game" (in Bruton, 2019).

Inarguably, Baker's skills are impressive. But with this milestone of inclusion, we see major corporate sponsorship but with minimal male 'gatekeeper' support. In Baker's story, a pivot can be seen from the previous milestone of *Getting Nowhere Faster*. In this instance, Baker was able to showcase skills through two major outlets, *Thrasher Magazine* and Street League, and translate that to a significant endorsement from Nike. And the Olympics also played a role in Baker's rise. Before 2015, Street League did not have women's events. It was compelled to do so because the requirement of the Olympics is that any organization that wanted to be an official Olympic qualifying contest needed to have women's divisions. Once Baker was able to showcase skill through Street League, Baker joined up with agent Yulin Olliver. And Olliver is part of this evolving network supporting women's skateboarding. These expanding networks have enabled other women to get major endorsements including Nora Vasconcellos on Adidas, Samarria Brevard on Enjoi, and Mariah Duran on Mtn Dew.

CONCLUSION

The Olympics have ushered in a new era in skateboarding with respect to who has power to determine what constitutes 'core' or 'authentic' ways. As we have shown, the debate about 'authenticity' has also been a debate about the gender boundaries of skateboarding. In this chapter we have examined the history and some of the mechanisms of boundary maintenance and women's exclusion from the core networks of skateboarding. Exclusion happens when there are inequitable structural opportunities and when certain group's norms and values are marginalized. We've shown how the normative gender structure of skateboarding, the media representation of skaters, and leadership positions in the industry have privileged men and masculinity. In response to being marginalized, women have made their own networks in order to have their voice count in creating skateboarding traditions and value systems.

Currently, although not close to an exhaustive list, some of these groups included, Girls' Riders Organization, No Limit, Girls Skate Australia, Skirtboarders, Skate Like a Girl, Chica Rider, Unity Skateboarding, and Skateistan (cf. Beal, 2013; MacKay, 2016; Thorpe & Chawansky, 2016). It should be noted that the hierarchy of gender in skateboarding has not been a simple binary of male vs female, but a privileging of cisgender heteronormativity. Thus, in response to the strict codes of authenticity (by all genders) was to create more welcoming spaces and narratives which have proliferated in diverse ways. For example, there are now groups who are explicitly promoting queer sensibility such as Doyenne, Unity Skateboarding, Pave the Way, and Skateism. In 2018, Pushing Boarders, a conference bridging academic and practitioners of skateboarding, was held to open lines of conversations about varied types of skate communities, commercial viability, and skateboard activism. These groups, and others like them, have broadened the definition of what constitutes a legitimate skateboarder. Although the Olympics are integral in providing economic and leadership opportunities for some women, we question whether the IOC can radically shift gender norms. We argue that grassroots groups play a crucial role in challenging the normative structures and traditions of skateboarding. The newly evolving women's networks include media production, community organizations, and some key industry players. The groups work to create spaces where more women and noncisgendered folks' concerns are addressed and where their voices are central. In turn, these spaces and communities serve to develop a broader range of skateboarders whose interests challenge the traditional boundaries of 'core' networks.

REFERENCES

Atencio, M., Beal, B. & Wilson, C. (2009). Distinction of risk: Urban skateboarding, street habitus, and the construction of hierarchical gender relations. *Qualitative Research in Sport and Exercise* 1, 1, 3-20.

Atencio, M., Beal, B., Wright, E. & McClain, Z. (2018). *Moving Boarders. Skateboarding and the Changing Landscape of Urban Youth Sports*. Fayetteville: The University of Arkansas Press.

Bäckström, Å. (2013). "Gender Manoeuvring in Swedish Skateboarding: Negotiations of Femininities and the Hierarchical Gender Structure." *Young, 21*, 1, 29-53. doi:10.1177/1103308812467670.

Bailey, R. (2005). Evaluating the relationship between physical education, sport and social inclusion, *Educational Review, 57*, 1, 71-90. doi: 10.1080/0013191042000274196.

Baker, L., 1/5/2019 personal interview.

Batuev, M. & Robinson, L. (2017). How skateboarding made it to the Olympics. *International Journal of Sport Management and Marketing* 17, 381-402.

Beal, B. (1996). Alternative masculinity and its effects on gender relations in the subculture of skateboarding. *Journal of Sport Behavior, 19*, 204-220.

Beal, B. (2013). *Skateboarding: The Ultimate Guide*. Santa Barbara, CA: ABC CLIO Extreme Sport Series, series editors Holly Thorpe and Douglas Booth.

Beal, B. & Weidman, L. (2003). Authenticity in the Skateboarding World. In Rinehart, R. E. & Sydnor, S. (Eds.), *To the Extreme. Alternative Sports, Inside and Out* (pp. 337-352). Albany: SUNY.

Beal, B. & Wilson, C. (2004). 'Chicks dig scars': Transformations in the subculture of skateboarding. In Wheaton, B. (Ed.), *Understanding lifestyle sports: Consumption. Identity, and difference.* (pp. 31-54). London: Routledge Press.

Borden, I. (2019). *Skateboarding and the City: A complete history*. London: Bloomsbury.

Bruton, M. (2019, March 10). Skateboarding's super agent helps clients soar as brands too. *Ozy*. Retrieved from https://www.ozy.com/the-huddle/skateboard ings-super-agent-helps-clients-soar-as-brands-too/90575?fbclid=IwAR32Bii Axy6_sLGQe8MLNPXb0h-EoJ1Or8jf4fUmCTj0ha9Wrdpmkk1qx-g.

Bullion, L. (2018, August 21). My experiences in skateboarding. *Jenken Magazine*. Retrieved from: http://www.jenkemmag.com/home/2018/08/21/my-experiences-in-skateboarding/.

Chivers-Yochim, E. (2010). *Skate life: Re-imagining white masculinity*. Ann Arbor: University of Michigan Press.

Collins, M. (2004). Sport, physical activity and Social exclusion. *Journal of Sport Sciences, 8*, 724-740. doi.org/10.1080/02640410410001712430.

Collison, H., Darnell, S., Giulianotti, R. & Howe, D. (2017). The Inclusion Conundrum: A Critical Account of Youth and Gender Issues Within and Beyond Sport for Development and Peace Interventions. *Social Inclusion 5*, 2, 223-231. doi: 10.17645/si.v5i2.888.

Cunningham, G. (2015). *Diversity and Inclusion in Sport Organizations: A multilevel perspective*. New York: Routledge.

Donnelly, M. (2006). Studying Extreme Sports: Beyond the Core Participants. *Journal of Sport and Social Issues 30*, 2, 219-224.

Donnelly, P & Coakley, J. (2002). *The role of recreation in promoting social inclusion*. Toronto: Laidlaw Working Papers Series.

Dupont, T. (2014). From core to consumer: The Informal Hierarchy of the Skateboard Scene. *Journal of Contemporary Ethnography, 43*, 5, 556-581.

Dupont, T. (2016). *Skateboarding through Life: Subcultural Careers and Exits from Skateboarding*. PhD. Dissertation from SUNY Buffalo.

Elling, A. & Knoppers, A. (2005). Sport, Gender and Ethnicity: Practises of Symbolic Inclusion/Exclusion, *Journal of Youth and Adolescence*, 34, 3, 257-268. doi: 10.1007/s10964-005-4311-6.

Frisby, W. (2011). Promising Physical Activity Inclusion Practices for Chinese Immigrant Women in Vancouver, Canada, *Quest, 63*, 1, 135-147, doi: 10.1080/00336297.2011.10483671.

Giannoulakis, C. (2016). The "authenticitude" battle in action sports: A case-based industry perspective. *Sport Management Review, 19*, 171-182.

Hawk, T. 1/20/2019 personal interview.

Higgins, M. (2011, May 13). Gender Gap. *ESPN*. Retrieved from http://www.espn.com/action/news/story?page=cara-beth-burnside-and-action -sports-gender-bias.

Kossek, E., Su, R. & Wu, L. (2017). "Opting Out" or "Pushed Out"? Integrating Perspectives on Women's Career Equality for Gender Inclusion and Inter-

ventions, *Journal of Management* 43, 1, 228-254. doi: 10.1177/01492063
16671582.

McKay, S. (2016). Spreading the Skirtboarder stoke: Reflexively blogging fluid
femininities and Constructing new Females Skateboarding Identities. In
Lomabard, K. J. (Ed.), *Skateboarding: Subcultures, Sites & Shifts.*
Routledge, 121-135.

Messner, M. (2002). *Taking the Field: Women, Men & Sports.* Minneapolis:
University of Minnesota Press.

O'Connor, P. (2018). Beyond the youth culture: Understanding middle-aged
skateboarders through temporal capital. *International Review for the Sociology of Sport,* 53, 8, 924-943. doi: org/10.1177/1012690217691780.

Olliver, Y. 1/14/2019 personal interview.

Porter, N. (2003). Female skateboarders and their negotiation of space and identity. *Journal for Arts, Sciences, and Technology,* 1, 75-80.

Pulley, A. (2015, March 4). These females skateboarders are changing the sport
for the better. *East Bay Express.* Retrieved from: https://www.eastbay
express.com/oakland/reinventing-the-wheels/Content?oid=4210451.

Pushing Boarders (2018). https://www.pushingboarders.com/talks.

Rannikkoa, A., Harinena, P., Torvinena, P., Liikanenb, V. (2016). The social
bordering of lifestyle sports: inclusive principles, exclusive reality, *Journal
of Youth Studies,* 19, 8, 1093-1109. http://dx.doi.org/10.1080/13676261.20
16.1145640.

Rinehart, R. (2005). "Babes" & Boards: Opportunities in the New Millennium
Sport? *Journal of Sport and Social Issues, 29,* 232-255.

Savage, E. (2017 January). In The 1980s, This All-Girl Skateboard Gang Took
Over the Streets Of LA. *Bust.* Retrieved from https://bust.com/living/18944-
hell-on-wheels.html.

Spaaij, R., Magee, J. & Jeanes, R. (2014). *Sport and Social Exclusion in Global
Society.* Routledge.

Steamer, E. 2/20/19 personal interview.

Synder, G. (2017). *Skateboarding LA: Inside Professional Street Skateboarding.*
New York: New York University Press.

Thorpe, H. & Chawansky, M. (2016) The "girl effect" in actions sports for Development: The case of female practitioners of Skateistan, in Thorpe, H. &
Olive, R. (Eds.), *Women in Action Sports Culture: Identities Politics and Experiences*, 133-152.

Thorpe, H & Olive, R. (Eds.) (2016). *Women in Action Sports Culture: Identities
Politics and Experiences.* London: Palgrave-MacMillan.

Travers, A. & Deri, J. (2010). Transgender inclusion and the changing face of lesbian softball leagues. *International Review for the Sociology of Sport, 46,* 4, 488-507.

Wheaton, B. & Beal, B. (2003). 'Keeping it real': subcultural media and the discourses of authenticity in alternative sport. *International Review for the Sociology of Sport*, 38, 2, 155-176.

Wheaton, B. & Thorpe, H. (2018). Action Sports, the Olympic Games, and the Opportunities and Challenges for Gender Equity: The Cases of Surfing and Skateboarding, *Journal of Sport and Social Issues,* 42, 5, 315-342. doi: 10.1177/0193723518781230.

Whitaker, L. 1/17/2019 personal interview.

White, A. 3/4/2019 personal interview.

No Comply.
The Resilience of Skateboarding Culture

Sebastian Schweer

INTRODUCTION

In 2002 the Swedish skateboarder Pontus Alv began producing experimental and at times irritating skateboard-art-videos in which he processed his father's and his grandparents' death. The skateboarding portrayed in his videos did not match the criteria of mainstream skateboarding and took place at unknown Scandinavian spots or at self-build concrete ramps, so called *do-it-yourself spots* (*DIY spots*), erected in industrial wasteland.

A couple of years later Alv is one of the most famous people in the skate world and owner of the highly successful brand Polar Skate. His rather unorthodox skateboarding style has spread internationally. The reasons for both, Alv's popularity and that of his interpretation of skateboarding, will be subject to the following analysis. I will argue that we are witnessing a reaction of the skateboarding culture to the tendencies that push skateboarding towards a regular, that is regulated, sport. This reaction can be understood as resilience.

HETERODOX SKATEBOARDING

The title of the promo video from the new skateboard brand *Polar Skate* "No Complies & Wallrides+shuvits" (Polar Skate Co., 2012a) exemplifies the dissemination of a new skateboarding style I will henceforth call *heterodox skateboarding*. It is characterized by a rather high trick frequency, a creative and sometimes even chaotic trick execution and manoeuvers that until recently were only to be found in the 'nerdy' periphery of skateboarding culture. These tricks include *wallrides*,[1] *wallies*,[2] *slappies*[3] as well as *no complies*,[4] *shuvits*[5], *power-slides*,[6] *boneless ones*[7] and *fastplants*.[8] Many of these tricks, which were uncommon around 2000, are now part of a skateboarder's standard repertoire.[9]

Outlining *heterodox skateboarding* one can state, firstly, that it entails a more intense contact with the urban space: hands and feet touch the ground more often

---

1 While *wallriding* a skateboarder pushes against a steep or vertical wall. The difficult part is to not collide with the obstacle, but to ride along it.

2 A *wallie* is a jump that includes the object one is to overcome. The skateboarder collides with the obstacle in a controlled way so that it is used as a ramp.

3 A *slappie* or *slappie grind* is a motion where a skateboarder pushes hard against a curb in order to lock in his trucks so that he can get to grind it without using the jumping technique called *ollie*. In the early nineties this trick was highly popular but then disappeared almost completely. It resurrected around 2010.

4 While performing a *no comply*, the skateboarder places his front foot on the ground in order to jump off only with his back foot. This trick can be performed in a myriad of ways and can be understood as the emblem of *heterodox skateboarding*.

5 A *shuvit* is a trick where the board is turned 180° around its longitudinal axis. This trick may be 'popped' (*pop shuvit*) which means that the board lifts off the ground or it may just slide over the ground (*shuvit*). The latter is highly popular within *heterodox skateboarding* as it can be performed while skating high speed.

6 A *powerslide* is performed mostly in order to limit one's speed while riding very fast, for instance a *downwhill*. The skateboarder pushes his board's back (*tail*) so that all four wheels are across the skating direction, slide over the ground and hence break.

7 While performing a *boneless one*, the skateboarder grabs the board and jumps off using his front foot.

8 A *fastplant* is a trick where the skateboarder jumps off and then places his back foot on the obstacle (which may also be the coping of a ramp) and grabs his board.

9 Speaking about a standard trick repertoire is of course problematic since the skateboarding culture and its participants are highly diverse and differentiated. But since I want to shed light to a change of style within the skateboarding community from a sociological meta-perspective I necessarily have to make certain generalizations. The popularity of the aforementioned 'new' tricks will be verified through the analysis of popular videos, discussions in the internet and company logos. What I want to do is to carve out a tendency of development but this does not imply that the skateboarders in 2019 skate according to certain fixed rules. The *orthodox* and *heterodox* skateboarders are to be understood as ideal types in the Weberian sense and do not exist in a pure form; they open up a spectrum.

than in the orthodox skateboarding style and one does not only jump over obstacles but skates with speed and technique against them. Popular skatespots are no longer those with the smoothest surface, but instead those with a rough ground or short and dangerous landing,[10] guaranteeing the highest reputation.

Secondly, *heterodox skateboarding* tricks are often being performed in a rapid succession (*line*) which is possible due to the fact that for example shuvits, wallrides or powerslides can be performed without demanding much energy and while skating very fast.

But neither the aforementioned tricks nor the general style of heterodox skateboarding are without precedent. Already in 2001 professional skateboarder Jason Adams was skating in a way that can be considered heterodox long before it became popular and a mass phenomenon. Indeed, at the beginning of the 21st century *heterodox skateboarding* was only to be seen at the margins of skateboarding culture and it was unlikely that professional skateboarders embraced this particular style and choice of tricks. That is why I refer to this style as heterodox. The fact that this peripheral approach to skateboarding now became a mass phenomenon is indicated by the comments posted beneath Jason Adams' part in the video "Label Kills" (Black Label, 2001), released in 2001, which can be viewed on YouTube.

"Ed Fisher (2010): [...] people are doing a lot of these tricks now.
Maxime Bel: this was jason adams attempt to subtly communicate that he was a time traveling [sic] skateboarder from the year of 2015." (Ed Fisher, 2010)

These comments suggest that the acceptance of Adam's *heterodox* style has increased since 2001 and entered mainstream skateboarding.[11] The question I want to dwell on is: why and how did this skateboarding style, which in 2000 was only a peripheral phenomenon, gain such a momentum? In this paper my approach is zooming out. Firstly, I will trace the development of skateboarder, art-

---

10 The *GX1000* crew from San Francisco would be one example of this style. In their skating the focus does not lie on a single trick but rather on the question whether they survive the following breakneck *downhill*.

11 As a proof for the popularity of *heterodox skateboarding* one can also consult the cover photos of *Thrasher Magazine*, the most influential skateboard medium. A *Thrasher* cover shot is considered an accolade for every skateboarder and the same is true for the covered tricks. In the April issue 2004 Ishod Wair was pictured with a *no comply-wallie* (Thrasher Magazine 2014), in the October issue 2015 Jake Johnson got the cover shot performing a *no comply* (Thrasher Magazine, 2015b).

ist and entrepreneur Pontus Alv, since I argue that he plays a major role in popularizing *heterodox skateboarding*.

Secondly, I will relate the growing popularity of *heterodox skateboarding* with the emergence of event formats pushing the sportisation of skateboarding such as *Street League Skateboarding* and *Battle at the Berrics*.

Thereafter I try to provide an explanation that does not argue on the actor's level but understands skateboarding culture as an emergent phenomenon. The formation and popularization of *heterodox skateboarding* will hence be understood as an expression of skateboarding culture's resilience against the accelerating sportisation. I will conclude by positioning my findings in a macrosocial perspective using the resonance theory as developed by sociologist Hartmut Rosa.

PONTUS ALV: A SKATEBOARDER'S EVOLUTION

Pontus Alv, born 1980, is a professional skateboarder who already as an adolescent had contracts with US skateboard companies and was represented in videos such as "5ive Flavors" by *Mad Circle* (Mad Circle Skateboards, 1998) and "Gumbo" by *Arcade Skateboards* (Arcade Skateboards, 1999). One must stress that by the end of the 1990s it was rather uncommon for European skateboarders to be sponsored by US companies. Alv was a successful skateboarder whose bag of tricks and skate style was representative for US West Coast street skating in the late 1990s. The places he mostly chose to skate at for his videoparts were the iconographic spots in San Francisco.

Pontus Alv left *Arcade Skateboards* in order to ride for the European skateboard company *Cliché Skateboards* and he had his own part in their video "Europa" (Cliché Skateboards, 2000), which was released in 2000. Like the video's name suggests, Alv chose to skate almost exclusively European spots, however his skate style remained conventional. Since Alv quit *Cliché* in 2003, he was not featured in their video "Bon Appetit" (Cliché Skateboards, 2004), which was released in 2004. The footage he collected during his time at *Cliché*, which was filmed by French filmer Fred Mortagne, was released as a so-called *b-side* (Thrasher Magazine, 2015a) and displays a change in Alv's skate style. One can see a more creative approach as Alv enlarged his repertoire which now included many *wallride* and *wallie* variations as well as *no complies*.

During this period of time he chose to move back to Malmö where he began to work on his own skate film. He decided to do so because he never felt that his own interpretation of skateboarding was represented in the aforementioned videos:

"For once in my career I wanted to show people who I really am and what I believe and stand for. All my past video parts before strongest [i.e. his first video 'The Strongest of the Strange', S. Schw.] never showed me. It showed me through the image and eyes of a company. I always felt like I worked so hard with my skating but when I saw the final result in the end I always felt like there were things missing. So this is why I decided to make my first film to show my beliefs and my ideas of what skateboard is and isn't for me." (theoriesofatlantis, 2014)

From this follows that Alv's early *orthodox* way of skateboarding did not necessarily emerge naturally but was shaped by the demands of the skateboard industry. Jason Adams has similar experiences concerning his choice of tricks. Adams, a lover of *slappy grinds,* never performed them in his role as a professional skateboarder, but solely in his free time. Only when he began riding for the skateboard company *Black Label* he felt free to include *slappies* into his videoparts since the owner, John Lucero, encouraged him to do so.[12]

Deriving from these examples one can see the codification of the diverse and multifaceted movement practice: the way professional skateboarders choose to present themselves and their skateboarding obeys to the (assumed) taste of the customers and hence perpetuates the orthodox way of skating, since ignoring or even undermining this codification can lead to the marginalization within mainstream skateboarding and this carries an economic risk for both, the sponsoring skateboard company and the professional skateboarder.

Pontus Alv took both risks, i.e. being marginalized within the skateboard community and being stripped of his source of income when he released his first self-made video in 2005. The video is titled "Strongest of the Strange" (Pontus Alv, 2005), with reference to a poem by Charles Bukowski. It was supported by

---

12 "Oh, for sure I was doing them [*Slappies*, S. Schw.] then, especially in the early 90s. You know what was going on in skateboarding. It was hip hop, urban, white shirts, baggy pants, that kind of bullshit, and I was still like: I like punk rock, I'm from the suburbs. I grew up with The Faction and Black Flag and all that kind of stuff...I never grew out of it. (In the 90's) one of my closest friends was Tim Brauch and he had the same attitude. We'd have slappy sessions, we kind of had that need for rebellion within skateboarding, that and San Jose pride was really heavy. I embraced it. I don't think that was really seen until later when I rode for Black Label. With the other companies I was just trying to fit in, but (John)Lucero was the first to really stress 'do whatever you want', so I'd show him video and be like: 'look at this (slappy) trick...I did all this stuff on a curb', and he'd love it." (Ackbar & Adams, 2014).

the fashion company Carhartt and in Switzerland, Austria and Germany it was attached as a free DVD to the issue 34 of the core skateboard magazine BOARDSTEIN. The video, a mixture of skateboard video and art movie produced between 2002 and 2005, gained much attention. Here one can identify all those topoi for which Alv eventually became recognized: an artistic and utterly personal approach towards skateboarding culture, many unknown Swedish spots (opposed to the iconic US-American sites at which he skated during the beginning of his career) and a strong focus on the history and evolution of the featured DIY spots, which are lovingly portrayed including their names and their date of 'birth' (and 'death'). The tricks can at large be subsumed under the umbrella of heterodox skateboarding.

The artistic approach is supported by a guest part of US skateboarder Scott 'Black Arm' Bourne, known for his aggressive and creative skateboarding style and his artistic way of life. The soundtrack to his black and white part is the reading of a Bukowski poem.[13] A graffiti sprayed on a DIY ramp may exemplify the state of mind portrayed in the video with respect to Alv's experiences within the skateboard industry: "NO RULES, NO FUCKING RULES".

Alv's second video "In Search of the Miraculous" (Polar Skate Co., 2010) not only sparked the interest of a huge part of the skateboarding community but has had a lasting effect on skateboarding culture. Kingpin Magazine concedes that "[…] his independent films, such as 2010's In Search Of The Miraculous, have left an indelible mark on the sport" (Kingpin Skateboarding).

The abovementioned combination of heterodox skateboarding, artistic film style, DIY culture as well as the personal component, which culminates in a scene in which Alv portrays himself next to the dead body of his grandfather, attracted widespread attention. In this video one finds another confrontation with the skateboard industry: in one scene a very young Pontus Alv is being interviewed after he won a skateboard contest. The interviewer asks about Alv's performance:

"Interviewer: This went splendid, Pontus!
Alv: Yeah. It went good, I placed first. So I am very pleased with myself.

---

13 Scott Bourne currently lives Paris and stylizes himself as an old-style writer rejecting modern technology, using only old typewriters or writing by hand. He published poetry (Bourne, 2015) and a novel (Bourne, 2013). He and Alv got to know each other during a *Carhartt* sponsored trip to Ulan Bator. They have in common an unusual skate-style, a sometimes ostentatious stylization as artist and the support of *Carhartt*.

Interviewer Why did you win?
Alv: I got something called a line… You know… When you ride a special route… So I
practice this line… So I win… and don't miss." (Polar Skate Co., 2010, 47:58)

Following this scene one can hear a sigh in the soundtrack which can be understood as a rejection of young Alv's competitive interpretation of skateboarding
and thereupon the part of the matured, *heterodox* Alv begins.

This composition addresses skateboarding's tendency towards sportisation
which Alv has rejected. Within the frame of professional competitive skateboarding it is not uncommon to practice a certain trick time and again. This interpretation of skateboarding does not significantly differ in any meaningful way
from other competitive sports.[14]

Alv's second video ends with a likely illegal break-in into an industrial site
where the featured skateboarders use a huge boiler in order to skate it as a
fullpipe. This shows that trespassing and violation are also part of *heterodox
skateboarding*.

Back to the video's history of reception: in 2011 "In Search of the Miraculous" received awards at the International Skateboard Film Festival in Los Angeles in the categories "Best Documentary", "Best Soundtrack" and "Best Director" (Schwinghammer, 2011). In the course of this resounding success Alv
founded his company Polar Skate in 2012, which quickly became one of the
most successful skateboarding labels and figurehead of heterodox skateboarding
style.

That Alv's company is inherently connected to this skateboarding style is exemplified through the fact that a famous design of *Polar Skate* is a sculpture
reminiscent of Henry Matisse's "Blue Nude" performing a *no comply*. In addition, *Polar*'s first promo videos are named after tricks which are an integral part
of *heterodox skateboarding*: "No Complies & Wallrides+shuvits" (Polar Skate
Co., 2012a) and "Wallrides. Oh Yeah, Oh Yeah Oh Yeah" (Polar Skate Co.,
2012b). The featured skateboarding complies with the titles.

The great and positive response to Alv's videos can inter alia be explained by
the artistic style, the innovative form of skateboarding, the *DIY spots* and the

---

14 Nyjah Huston, role model of *orthodox* mainstream skateboarding and a likely Olym-
    pic participant in 2020, describes the training routine he underwent already at the age
    of 8: "I would go through these like hour, two, three hours long routines of just prac-
    ticing tricks and after that I'd be like: Ok, now I can learn something new" (The Nine
    Club, 2018, 14:00).

well curated soundtrack, but this alone does not sufficiently explain the thorough impact Alv and *heterodox skateboarding* has had on the skateboarding culture as a whole. To understand this phenomenon, one needs to consider further details in order to understand Alv's success and that *of heterodox skateboarding* as part of a bigger picture, so that one may answer the following question: why did *heterodox skateboarding* become popular around 2010, that is with the release of "In Search of the Miraculous", and not earlier, promoted, for instance, already in 2001 via aforementioned Jason Adams or other *heterodox* skateboarders?

THE POLE OF SPORTISATION

Besides the *X Games* which for the first time took place 1995 in Newport, Rhode Island and presented skateboarding as a mass-compatible sport in mainstream TV, the year 2008 can be considered a watershed within skateboarding culture. Firstly, the *Maloof Money Cup*, until then the contest with the highest prize money in skateboarding ever, that is 160.000 US$ (NBC Washington, 2011), was inaugurated. This supported skateboarding's approximation of other professional sports since from then on, substantial sums could be won at the events.

Another format which would set out to become a highly successful event series is *Battle at the Berrics* (BATB). This series was also introduced in 2008. Here, 32 skateboarders compete against each other in pairs of two. The concept is simple and highly competitive: skateboarder 1 presents a trick performed on flatground only, skateboarder 2 tries to do the same trick. If they fail, they collect one letter. The one who first accumulates five letters (SKATE) loses.[15]

The event is organized by the company *Berrics* which is a portmanteau made of the founder's names, Steve Berra and Eric Koston (Berra, Eric). They acquired a warehouse facility in Los Angeles and set up a skatepark, which chosen skateboarders can use, avoiding the hassle of street skateboarding.[16] Their website is "one of skateboarding's most trafficked websites" (Jenkem Magazine, 2014) and entails an online shop as well as many different video formats. Most refer to the semantic field 'military', since the name *Berrics* is a (rather imprecise) homophone to barracks. Hence video formats bear names such as Battle Commander, Canteen, New Recruit or Shoot all Skaters. The most important – that is, most successful – format is the Battle at the Berrics. As is customary in a

---

15 The format derived from the game HORSE known in basketball.
16 Rough surface, intervening securities, wind, pedestrians, parked cars blocking the run up, furious residents, to name but a few.

barrack and in regular sports, a rather strict set of rules applies. These rules are being read out aloud prior to every duel by the referee and it is worth quoting them at length:

"BATB X Rules
This is flatground only but that doesn't mean everything on flatground counts.
No feet on the ground so that means no no-complies.
No handplants.
No bonelesses.
No grabs.
No doing tricks that slide on the ground if your opponent popped his trick. [...]
Let's keep it clean, let's keep it lean. This is battle of the Berrics and there's only gonna be one winner so may god have mercy on your souls." (The Berrics, 2017)

In spite of the ostentatious ironic way in which the referees, who are mostly professional skateboarders themselves, read out the rules, they are applied in a very strict sense: the tricks have to be executed cleanly and are limited to a clear spectrum from which deviations like touching the board with a hand (grabs, bonelesses, handplants), touching the ground with a foot (no complies, fastplants) are not accepted. In this context the literal meaning of 'no comply' gains a symbolic level since the exclusion of this trick via BATB rules exemplifies the codification and quantification of skateboarding in favor of clear comparability. It may hence not be a coincidence that this trick became emblematic for heterodox skateboarding.

Following the far-reaching changes induced by the *Maloof Money Cup* and BATB, one has to mention the event series named *Street League Skateboarding* (SLS), which was inaugurated in 2010, the same year in which the *X Games* took place in Europe for the first time.

Not only did SLS considerably raise the prize-money, but it introduced an unprecedented way of rating the skateboarders: for the first time, every trick has a clear score, which is shown in real time on the huge screens in the event hall.[17] This rating system is called *Instant Scoring Experience* (ISX) and is of great importance for the Olympic contest in 2020, since now for the first time in skateboarding history there seems to be an 'objective' way of measuring the hard to grasp movement practice.

This is the bigger picture within which Alv's skate and art videos were celebrated and in which a skateboarding style is presented that can be understood as

---

17 For a more detailed, alas German, discussion of SLS cf. Schweer, 2014, p. 117 ff.

an inversion of the BATB rules. As mentioned above, famous tricks of hetero-dox skateboarding include *wallrides*, *no complies*, *slappy grinds* as well as *bone-less* and *fastplant* variations, all of which are decidedly excluded via BATB rules. Other components of heterodox skateboarding are quick and creative lines in which many – often simple – tricks are combined so that the focus is not on a certain singular mega-trick but on the line as an emergent whole with an empha-sis on the skateboarder's style. This can be understood as an inversion of the way a skateboarder has to skate if they want to score high at SLS, where one has to perform a clear trick with a high level of difficulty.

Against this backdrop I want to put forward the thesis that *heterodox skate-boarding* is a critique on the trend towards sportisation which was popularized and accelerated by the abovementioned events and the upcoming Olympic Games in Tokyo 2020.

The huge resonance for *heterodox skateboarding* indicates a resilience of the skateboarding culture that can be understood as a resistivity in existential crisis situations. Through the pressure of quantification and the codification of the trick-repertoire, certain practices within the skateboarding culture are in danger of disappearance such as: DIY culture, the spontaneous cruising through urban spaces and the playful, creative and spontaneous component of skateboarding all of which are characterized by a high degree of "participant control" (Beal & Weidman, 2003, p. 344) and self-efficacy.

Hence skate styles, tricks and preferences for spots which evade the demands of sportisation, at least temporarily,[18] are emerging. The choice of spots can be considered a part of skateboarding culture's resilience insofar as the sites are not being chosen for their smooth surface or easy access anymore, for instance

---

18 On the *Berric*'s Instagram account it was asked whether or not the *no comply* should be included at *BATB* 11. The numerous comments show that there is no consensus within the skateboarding community. It is interesting to look at the arguments that are made against the inclusion of the *no comply*. Many point out that this trick has many, often confusing varieties and hence does not fit into a competition in which tricks have to be accurately executed and replicated. At the same time many complain that the *no comply* is not even a real trick. It is questionable whether the owners of *Berrics* gathered their consumer's opinion in order to evaluate if the rules should really be changed. The new Instagram algorithm which measures the time users spend looking at a post and how they interact may have played a role as the predictable controversy evolving around the *no comply* is a sure way in order to comply with the requirements of aforementioned algorithm in order to increase the relevance and profitability of the *Berrics*.

skateparks or -plazas, but for their roughness and resistance against an easy us-age. In this respect Alv states that a given DIY spot has to be built preferably tough so that it won't be boring too quickly. Hence the DIY culture with its small or non-existing budget and the imperfect, individual and idiosyncratic ramps can be considered a counter-world to the clean, smooth and crisp skate-plazas on which events like SLS and BATB take place.

Skateboarding culture's resilience comes into view only through a socio-cultural perspective that abstracts from a skateboarder's individual motivation: one must not mistake the fact that a skateboarder integrates the *no comply* into their repertoire for a deliberate opposition to the BATB rules, the SLS scoring system or the tendency towards sportisation in general.[19] The subject's individual disposition is not the central issue. I have tried to show that skateboarding culture's resilience, manifested through the popularity of *heterodox skateboarding*, emerged when central core values are under attack from the growing influence of the competitive and professionalizing tendencies within the skateboarding field. To be sure, the counter practice, which in my case is *heterodox skateboarding*, needs amplifiers such as Pontus Alv in order to gain momentum. But the success and the resonance cannot be explained sufficiently, if one only focuses on the, forgive me the pun, polarizing multipliers. As I have shown, one has to view the entire constellation within the skateboarding field with its specific discourses and developments. From here one can understand that only by taking into account the abovementioned changes within mainstream skateboarding one can grasp the rise of *heterodox skateboarding* in general and *Polar Skate* in particular.

When one understands resilience as a reaction to skateboarding's sportisation then one has to reject Cantin-Brault's thesis that skateboarding's inclusion in the Olympic Games 2020 will be the "final nail in the coffin of its [i.e. skateboarding's, S. Schw.] reification" (Cantin-Brault, 2015, p. 65). Rather, the skateboarding culture differentiates itself because of the tendency towards sportisation, new styles, such as *heterodox skateboarding*, emerge and can be read as a critique on the interpretation of skateboarding as a regular sport. These resilient tendencies are by no means immune to commercialization. The opposite is true: *heterodox skateboarding* as artistic critique (cf. Boltanski & Chiapello, 2006) provides the market with a new reservoir of authenticity and hence poses a great investment opportunity. Thus it is not resistant, as it does not escape the logic of capital (which skateboarding culture never did), but only resilient. The commercial suc-

---

19 Skateboarders who began skateboarding after 2010 may view the *no comply* and other elements of *heterodox skateboarding* as a natural part of their repertoire.

cess of *heterodox skateboarding* not only manifests itself through the growth of companies such as *Polar Skate* but also through the fact that this style is taken up by fashion companies, for example *Supreme*. Other companies such as *Converse Shoes* push this trend and they have good reason to do so: their rediscovered shoe model Chucks can be considered the standard equipment for heterodox skateboarders. Unsurprisingly, *Converse Shoes* support Alv's skate- and art projects.

The other, mainstream oriented pole is represented inter alia by *Nike Skateboarding*, who contracted many of the most popular skateboarders, some of whom will likely be Olympic athletes in 2020. The trick is that *Converse Shoes* is owned by *Nike* and hence skateboarders who want to be either the creative, rebellious and chaotic heterodox skateboarder or those who prefer to be the clean and sleek mainstream (orthodox) skateboarder spend their money on the same company. With that being said I want to come back to Cantin-Brault, who assumes that there is an essence to the skateboarding culture, something that in its original purity has not (yet) been part of what he calls "ideology". He writes:

"Skaters need to find recognition in celebrating their roots, which are not to be found in a reified, quantified and ideological soil. A professional skater is not like the professional athlete of an organized sport: he is not in direct competition with others but only with himself, pushing his limits and the limits of skateboarding's constellation." (Cantin-Brault, 2015, p. 65)

Firstly, there are professional skateboarders, especially those who will eventually compete in the Olympic Games, who are decidedly in competition with other skateboarders (*and* themselves). Secondly, one can state that those core values of skateboarding culture such as intrinsic motivation, creativity, risk appetite, to name but a few, have indeed been part in forming our recent ideology which Boltanski and Chiapello call the "new spirit of capitalism" (Boltanski & Chiapello, 2006). One could even go further by saying that the skateboarder is, at least in the Western hemisphere, a role model for the recent post-Fordist ideology (Schweer, 2014, p. 157 ff.).[20] In this regard, Jamie Thomas, a skateboarding legend and entrepreneur, stated: "Skateboarding and my pro career were like

---

20 Cantin-Brault's notion of ideology is inspired by Theodor W. Adorno and refers to the norms that were hegemonic during the era of Fordism, that is until around 1970. He writes: "Ideology is the term Adorno uses to indicate a social organization that seeks unity, conformity, totality" (Cantin-Brault, 2015, p. 57).

boot camp for business. [...] Trying tricks, envisioning outcomes, persevering – that's exactly like business" (Higgins, 2006).

Cantin-Brault does not disclose what exactly these roots are and when one should locate them chronologically. He defines them negatively: not reified, not quantified, and not in "ideological soil".[21]

But even if one traces back the history of skateboarding to its beginning, one will not find primal, supposedly not-contaminated roots since skateboarding immediately became a commodity. As early as 1962 Larry Stevenson advertised his *Makaha Boards* in his magazine *Surf Guide* since he quickly realized that customers interested in surfing would also be grateful consumers for the new skateboard-related products (Mortimer, 2008, pp. 17-18). Sean Dinces analyzes the complex interplay between commodification and its refusal during the 1970s:

"More specifically, while the subcultural representations of skateboarding – magazines and videos, for example – have relied on an ongoing and shifting negotiation between the refusal and embrace of commodification, this contingent and 'flexible' negotiation is precisely the mechanism by which the sport has maintained its profit-generating capacity across different historical moments. Not long after a select cadre of Southern California skaters cemented a loudly rebellious image for the sport in the 1970s, certain members of that very group began to capitalise financially and professionally on their capacity to craft a subcultural mantra that was both 'authentic' and marketable beyond the confines of their original clique." (Dinces, 2011, p. 1514)

Using the example of Stacy Peralta's self-staging and marketing strategy,[22] Dinces also shows that even the skateboarder-owned company, which until this day is a highly regarded proof of a company's authenticity, was a deliberately created 'myth' in order to successfully and credibly balance between authenticity and commodification. Iain Borden qualifies the idea of a circulation of commodities within the skateboarding culture as a "self-delusional ideology" (Bor-

---

21 He refers to Henry Sanchez' video part in the 1992 video "Tim and Henry's Pack of Lies" which qualifies as an example for the "unreified behavior in the history of skateboarding" (Cantin-Brault, 2015, p. 59). While it is true that this part came out in a time when skateboarding was at a low and only 'hardcore' skateboarders stayed true without hoping to earn a significant amount of money, it is also true that this part was the cornerstone of Sanchez' career as a professional skateboarder.

22 Key to Peralta's project of constructing the subcultural character of skateboarding was his creation of a new version of 'authenticity' for both skateboarders and skateboard companies (Dinces, 2011, p. 1519).

den, 2001, p. 157). Against this background it is questionable whether skateboarding has non-reified roots and when one should situate them chronologically. Of course there have been (and still are) specific constellations, in which the skateboarding culture confronted and trespassed certain norms, rules or laws. But deriving a, say, rebellious essence from a historical specific configuration falls short of understanding skateboarding's dynamic and contingent character as well as its macrosocial embeddedness.[23]

CONCLUSION

Before concluding with an outlook, I quickly want to summarize the arguments I unfolded above. The 'new' skateboarding style I have coined as *heterodox skateboarding* existed long before its popularization in the periphery of skateboarding culture. It was appreciated by connoisseurs without having a noteworthy impact on the skateboarding community. Pontus Alv adopted this style through his artistic approach towards skateboarding and produced videos that, at that time, broke every rule of professional skateboarding: Moving away from San Francisco to Europe (Malmö) and quitting his US sponsors, Alv left the center of the skateboarding industry on both levels: symbolically and geographically. He then filmed at many Swedish spots that were unknown for the international skateboard community, featured many non-famous skateboarders and, due to his artistic approach, implemented arty, heavy and partly unsettling sequences into his videos.

Despite this new, unapologetic and, one could say, heretical approach, his first work "The Strongest of the Strange" attracted much attention and his second video "In Search for the Miraculous" even more so. Via receiving awards in the categories "Best Documentary", "Best Soundtrack" and "Best Director" at the International Skateboard Film Festival in Los Angeles Alv was ennobled by the very center of the skateboarding industry he had previously left.

The success of Alv with regard to *heterodox skateboarding*, his videos and his company can only be understood if it is connected to the newly established event series *BATB* and *SLS*, which represent a major turn within the skateboarding culture towards sportisation. Alv's second award-winning video was released after the introduction of competitive formats such as *BATB* and *Maloof Money Cup* were established and simultaneously with the inauguration of *SLS* in 2010.

---

23 Including factors such as the specific political, economic, legal, cultural, geographical, subcultural and discursive context.

Hence *heterodox skateboarding* became popular at a time when core values of skateboarding culture came under attack and therefore one can understand this style, which (at least temporarily) evades quantification, as an expression of the culture's resilience. Thus Alv is a major figure within this shift in the skateboarding culture but he only became that influential as he was there at the right time and the right place. He is hence to be understood more as an expression and less as an initiator of an emergent phenomenon, that is, resilience.

In order to avoid exaltation of *heterodox skateboarding* one must say very clearly that it does not curb the tendency towards sportisation. What it does is providing a counter model that will offer both professional and amateur skateboarders an alternative movement practice, an alternative style and alternative products.

While in 2020 the first Skateboarders will enter the Olympic stadium in Tokyo with their jerseys which display their national identity, there will still and simultaneously be skateboarders out in the streets who ignore traffic laws, societal norms as well as national origin and trespass private property. Both forms will be part of the same differentiated culture.

OUTLOOK

I have pointed out the affinity between an accelerated world and the flexible skateboarders elsewhere (Schweer, 2014, p. 58). Due to the *time-space-compression* diagnosed by David Harvey skateboarders can be considered a historically fitting movement culture. I want to follow up on this line of thought by applying the concept of resonance developed by sociologist Hartmut Rosa (Rosa, 2017). Due to limited space, I have to draw a rather rough sketch focusing on just a few of Rosa's terms. He assumes that his concept of resonance provides an answer to both a steadily accelerating capitalist society and the accompanying (supposedly increasing) feeling of alienation. Rosa writes: "If acceleration is the problem, then resonance may be the solution [all quotes by Rosa are my translation, S. Schw.]" (Rosa, 2017, p. 13). He emphasizes that deceleration is not the solution, which is of importance for the transfer to the movement practice skateboarding. Rosa, who understands the resonance-theory as an actualization of Critical Theory, advocates that resonance is the counter-term to alienation, understood as a state "in which the 'appropriation of the world' [*Weltanverwandlung*] fails, so that the world consistently appears as cold, rigid, rejecting and non-responsive" (ibid., p. 316). According to Rosa, depression and burnout are conditions which are characterized by the fact that the subject does not experience feelings of "self-efficacy" (ibid., p. 316). One could conclude that a highly accessible environment would enable experiences of resonance but the opposite is true. Rosa writes:

"For resonance requires the existence of the not-appropriated, unfamiliar and even mute; only on this basis another can become audible and hence answer. [...] Resonance-capability is grounded in the prior experience of the unknown, irritating and unavailable, but especially in the indisposable, that which evades the access and the expectation." (ibid., p. 317)

Rosa exemplifies this seemingly counterintuitive thesis by stating that only through the confrontation with something unfamiliar a "dialogical process of appropriation" (ibid., p. 317) can evolve. Without resistance or experience of the unknown one only hears one's own echo. Against this roughly sketched theoretical background *heterodox skateboarding* gains another level of meaning: With Rosa one can state that the 'appropriation of the world' qua skateboard enables a non-alienated experience. This skateboarding style popularized by Alv makes a skateboarder's appropriation of the world possible in two ways: firstly, through the self-made concrete ramps (*DIY-Spots*) which are erected in the public space. By transforming urban spaces in a very 'concrete' way, skateboarders experience a high level of self-efficacy. Their ramps are often built so that skating them is extra hard since a too easy to skate (i.e. assimilate) ramp would soon lose its charm. Alv states:

"If you build something that you can do everything first try then it's no fun. If you build something that you can barely grind the first time, well then you have to work your way up and after, like, a couple of weeks sessioning you gonna be a master of it." (Jeanfeil, 2009, 1:00)

This can be considered an empirical prime example which shows that a satisfying experience of resonance only emerges through the existence of something that resists and that is being appropriated in a dialogical process.

Secondly, heterodox skateboarding enables experiences of resonance since compared to orthodox skateboarding, this style comes into contact with the environment in a more frequent and intensive way. Hands and feet touch the ground way more often and one does not only jump over obstacles but skates against them. The spot preferences, which decidedly include rough, hard to skate, idiosyncratic and weathered sites, also facilitate experiences of resonance, since one has to conquer the spots against a more resistant environment.[24] Also the shoe models preferred by heterodox skateboarders are decidedly slim and without air pads or cushion which facilitates more board control but also a more intense and at times painful impact. In short, the resistant environment is experienced in a more direct way. Following this argument, the plazas at which SLS events take place with their smooth surface and the perfectly built obstacles that are carefully designed for skateboarding purposes do not facilitate experiences of resonance. They pose a highly codified and sterile terrain which was built for the purpose of performance measurement. Here the critical impetus of the appropriation of the world's streets and industrial sites via skateboarding is being lost. From this follows a theoretical argument for street skating[25] in general and for *heterodox skateboarding* in particular, since according to Rosa an "irrevocable moment of unavailability" (Rosa, 2017, p. 295) is inherent to experiences of resonance.

I want to conclude by embedding skateboarding into a macrosocial panorama: a skateboarder making experiences of resonance end self-efficacy through the movement practice skateboarding has found a way to undergo something one could emphatically call an authentic – that is, non-alienated – (bodily) experience. Rosa stresses that his is a highly pressing and current issue:

"One does not really need to investigate the countless medical, gymnastic and in many cases esoteric practices or guidebooks who promise us to be able to once again feel the own body (and let it answer) [all italics in original, S. Schw.] in order to attribute at least some plausibility to the notion of 'resonance-blockades' in the body condition. In fact, the history of modernity is significantly determined by the sometimes even politically articulated concern about the gradual loss of the sense for the corporeality of our existence." (ibid., pp. 71-72)

Against this background one can understand the popularity of and the great interest in so called *b-side* videos. These rough cuts do not have a soundtrack other than the noises the skateboarder and their environment make and are rather lengthy, i.e. 7-20 minutes. They show the countless slams, bails and encounters

---

24 A radical extension of the concept of a skatespot can be seen in Dane Brady's video part in the 2016 *Polar* video "I like it here inside my mind. Don't wake me this time" (Polar Skate Co., 2016). Brady skates inter alia on lawns, cars, clay soil or through water-filled fountains.

25 What qualifies as street skating is the usage and appropriation of urban spaces that were not built for skateboarding and hence have to be 'misused'.

with securities or bystanders a skateboarder endured until they are finally able to land the envisioned trick. The, at first surprising popularity of the format, is another supporting argument for the plausibility of the resonance theory, at least in the case of skateboarding. In these videos one can witness how a skateboarder is appropriating a resistant urban environment and is making, through this *trial-and-error dialogue*, an experience of self-realization, freedom and self-efficacy, that is, an experience of resonance.

On the other hand, the *b-sides* expose the dialectical flip side of skateboarding. Skateboarders are in their autonomy necessarily intrinsically motivated, flexible, risk-prone post-Fordist subjects. What is thus also exhibited in these videos is a relentless self-discipline and self-drill of a person who has to generate media content in order to maintain a relevant figure within the field of skateboarding.

The potential for an authentic and resonant experience and the self-exploitation and reification are dialectically interwoven.

REFERENCES

Ackbar, D. & Adams, J. (2014). Talking Slappies With Jason Adams. http://park ingblockdiaries.blogspot.de/2014/03/talking-slappies-with-jason-adams.html (12.03.2018).

Arcade Skateboards (1999). Gumbo.

Beal, B. & Weidman, L. (2003). Authenticity in the Skateboarding World. In Rinehart, R. E. & Sydnor, S. (Eds.), *To the Extreme. Alternative Sports, Inside and Out* (p. 337-352). Albany: SUNY.

Black Label (2001). Label Kills.

Boltanski, L. & Chiapello, È. (2006). *Der neue Geist des Kapitalismus*. Konstanz: UVK.

Borden, I. (2001). *Skateboarding, Space and the City. Architecture and the Body*. Oxford: Berg Publishers.

Bourne, S. H. (2013). *Room with no windows*. Amsterdam: 19/80 Editions.

Bourne, S. H. (2015). *Orgy Porgy. Short Stories and True Tales*. Amsterdam: 19/80 Editions.

Cantin-Brault, A. (2015). The Reification of Skateboarding. *International Journal of Science Culture and Sport* 3, 1, 54-66.

Cliché Skateboards (2000). Europa.

Cliché Skateboards (2004). Bon Appetit.

Dinces, S. (2011). 'Flexible Opposition': Skateboarding Subcultures under the Rubric of Late Capitalism. *The International Journal of the History of Sport* 28, 11, 1512-1535.

Ed Fisher (2010). jason adams – label kills. https://www.youtube.com/watch?v=pArrVpJdvSs. (05.03.2018).

Higgins, M. (2006). In Board Sports, Insider Status Makes Gear Sell. http://www.nytimes.com/2006/11/24/sports/othersports/24brands.html?pagewanted=all&_r=0.

Jeanfeil (2009). Pontus Alv New Full Part – His Shoe is out!!!. https://www.youtube.com/watch?v=BmcDLGmlRp8 (18.03.2018).

Jenkem Magazine (2014). THE BERRICS ACQUIRES THE SKATEBOARD MAG – Jenkem Magazine. http://www.jenkemmag.com/home/2014/10/16/the-berrics-acquires-the-skateboard-mag/ (16.03.2018).

Kingpin Skateboarding: Pontus Alv. https://kingpinmag.com/people/pontus-alv#8ECGcbIu65uyxvd3.97 (14.03.2018).

Mad Circle Skateboards (1998). 5ive Flavors.

Mortimer, S. (2008). *Stalefish. Dirtbag skate culture from the dirtbags who made it*. San Francisco: Chronicle Books.

NBC Washington (2011). Skate Park Opens This Weekend in D.C. https://www.nbcwashington.com/the-scene/events/Skate-Park-Opens-This-Weekend-in-DC-129182168.html (Zugriff am 12.03.2018).

Polar Skate Co. (2010). In Search of the Miraculous.

Polar Skate Co. (2012a). No Complies & Wallrides+shuvits.

Polar Skate Co. (2012b). Wallrides, Oh Yeah, Oh Yeah, Oh Yeah.

Polar Skate Co. (2016). I like it here inside my mind. Don't wake me this time. https://www.youtube.com/watch?v=abTTtyAPeN4 (17.03.2018).

Pontus Alv (2005). The Strongest of the Strange.

Rosa, H. (2017). *Resonanz. Eine Soziologie der Weltbeziehung*. Berlin: Suhrkamp.

Schweer, S. (2014). *Skateboarding. Zwischen urbaner Rebellion und neoliberalem Selbstentwurf*. Bielefeld: trancript.

Schwinghammer, S. (2011). Pontus Alv räumt bei Skateboard Film Festival ab. https://skateboardmsm.de/news/international-skateboard-film-festival.html. (13.03.2018).

The Berrics (2017). BATB X Finals. Championship Battle. http://theberrics.com/battle-at-the-berrics-10/championship-battle-batbx/ (13.03.2018).

The Nine Club (2018). Nyjah Huston | The Nine Club With Chris Roberts – Episode 86 – YouTube. https://www.youtube.com/watch?v=Aqmjl5NxhH0 (16.03.2018).

Theoriesofatlantis (2014). Pontus Alv. http://www.theoriesofatlantis.com/inter view/2014/7/30/pontus-alv (15.03.2018).

Thrasher Magazine (2014). http://www.thrashermagazine.com/articles/magazine /sneak-peek-april-2014/ (14.03.2018).

Thrasher Magazine (2015a). BFFS: Pontus Alv. https://www.youtube.com/ watch?v=zpiodfppk44 (16.03.2018).

Thrasher Magazine (2015b). https://shop.thrashermagazine.com/magazines/back -issues/2015-back-issues/thrasher-magazine-october-2015.html (14.03.2018).

The Role of Online Media Content in Skateboard Culture

Katharina Bock

INTRODUCTION

Long gone is the time when scene-based cultural processes of self-discovery and community building were only thought of as existing offline: the Internet provides individuals and members of communities with opportunities for participation and collaboration as well as for managing information, identity and relationships (cf. Hettler, 2010, p. 12ff.). Youth scenes thus offer a variety of possibilities for presenting, staging, stylising and orienting oneself and establishing oneself in a community (cf. Hugger, 2014, p. 21). The skate scene makes use of this too. It should, however, be borne in mind that this is a community of like-minded people who are connected by similar preferences when it comes to body models, signs and gestures from sports and pop culture. Their core interest and the activities associated with this are explicitly oriented towards physically tangible spaces. Here, scene members are acquired through physical, sporting exercise, and thus get the opportunity to showcase skills and qualities that are valued by significant other members. At the heart of the skaters' interest is "collective physical action and moods and feelings generated or strengthened thereby" (Alkemeyer, 2010, p. 332).

Based on precisely this specific thematic point of interest – namely, that which is relevant to the body and to sport – the question arises as to how online media and the content of these channels contribute to the skate scene? This question will be investigated by exploring and discussing the meanings, potential and limits of scene-relevant online media and content.

THEORETICAL FRAMING

The skate scene can be viewed as a body- and sports-focussed community with an extreme affinity to the media that reacts to the effects of modernity in a special way. Among the hallmarks of this modernity are phenomena that are primarily dealt with by using the terms globalisation and individualisation (cf. Hitzler, 1998, p. 81). The main driving force behind globalisation is technological innovation, especially those innovations in the field of information technology (cf. Ferchhoff, 2011, p. 74ff. and Beck, 1997). This in turn is associated with a shift in the media sector, which is characterised by terms such as digitisation, convergence, pluralisation and diversification (cf. Hugger, 2014, p. 13f.). At the same time, modernity has brought about a social shift, which has resulted in massive developments in terms of individualisation and, with this, the dissolution of pre-existing forms of social living (cf. Beck & Beck-Gernsheim, 1994, p. 11). This means that the opportunities, risks and uncertainties of life, which were previously defined within the familial network or by means of recourse to social classes, must now be perceived, interpreted, decided and processed by individuals themselves. However, in view of the great complexity of the social contexts, individuals are often hardly in a position to make these decisions that are becoming necessary in a well-founded manner (cf. ibid., p. 15). This impacts not only the lifestyle of the individual, but also the forms of communal living. In an attempt to cope with the consequences of mass emancipation and liberation and to deal with the experience of uprooting, new patterns of community building have emerged along with alternative concepts of communal living and of dealing with one another (cf. Hitzler, 1998, p. 84). An essential hallmark of these new communities, also referred to as "post-traditional" (Hitzler, Honer & Pfadenhauer, 2008), is that their power to form communities is no longer based on the similarity of social situations, but on the similarity of life goals, interests and aesthetic forms of expression (cf. ibid., p. 8). These new communities thus promise those individuals who have been liberated from binding, reliable patterns of thought and behaviour and at least a relatively secure and unquestionable way of dealing with each other, in that they find their own interests assessed as common (cf. ibid., p. 30).

Such alternative processes of self-discovery and community building are not only to be thought of as offline phenomena; rather, online media and content play a crucial role in their construction – more precisely: in the construction of scene-specific bodies of knowledge. These bodies of knowledge are used in communicative exchange – both off- and online – and serve to generate competent membership (cf. Maeder & Brosziewski, 1997, p. 340). Here, bodies of knowledge can include anything that can be described through language or to which one can refer by means of communication (cf. Maeder, 2007, p. 683). Taking one's cue from Blumer (1981, p. 81), these can be objects, situations, places, events, particular persons and their actions, but also online media content. For the purposes of symbolic interactionism (Blumer, 1981), scene-related action can be understood as significant, interpretative social action, and media use, as meaningful and deliberate use and exploitation by skaters (cf. Renckstorf, 1989, p. 314) of online media offerings that relate to the scene. The following section pays special attention to these offerings.

SCENE MEDIA ONLINE: CONTENT, MEANINGS, POTENTIAL AND LIMITS

Not least against the background of my own experiences accessing the field (cf. Bock, 2017), it becomes apparent that knowledge of important scene media and their content is indispensable in order to be able to have a say and to belong. Current topics and trends as well as insights into the historical development of the scene, together with its important stages, are for the most part exclusively accessible via scene-based media products (e.g. e-zines and their editorial content, skate videos, tutorials, scene-related advertising content) and infrastructures (e.g. scene-specific websites, video portals), which will be examined in more detail below.

E-Zines, Video Portals, Websites

In the German-speaking region (but not exclusively), well-known e-zines, some of which also appear as printed monthly or quarterly issues, include SOLO skateboard magazine (Soloskatemag.com), Monster Skateboard Magazine (Skateboardmsm.de), the magazines Place (Placeskateboarding.de), Thrasher (Thrashermagazine.com) and Kingpin (Kingpinmag.com), TransWorld SKATE-boarding magazine (Skateboarding.transworld.net), the Free Skateboard Magazine (Freeskatemag.com), Concrete Wave Magazine (Concretewavemaga-zine.com), and The Skateboard Mag (Theskateboardmag.com). When look at such zines, it becomes apparent what their most frequent editorial content is: interviews with well-known (mostly male) skaters, reviews of skate spots, reports on events, tours or video productions, and articles featuring retrospectives or current trends. In addition, person profiles introduce important skaters and newcomers, provide information on the moves they can do, their scene knowledge and their preferences regarding spots, tricks, brands, etc. In this way, fitting templates with which to identify are made available, and scene members are indirectly taught to value the knowledge, performance and style above all of male professional skaters to a special degree. Because when it comes to choosing what skateboarding tricks to perform, it is always about belonging to those "few [male] skaters" who master the "damn hard" and particularly "stylish" tricks (cf. Bock, 2017, p. 154f.). This is probably the reason why we do not get a sense here of the images of less high-performance, more uncool (because they are simply not as stylish or because they are more feminine) scene members.

This textual editorial content is interspersed with sometimes highly aestheticised photos, video stills, and advertisements by scene insiders and external actors as well as social media icons (above all from Facebook, Instagram, Twitter), who sometimes call upon people to share ("share this") or follow ("follow us") the content in question. Often the e-zines also have their own video sections in which current videos are made available, discussed and rated (on this, see for example Soloskatemag.com/category/videos, Skateboardmsm.de/tv, Kingpinmag.com/videos, Concretewavemagazine.com/videos, Theskateboardmag.com/video or Freeskatemag.com/category/videos). Video clips, films or documentaries are also listed on video portals within the scene (for example Skatevideosite.com, Skimthefat.com, Hellaclips.com or Skatevideomagazine.com) and can be rated there. But video platforms outside of the scene (especially Youtube.com and Vimeo.com) also make moving images available that are relevant to the scene, and many of the zines mentioned are actually represented there with their own channels.

In addition, on websites such as Skatecheck.de, Boardstation.de, Boardstein.com, Boardmag.com, Skatemap.de or Everskate.com (which are not only published in German), one can find all kinds of news and (additional) information from and for the scene. This includes, for example, dictionaries and lexica with facts and figures on history of the scene; calendars and updates providing information about trendy meeting points and events; trick tutorials; and skate spots and important (local) skate shops. For example, a ranking of the "Top 30 Skateboard Websites & Blogs For Skateboarding Enthusiasts" can be found at Blog.feedspot.com.

What's more, websites of online skate shops offer a wide range of materials for kitting out one's body. So, for example, Skatedeluxe.com, Titus.de and Boardjunkies.de offer both skate-specific equipment (decks, grip tapes, wheels, trucks etc.) and clothing, shoes and accessories from various manufacturers and brands. Kitting oneself out with these materials is an expression of belonging to the skate scene. The choice of particular designs, brands and manufacturers moreover serves as a means of stylisation and thus also of internal differentiation. The use of materials is also an expression of a preference for certain manufacturers and their brand images. The content of the online media (including the offerings of the online skate shops) is accordingly not aimed simply at skaters; it is aimed at fans of particular boarders, products or companies, as skater and videographer Pascal Richter explained to me. Motivation and identification with role models determine the core business of skateboarding companies; the scene's media outlets in turn finance themselves through adverts of these very companies, as I was told by Pascal Richter and Ole Tremp, editor-in-chief of an important German-language skate magazine. Without motivated skaters, the result would be no economic success for companies.

Quite a few skaters are critical of such developments of commercialisation. At the same time, however, this also creates career opportunities; namely, when the physical ability and movement skills of outstanding individual scene members are acknowledged through sponsorships from major clothing and equipment manufacturers (cf. Buckingham, 2009, p. 136). Additional career opportunities are opening up in the quasi-journalistic field; namely, in the production of editorial (online) content. Editor-in-chief Ole Tremp, for example, reports that he was initially sponsored by a relatively large number of companies (due to his boarding achievements), that he got around a lot, and was often in America. And through this, he then started to write texts or do interviews for his magazine – as a skater, freelance, so to speak. He also wrote for other (well-known) skateboarding magazines. And, finally, he was approached and asked if he could imagine setting up a new editorial department for one of those magazines. That's what he did – and he's still there today.

Skate Videos

Whereas in the 1990s VHS cassettes (then later DVDs) were responsible for the distribution and multiplication of audiovisual (re)presentations of the skate scene, video content is now almost exclusively distributed through online media via the distribution channels already mentioned.[1]

---

1   Crucial for the dissemination of skate videos at that time was "411 Video Magazine", founded in 1993, which is regarded as the source of information par excellence. New tricks and trends were disseminated here at regular intervals; in addition, profiles of companies and boarders were published – with worldwide success (Brooke, 2001, p. 146 f.; Gausepohl, 2012).

The video market is as heterogeneous as the skate scene itself. There are commercial and non-commercial videos, small clips and large productions, says Pascal Richter. Markus Kannenthal, like Richter also a long-time skater and videographer, adds: the diversity ranges from genre-specific videos in the hip-hop, rocker or mega ramp styles to contest and tour videos produced by television stations (e.g. MTV or ESPN). There are also documentary approaches and video art productions. Skate videos in the documentary style are a "matter of the heart", describes Kannenthal, and are therefore quite unstructured in terms of conception, planning and implementation. They are designed in a patchwork-like manner and constitute a conglomeration of experiences and impressions of local skate culture. The film "Radio Active Kids" (2009), for example, represents the local Berlin scene. An extremely important piece of film documentation in this regard – and still today, for that matter – is "The Bones Brigade Video Show" by the skateboard company Powell-Peralta, from 1984. This video sparked enormous enthusiasm in its day and made audiovisual (re)presentations of the scene indispensable from that point on.[2] Since then, the following remained, as the documentary "Skate on Film" (2012) puts it: "Like the album is to the musician or the building to an architect, the video is to the skateboarder".

Among the most common and popular formats, however, are "classic" skate videos. These, as explained to me by Kannenthal and Richter, focus on sport, taking no specific approach. Depending on the type, these may involve a short clip (i.e. one rider, three minutes and tricks, tricks, tricks) or a longer production (between 20 and 40 minutes long, six to ten riders from one skate team showing their tricks). The production and distribution of these "classic" videos serve primarily commercial interests, because these are promotional films whose protagonists are financed by sponsorships within the scene or those of well-known sporting goods manufacturers. Even the energy and soft drink industry, far removed from sport, is now represented in skateboarding with numerous sponsorships (cf. Schweer, 2014, p. 154). Furthermore, a large number of home video productions of local heroes circulate online, in which they showcase their sporting abilities in their immediate, home environments. Often these are "'sponsor me' videos" (Buckingham, 2009, p. 140), which are produced and distributed in the hope of sponsorship contracts and a related professional career. This offers scene members opportunities to use their own media experience and opens up

---

2   Videos like these "showed skaters in the streets of Los Angeles and Santa Barbara jumping over cars, riding up the walls of buildings, over hydrants and planters, onto benches, flying over steps, and sliding down the free-standing handrails in front of a bank" (Borden, 2001, p. 182).

new, additional paths of expression and communication (cf. Witzke, 2005, p. 325). And finally, there is also a considerable volume of video tutorials, which will be discussed in more detail in the next section.

What makes videos so popular? For a start, moving pictures have a clear advantage over static photographs, because they exert a much greater level of fascination for members of the scene: "What do I want with a frozen picture of someone standing mid-air or something? I think, yeah like, where does he come from, where is he going, how does he balance it out, what does he look like afterwards?" says the Swiss ex-professional skateboarder Dirk Steffens. "Living impressions" such as these can "only be seen in the flesh or in moving images", he adds. They also serve as motivation before boarding, because they "actually show you where you want to go, how it looks when it's perfect", Steffens continues. That's why he always used to watch some such videos as motivation before boarding, because then he was "itching to do that too". Consequently, video consumption also helps one get ideas for one's own skating. Most of the time these are US skaters "you could never go to visit or see live, but you have them on video", says Steffens. "And then you see this guy and you say, 'damn, he's cool, he's exactly my idea of awesome'. And that's great – then you can watch him and get motivation and ideas from him", explains Steffens. It is not least for this reason that, as editor-in-chief Tremp describes it, skate videos are "the most direct medium for enabling one to orientate oneself, so to speak, by one's role models" – in terms of tricks, bodily styling and "just the whole shebang, all this slang and stuff".

Videos also have a trendsetting function, because consumption is also about finding out "what new tricks there are" or "who did what and where", says Tremp. Information like this is especially important because skateboarding is often about so-called "NBDs". NDBs ("never been done") are tricks that have never been performed at a particular spot before, as Sandro Volkmann, a long-time skater who is now responsible for a Berlin skate team, explains. Skate videos are nothing less than essential here, because it is only through their consumption or by reporting about them that scene members are kept completely up to date about NBDs. What is also expressed here is the focus on contests or competition that is typical for the skate scene, which is transmitted into the online arena through the medium of video, because to stand in front of the camera in a professional capacity means to pitch oneself against other scene members. Skate videos thus not only serve to merely document the progress of one's own performance, but also enables one to compare oneself with others.

Tutorials

The web has long been used to gain knowledge about the body and skate tricks. 'Amateur forms of teaching' have evolved for this purpose – that is to say, instructions on how to pick up skateboarding tricks provided by experienced members of the scene through demonstrating and explaining certain movements. This knowledge of the body and movement is so important for the skate scene, not least because in the course of it being illustrated, female and male skaters are given the opportunity to display skills and qualities that are valued by significant others in the scene. Knowledge of the body and its movements can be used in this way to accumulate symbolic capital in the form of group membership, solidarity, recognition, respect or friendship (cf. Bourdieu, 1992, p. 64ff.) – needs that adolescents, especially, have to satisfy.

Receiving such tutorials is supposed to not only make it possible to understand the physical gestures that are so important for the skate scene, but actually to enable skating at all. What is 'promised' are the most precise insights into individual sequences of movements – insights that are made possible in a manner that only seems to exist online. However, the question arises here as to what such forms of teaching provided by online media are actually capable of achieving, especially if they are attempting to convey a strictly speaking long-winded process of internalisation (cf. ibid., p. 55) of complex body movements using a piece of sports equipment. In order to investigate this, one such tutorial will be examined in more detail below.

The navigation bar of the website of a well-known German e-zine leads to an introductory explanation of what the editorial staff considers as the basic knowledge of skateboarding. It says: if you want to start skating but don't really know how this skateboard business works, you'll get just what you need here. In the "Flat", "Curb" and "Transition" sections, experts give tips on the tricks that beginners should be able to manage.[3] There are 21 trick tip videos to choose from, the first of which tackles mediation of the most fundamental of all skateboarding tricks, the "Ollie". These videos promise their consumers that they can execute these tricks. The content sequence, including verbal and non-verbal actions, is recorded in a shot list (cf. Korte, 2005)[4], which I repeatedly reference in the fol-

---

3   Here, too, one can read "male experts" and "male beginners" (i.e., using the grammatically male form in German), which again creates the impression that members of the skate scene are exclusively male.

4   One shot constitutes the smallest unit of film, bookended by two cuts or fades (cf. Bienk, 2008, p. 52).

lowing section and is made available as an extract complimenting this piece. There are two special media technology applications – "Slow Motion" and "Re-play Last 3 Seconds" – that greatly facilitate the creation of such a list. These allow one to consume the movement sequences at a slower speed, re-watching any number of times, and thus providing detailed insights.

The video starts. After a few introductory shots (s1 to s6), a young man suddenly comes racing into the frame from the left, takes a run-up with a skateboard in his hand, drops it to the ground then steps onto it with his right foot, shortly afterwards placing his left foot on the board too, and then rolls out of the picture on the right-hand side (s7). After two other similar performances (s8, s9), the same young man, on screen, turns to the camera: "Hi. Um, my name is Felix Nürnberg. Today I'm gonna explain the ollie to you. Basically, you just put your back foot directly on the tail". (The young man is wearing a dark-grey hooded jumper, dark-grey, loose-fitting jeans and sports shoes with a flat sole.) Felix is sitting on a small wall in a park. The skateboard is lying across his lap. During his explanation, he hits one of the two ends of the skateboard with his right hand – evidently the "tail" (s10 to s13). "The front foot", he continues, smacking his left hand down on the other end of the skateboard, "goes in front of the shorties, like this – roughly like that – and then you just press down at the back – like this". Upon saying this, he smacks his right hand down on the right end of the skateboard, causing the opposite (left) end of the skateboard to tilt upwards (s14 to s16). "And then you pull forward until you get to the nose". Meanwhile, twice in a row, he moves his left hand over the surface of the skateboard to its other end – in the direction of the "shorties", that is, towards the "nose".

"The whole thing together should then look like this". He is speaking off camera. You can see him coming into the frame on the skateboard from the right. Standing on the rolling skateboard, he squats slightly and then transports himself and the skateboard about half a meter up into the air. He subsequently lands on, or with, his skateboard and rolls out of the frame to the right (s17 to s18).

"Then you stand in the air, land again", says the expert, now back in frame. He sits and holds the skateboard, initially at chin height. He then brings it down and lays it on his lap. Immediately afterwards, he places his hands on the two ends of the skateboard (s19), and then says, "and keep rolling". He simultaneously enters the picture from the left. Standing on the rolling skateboard, he squats slightly and steps on the back end of the skateboard with his right foot, whereupon its front-end tilts upwards, and he then transports himself together with the skateboard about half a meter up into the air. Mid-air, the young man shifts his left foot a little towards the front end of the skateboard, and this then tilts down and lands back on the ground. After this, the young man rolls along further on the skateboard (s20). The detailed steps of the movement are captured in Figure 1 below.

Figure 1: Movement Ollie (Screenshots S20)

Felix adds that it's best to practice the whole trick in motion (s21). In the shots that follow, he repeats his explanations once more, briefly: "Yep: rear foot on the tail, front foot on the shorties, up to the shorties. Down at the back, pull up at the front, then up. That's it, basically. Have fun practising!" (s25 to s28). The ollie is then demonstrated by the expert several more times in the remaining shots using varying aperture sizes, camera angles and axial ratios (s29 to s37).

What is it that we are being taught here? First of all, we are getting detailed insights into a body movement that is important for the scene, which we can watch as many times as we like thanks to the capabilities of media technology. We learn that this bodily movement is the "Ollie" – which is generated by a transfer of weight due to stepping on the rear end of a skateboard. On top of this, we get pointers as to the skater's physical styling: hoodies, loose fitting jeans and sports shoes with a flat sole. We also learn something about the scene's specific lexicon and its usage. In skateboarding, a clear distinction is made between three areas: "flat", "curb" and "transition". And "nose", "tail", and "shorties" describe parts of a skateboard.

These online instructions can now be compared with the acquisition of skating-specific bodily movements in the offline world in order to highlight what it means to learn to skate in a 'physically-tangible' way. The ethnographic record cited below reports on a skateboard training session conducted by an experienced member of the scene. The excerpt of the text comes in at roughly the last third of the report. Amongst other things, the following has already been described up until this point in the text; warm-up exercises to get the sweat going, a 'test of courage', fall and balance exercises, practising changes of foot placements and jumping movements (cf. Bock, 2017, pp. 82-87).

"I also quickly realise how important it is to always bend the upper body forward slightly while boarding. But I don't pay close attention to this. For a brief moment, my centre of gravity is shifted a little too far back and so I immediately lose control of the 'skateboard', because it slips away under my foot. The fact that my other foot is still on the ground is of little use to me, as it is slightly offset to the rear and so only encourages the backward fall further. I fall several times in this manner, extremely painfully, to the ground. On one of these occasions, I fall directly on my coccyx, sending a horrible jerk through my entire spine. It's like I'm paralysed. I can't get up – it hurts so terribly. A few seconds go by. Then Jan [the training leader] comes up to me and asks if I have hurt myself. I can barely answer. 'Can you stand up?' I am not sure and reach for his hand, which he stretches out to help me. Back on my feet, I ask myself what I'm actually doing here. I quickly push the thoughts away again. I don't want to be a chicken. I pull myself together and carry on.

The previous exercises – run-ups, changing footing, squatting, braking – are now to be initiated with an attempt to jump onto our slowly rolling 'skateboard' and continue moving. I am very cautious and so I manage the first attempts pretty well. Because I feel somewhat advanced, I stupidly get a little cocky and nudge the 'board' a bit too much. During the run-up, I misjudge things and again do not pay enough attention to my upper-body posture. When trying to place my front foot on the 'board', it slips away under me once again and I fall back diagonally. I want to absorb my fall with my left hand – another fairly stupid idea, because by doing so I transfer my entire body weight onto my wrist. Lying on the ground, I immediately clutch my wrist with a firm grip and hope that the pain will subside. But it doesn't. It gets worse, with a stabbing pain. I feel sick for a second. Again, Jan comes to my aid. 'Wrist?' I can't answer and instead just nod at him. Again, he helps me up. 'Can you move your hand?' I don't know, and I'd rather not risk an attempt. [...] The trial training session will continue – but without me. I sit on the side-lines and wonder if I was in fact crazy to think I could actually learn to 'skate'. This here is the purest form of (self-inflicted) bodily assault! [...] The next day I can barely move. Every movement hurts, everything aches – shoulders, neck, arms, abdomen, thighs, calves, my wrist, which is now in plaster, and let's not forget my coccyx. I feel dreadful [...]" (Bock, 2017, p. 87ff.)

Contrasting the video tutorial with the body's real-world confrontation with the skateboard reveals some clear differences: the tutorial does not address the physical stress you are exposed to and the mental challenges you have to overcome when skateboarding (and again and again). It turns out that – long before any of the tricks 'touted' online can actually be practised – very basic skills (especially keeping balance, run-ups, braking and falling 'correctly') must first be acquired, internalised and/or put to the test. As becomes clear here, skateboard movements can only be acquired through a laborious, difficult, long-winded and physically stressful process. And forms of teaching that use online media, such as video tutorials, can only convey an idea (in snippet form) of what this acquisition process feels like. Perceiving the movements of body and board visually while at the same time hearing words of explanation does make it possible to grasp postures, movements and processes as well as the complexity of these and the fact that they occur simultaneously – but their interaction can only be fully understood and implemented through one's own bodily action (cf. Brosziewski & Maeder, 2010, p. 405). That is, the mere consumption of online tutorials does not enable you to skate – far from it– but rather, only seems to be able to convey ideas and the impulses behind movements.

FINAL OBSERVATIONS

The scene's online media and the content hosted there are an important part of the skaters' world of meaning, shaping it to a great extent. These platforms make available large and diverse bodies of knowledge. And the possibilities provided by digitisation in terms of the storage and multiplication of bodies of knowledge help stabilise their existence. (Incidentally, scene-based knowledge does not remain internal, but also becomes accessible to external actors, who can claim it, make it their own and, perhaps, even modify it.)

Online media therefore have a variety of functions in terms of promoting the scene's communicative processes and community building, thereby satisfying the individual needs of scene members in a special way, precisely because online media address the body. It enables scene members to develop their own skating by equipping oneself with scene-specific materials or physical styling. It gives information on the use of the scene-specific lexicon, provides ideas and motivation, acts as a trendsetter and supplies important templates with which to identify. The possibilities offered by scene-relevant online media and the content hosted there thus open up a variety of modes of expression, communication and scene participation. Platforms for self-expression and intra-scene competition are created, media skills can be acquired and commercial interests might be pursued, whilst career opportunities announce themselves.

Despite all the potential offered by digital distribution channels, it simultaneously shows how snippet-like, abridged and selected the skate scene appears online – for example in the (re)presentation of a body of membership that essentially consists of high-performance, male skaters, but also with regard to the limited expressiveness and impact of online content. This makes it clear that 'true' membership of and participation in the scene is decided by competent physical action, a sense of togetherness and experiences in the offline world, which can at best be inspired and supplemented by online media offerings.

REFERENCES

Alkemeyer, T. (2010). Verkörperte Gemeinschaftlichkeit. Bewegungen als Medien und Existenzweisen des Sozialen. In Böhle, F. & Weihrich, M. (Eds.), *Die Körperlichkeit sozialen Handelns. Soziale Ordnung jenseits von Normen und Institutionen* (pp. 331-348). Bielefeld: transcript.

Beck, U. (1997). *Was ist Globalisierung? Irrtümer des Globalismus – Antworten auf Globalisierung.* Frankfurt/Main: Suhrkamp.

Beck, U. & Beck-Gernsheim, E. (1994). Individualisierung in modernen Gesellschaften – Perspektiven und Kontroversen einer subjektorientierten Soziologie. In Beck, U. & Beck-Gernsheim, E. (Eds.), *Riskante Freiheiten. Individualisierung in modernen Gesellschaften* (pp. 10-39). Frankfurt/Main: Suhrkamp.

Bienk, A. (2008). *Filmsprache. Einführung in die interaktive Filmanalyse.* Marburg: Schüren.

Blog.feedspot.com: Top 30 Skateboard Websites & Blogs For Skateboarding Enthusiasts. https://blog.feedspot.com/skateboard_blogs/ (Consulted on 19.03.2018).

Blumer, H. (1981). Der methodologische Standort des Symbolischen Interaktionismus. In Arbeitsgruppe Bielefelder Soziologen (Ed.), *Alltagswissen, Interaktion und gesellschaftliche Wirklichkeit. Band 54/55: 1, Symbolischer Interaktionismus und Ethnomethodologie; 2, Ethnotheorie und Ethnographie des Sprechens* (pp. 80-146). Opladen: Westdeutscher Verlag.

Boardjunkies.de. http://www.boardjunkies.de/ (Consulted on 19.03.2018).

Bock, K. (2017). *Kommunikative Konstruktion von Szenekultur. Skateboarding als Sinnstiftung und Orientierung im Zeitalter der Digitalisierung.* Weinheim, Basel: Beltz Juventa.

Borden, I. (2001). *Skateboarding, Space and the City. Architecture and the Body.* Oxford, New York: Berg.

Bourdieu, P. (1992). Ökonomisches Kapital – Kulturelles Kapital – Soziales Kapital. In Bourdieu (Ed.), *Die verborgenen Mechanismen der Macht. Schriften zu Politik und Kultur 1* (pp. 49-79). Hamburg: VSA Verlag.

Brooke, M. (2001). *The Concrete Wave. The History of Skateboarding.* Toronto: Warwick Publishing.

Brosziewski, A. & Maeder, C. (2010). Lernen in der Be-Sprechung des Körpers. Eine ethnosemantische Vignette zur Kunst des Bogenschießens. In Honer, A., Meuser, M. & Pfadenhauer, M. (Eds.), *Fragile Sozialitat. Inszenierungen, Sinnwelten, Existenzbastler. Ronald Hitzler zum 60. Geburtstag* (pp. 395-408). Wiesbaden: Verlag für Sozialwissenschaften.

Buckingham, D. (2009). Skate Perception: Self-Representation, Identity and Visual Style in a Youth Subculture. In Buckingham, D. & Willett, R. (Eds.), *Video Cultures: Media Technology and Everyday Creativity* (pp. 133-151). Basingstoke: Palgrave Macmillan.

Concrete Wave Magazine.com. https://concretewavemagazine.com/ (Consulted on 19.03. 2018).

Facebook.com. https://de-de.facebook.com/ (Consulted on 19.03.2018).

Ferchhoff, W. (2011). *Jugend und Jugendkulturen im 21. Jahrhundert. Lebensformen und Lebensstile.* Wiesbaden: Verlag für Sozialwissenschaften.

Freeskatemag.com. http://www.freeskatemag.com/ (Consulted on 19.03.2018).

Gausepohl, J. (2012). Skateboarder Mag will alle 411 Video Magazine Ausgaben online stellen – 50 sind schon da! http://www.boardstation.de/2012/06/2 9/skateboarder-mag-will-alle-411-video-magazine-ausgaben-online-stellen-5 0-sind-schon-da/ (from 29.06.2012) (Consulted on 21.01.2018).

Hellaclips.com. http://www.hellaclips.com/ (Consulted on 19.03.2018).

Hettler, U. (2010). Einordnung und Stellenwert von Social Media und Social Media Marketing. In Hettler, U. (Ed.), *Social Media Marketing. Marketing mit Blogs, Sozialen Netzwerken und weiteren Anwendungen des Web 2.0.* München: Oldenbourg.

Hitzler, R. (1998). Posttraditionale Vergemeinschaftung. Über neue Formen der Sozialbindung. *Berliner Debatte INITIAL,* 9, 1, 81-89. http://www.hitzler-soziologie.de/pdf/Publikationen_Ronald/2-40.pdf (Consulted on 07.11.2017).

Hitzler, R., Honer, A. & Pfadenhauer, M. (2008). Zur Einleitung: "Ärgerliche" Gesellungsgebilde? In Hitzler, R., Honer, A. & Pfadenhauer, M. (Eds.), *Posttraditionale Gemeinschaften. Theoretische und ethnografische Erkundungen* (pp. 9-31). Wiesbaden: Verlag für Sozialwissenschaften.

Hugger, K.-U. (2014). Digitale Jugendkulturen. Von der Homogenisierungsperspektive zur Anerkennung des Partikularen. In Hugger, K.-U. (Ed.), Digitale Jugendkulturen (pp. 11-28). Wiesbaden: Verlag für Sozialwissenschaften.

Instagram.co. https://www.instagram.com/ (Consulted on 19.03.2018).

Kingpinmag.com. https://kingpinmag.com/ (Consulted on 19.03.2018).

Korte, H. (2005). Sequenzprotokoll. In Mikos, L. & Wegener, C. (Eds.), *Qualitative Medienforschung. Ein Handbuch* (pp. 387-394). Konstanz: UVK.

Maeder, C. (2007). Ethnographische Semantik. Die Ordnung der Mitgliedschaftssymbole am Beispiel des Bergsports. In Buber, R. & Holzmüller, H. M. (Eds.), *Qualitative Marktforschung. Konzepte – Methoden – Analysen* (pp. 681-696). Wiesbaden: GWW Fachverlage GmbH.

Maeder, C. & Brosziewski, A. (1997). Ethnographische Semantik: Ein Weg zum Verstehen von Zugehörigkeit. In Hitzler, R. & Honer, A. (Eds.), *Sozialwissenschaftliche Hermeneutik. Eine Einführung* (pp. 335-362). Opladen: Leske + Budrich.

Monster Skateboard Magazine. https://skateboardmsm.de/ (Consulted on 19.03. 2018).

Owens, J. (2012). Skateboarder Magazine's 411VM Teaser Video. http://www. grindtv.com/skateboarding/skateboarder-magazines-411vm-teaser-video/ (from 26.06.2012) (Consulted on 10.02.2017).

Place Skateboard Culture. http://www.placeskateboarding.de/ (Consulted on 19.03.2018).

Radio Aktive Kids. A Berlin Skateboard Movie. Regie: Max Kähni, Maxim Rosenbauer. Deutschland 2009: Radiocinematics. DVD, 117:00 Minuten.

Renckstorf, K. (1989). Mediennutzung als soziales Handeln. Zur Entwicklung einer handlungstheoretischen Perspektive der empirischen (Massen-)Kommunikationsforschung. In Kaase, M. & Schulz, W. (Eds.), *Massenkommunikation. Theorien, Methoden, Befunde*. Sonderheft Kölner Zeitschrift für Soziologie und Sozialpsychologie (pp. 314-336). Opladen: Westdeutscher Verlag.

Schweer, S. (2014). *Skateboarding. Zwischen urbaner Rebellion und neoliberalem Selbstentwurf*. Bielefeld: transcript.

Skateboard Stories. Regie: Thomas Lallier. Frankreich: ARTE France/No One 2011. Dokumentarfilm, 52:00 Minuten. Ausgestrahlt auf ARTE am 16.06. 2011 um 21.50 Uhr.

Skatedeluxe.com. https://www.skatedeluxe.com/de (Consulted on 19.03.2018).

Skate on Film. Regie: Jared Prindle. USA 2012: ESPN/900 Films. Dokumentation, 22:02 Minuten. http://www.espn.com/video/clip?id=8121027 (Consulted on 10.02.2017).

Skatevideomagazine.com. https://skatevideomagazine.com/ (Consulted on 19.03. 2018).

Skatevideosite.com. http://www.skatevideosite.com/ (Consulted on 19.03.2018).

Skimthefat.com. Your Guide to Skateboarding Videos. http://www.skimthefat. com (Consulted on 19.04.2014).

Slap Magazine.com. http://www.slapmagazine.com/ (Consulted on 19.03.2018).

SOLO Skateboardmagazine. http://www.soloskatemag.com/ (Consulted on 19.03.2018).

The Bones Brigade Video Show. Regie: Stacy Peralta. USA 1984: Powell Peralta. VHS-Video, 28:00 Minuten. https://www.youtube.com/watch?v=BVu9G QD0j0s (Consulted on 10.02.2017).

Theskateboardmag.com. http://theskateboardmag.com (Consulted on 19.03. 2018).

Thrasher Magazine. http://www.thrashermagazine.com (Consulted on 19.03. 2018).

Titus.de. https://www.titus.de/ (Consulted on 19.03.2018).

Transworld Skateboarding Magazine. https://skateboarding.transworld.net/ (Consulted on 19.03.2018).

Twitter.com. https://twitter.com/ (Consulted on 19.03.2018).

Vogelgesang, W. (2010). Digitale Medien – Jugendkulturen – Identität. In Hugger, K.-U. (Ed.), *Digitale Jugendkulturen* (pp. 37-53). Wiesbaden: Verlag für Sozialwissenschaften.

Witzke, M. (2005). Jugendforschung mit Video-Eigenproduktionen. In Mikos, L. & Wegener, C. (Eds.), *Qualitative Medienforschung. Ein Handbuch* (pp. 323-332). Konstanz: UVK.

Youtube.com. https://www.youtube.com/ (Consulted on 19.03.2018).

Video Tutorial Ollie: Shot List

Time code	Shot (s)	Image layer (aperture size (as)[5], camera angle (ca)[6], people, action)	Verbal layer
...	...	...	
00:13	s7: Ollie	as: medium long shot (the young man is completely in shot) ca: high-angle shot (camera view from above)	
		an asphalted path surrounded by parkland action: A young man suddenly comes racing into the frame from the left, takes a run-up with a skateboard in his hand, drops it to the ground then steps onto it with his right foot, shortly afterwards placing his left foot on the board as well, and then rolls out of the picture to the right. The young man is wearing a dark-grey hooded jumper, dark-grey, loose-fitting jeans and sports shoes with a flat sole.	
00:15	s8: Ollie	as: medium long shot (the young man is completely in shot) ca: natural perspective (camera at eye level); horizontal pan (from left to right)	
		action: Again, the same young man comes racing into the frame from the left. Standing on the rolling skateboard, he squats slightly and then transports himself together with the skateboard about half a meter up into the air. After this, the young man rolls out of the picture to the right.	
00:17	s9: Ollie	as: medium close-up (the middle part of the young man is visible) ca: low-angle shot (camera at stomach level); tracking shot; fish eye lens	
		action: The same young man performs the same movement with the skateboard (from s8).	
00:20	s10: Felix	as: close-up (the young man's head and torso are visible) ca: slight low-angle shot (camera at stomach level)	"Hi. Um, my name is Felix Nürnberg. To-day I'm gonna explain the ollie to you."
		action: The same young man sits and speaks facing the cam-era.	
00:24	s11: Ollie	as: medium long shot (the young man is completely visible) ca: low-angle shot (worm's-eye view); tracking shot; fish eye lens	
		action: The same young man performs the same movement with the skateboard (from s8).	
00:26	s12: Felix	as: close-up (the young man's head and torso are visible) ca: slight low angle shot (camera at stomach level)	"Basically, you just put your back foot ..."
		action: The same young man speaks to camera. He sits.	

5 Aperture sizes (E) define the camera range and consequently the distance or proximity with which the audience interacts with the filmic events (cf. Bienk, 2008, p. 52).

6 Camera perspectives are defined according to the angle at which the camera is aimed at an object or a person (cf. Bienk, 2008, p. 57).

00:27	s13: Felix	as: medium close-up (man's upper body and lap are visible) ca: slight top-angle shot (camera view from above); camera zooms to the right end of the skateboard action: The young man speaks to camera. He sits and the skateboard is lying across his lap. During his explanation, he hits one of the two ends of the skateboard with his right hand – evidently the "tail".	… directly on the tail."
00:29	s14: Felix	as: close-up (the young man's head and torso are visible) ca: slight low-angle shot (camera at stomach level) action: The young man speaks to camera. The skateboard is still lying across his lap, while he's looking at it. To explain, he whacks his left hand down on the other end of the skateboard.	"The front foot …"
00:31	s15: Felix	as: medium close-up (man's upper body and lap are visible) ca: slight top-angle shot (camera view from above) action: The young man speaks to camera. He sits and the skateboard is lying across his lap. His left hand is still touching the front end of the skateboard – the "shorties". He then turns the topside of the skateboard to the camera, his hands still on that side.	… goes in front of the shorties – roughly like that – …
00:33	s16: Felix	as: close-up (the young man's head and torso are visible) ca: slight low-angle shot (camera at stomach level) action: The young man speaks to the camera. He is sitting and the skateboard is lying across his lap. Now he smacks his right hand down on the right end of the skateboard, causing the opposite (left) end of the skateboard to tilt upwards.	… and then you just press down at the back – like this – …
00:38	s17: Felix	as: medium close-up (man's upper body and lap are visible) ca: slight top-angle shot (camera view from above); camera slowly zooms out action: The young man speaks to the camera. The skateboard is still lying across his lap. The left end of the skateboard is still tilted upwards. Then, he moves his left hand over the surface of the skateboard to its other end – in the direction of the "shorties", that is, towards the "nose".	… and pull forward until you get to the nose."
00:42	s18: Ollie	as: medium long shot (the young man's body is fully visible) ca: natural perspective (camera at eye level); horizontal pan (from left to right) action (s8 repetition): The same young man is speaking off camera. You can see him coming into frame on the skateboard from the right. Standing on the rolling skateboard, he squats slightly and then transports himself and the skateboard about half a meter up into the air. He subsequently lands on, or with, his skateboard and rolls out of the frame on the right-hand side.	"The whole thing together should then look like this."
00:44	s19: Felix	as: close-up (the young man's head and torso are visible) ca: slight low angle shot (camera at stomach level) action: The young man speaks to the camera. He sits and holds the skateboard, initially at chin height. He then brings it down and lays it on his lap. Immediately afterwards, he places his hands on the two ends of the skateboard at the same time.	"Then you stand in the air, land again …"

00:47	s20: Ollie	as: close-up (only the young man's legs and feet on the skateboard are visible) ca: slight top angle shot (camera view from above); tracking shot	
		action: The young man is speaking off camera. He simultaneously enters the picture from the left. Standing on the rolling skateboard, he squats slightly and steps on the back end of the skateboard with his right foot, whereupon its front-end tilts upwards, and he then transports himself together with the skateboard about half a meter up into the air. Mid-air, the young man shifts his left foot a little towards the front end of the skateboard, and this then tilts down and lands back on the ground. After this, the young man rolls along further on the skateboard.	… and keep rolling."
00:50	s21: Felix	as: medium close-up (the young man's upper body is visible) ca: slight low-angle shot (camera at stomach level)	"It's best to practice the whole trick in motion, because …
		action: The young man speaks to the camera, alternately looking at the camera and the skateboard on his lap.	
00:55	s22: Felix	as: close-up (the young man's head and torso are visible) ca: tilt from the young man's lap to his face	… it's easier for you …
		action: The young man speaks to camera.	
00:57	s23: Felix	as: close-up (the young man's head and torso are visible) ca: slight low angle shot (camera at stomach level)	… when performing the ollie on the pad …
		action: The young man speaks to the camera, alternately facing the camera and the skateboard on his lap.	
00:59	s24: Ollie	as: medium long shot (the young man's body is fully visible) ca: slight top-angle shot (camera view from above); the camera zooms in	… or on the curb, aaand …"
		action: The young man enters the picture from the left. Standing on the rolling skateboard, he squats slightly and steps on the back end of the skateboard with his right foot, whereupon its front end tilts upwards, and he then transports himself together with the skateboard about half a meter up into the air. Mid-air, the young man shifts his left foot a little towards the front end of the skateboard, and this then tilts down and lands back on the ground. After this, the young man rolls along further on the skateboard.	
01:02	s25: Felix	as: close-up (the young man's head and torso are visible) ca: slight low-angle shot (camera at stomach level)	"Yep: rear foot on the tail, …
		action: The young man speaks off camera looking at the skateboard on his lap. To affirm his explanation he again whacks his right hand down on the right end of the skateboard – the "tail".	
01:05	s26: Ollie	as: medium long shot (the young man's body is fully visible) ca: low camera angle (worm's-eye view); tracking shot; fish eye lens	… front foot on the shorties, up to the shorties.
		action: The young man speaks off camera. He simultaneously enters the picture from the left. Standing on the rolling skateboard, he squats slightly and steps on the back end of the skateboard with his right foot, whereupon its front end tilts upwards, and he then transports himself together with	

		the skateboard about half a meter up into the air. Mid-air, the young man shifts his left foot a little towards the front end of the skateboard, and this then tilts down and lands back on the ground. After this, the young man rolls along further on the skateboard.	
01:08	s27: Felix	as: medium close-up (the middle part of the young man's body is visible) ca: slight low angle shot (camera at stomach level); the camera zooms out	Down at the back, pull up at the front, then up."
		action: The young man speaks to the camera. He sits holding the skateboard in his hands. To affirm his explanation, he again shows how his feet must move to perform the ollie successfully. Again, he whacks his right hand down on the right end of the skateboard, causing the opposite (left) end of the skateboard to tilt upwards. Then, he moves his left hand over the surface of the skateboard to the other end. After that he lifts the skateboard up diagonally to illustrate this movement.	
01:13	s28: Felix	as: close-up (the young man's head and torso are visible) ca: slight low-angle shot (camera at stomach level)	"That's it, basically. Have fun practising!"
		action: The young man speaks to the camera, alternately facing the camera and the skateboard on his lap.	
...	...	...	

Sport Instead of Play

From Skateboarding to the Sport of Competitive Skateboarding

Antoine Cantin-Brault

"Finally, there came a time when everything that men had considered as inalienable became an object of exchange, of traffic and could be alienated. This is the time when the very things which 'till then had been communicated, but never exchanged; given, but never sold; acquired, but never bought – virtue, love, conviction, knowledge, conscience, etc. – when everything, in short, passed into commerce. It is the time of general corruption, of universal venality, or, to speak in terms of political economy, the time when everything, moral or physical, having become a marketable value, is brought to the market to be assessed at its truest value."

Karl Marx, 1955, p. 30

INTRODUCTION: SKATEBOARDING AS AN ART FORM

It was once possible to identify skateboarding as an art form. Like art, skateboarding exercised complete control over its limitations; it was capable of endlessly reinventing and redefining its format through the exercise of free choice with regard to its terrains. It was also free in choosing its means of projecting itself into the world where, in turn, it articulated a form of critical understanding of the society it inhabited. Like art, it was creative, expressing itself through a form of violence and destructiveness that seemed a singularly appropriate answer to the forces of consumerism and utility. Skateboarding, like art, was not to be perceived by the general public as a fruitful form of activity, nor could it easily accommodate any clear and acceptable set of values. Skateboarding enjoyed negative freedom, true freedom. Freedom that is lived through the sacrifice of any willingness to conform to the limitations that render people and things serviceable within a given ideology.[1]

But to address the obvious: there are no art forms capable of being presented at the Olympic Games as art forms.[2] The sports represented at the Olympic

---

1   The following builds upon the work of a previous article on skateboarding (Cantin-Brault, 2015) wherein I situate myself within an Adornian conception of dialectics and freedom. The present article maintains this position. This conception of freedom must be understood against the illusions of a positive Hegelian freedom that posits that: "Now this is Freedom, exactly. For if I am dependent, my being is referred to something else which I am not; I cannot exist independently of something external. I am free, on the contrary, when my existence depends upon myself" (Hegel, 2001, p. 31). Hegelian freedom posits that to be free is to be able to install oneself into what is *other*, to conquer its meaning and grasp it within oneself. However, in doing so, as Adorno puts it, this freedom as thought proves that there is "coercion both of what is being thought and of the thinker, who must extract the thought from himself via concentration. Whatever does not fit a judgment will be chocked off; from the outset, thinking exerts that power which philosophy reflected in the concept of necessity. By way of identification, philosophy and society are interrelated in philosophy's inmost core" (Adorno, 1973, p. 233). Negative freedom is to linger beyond the necessary coercion of reason and to understand how society, as a mirror of philosophy, seeks to compel the individual to follow its determinism.

2   Ted Barrow, in a recent article (2019), has argued that skateboarding is not art. His argument seems to rely on a very narrow conception of art: "I define art as a language that functions on a purely symbolic level". Art is often not *purely* symbolic as it relies on forms that are comprehended as such. In any case, style – in skateboarding as in other forms of art as well –, is symbolic in that it is capable of signaling a general quality that transcends the immediacy of a particular event. In its resemblance to other forms of art such as graffiti, albeit in a more performative manner, skateboarding also transcends the immediacy of an environment shaped by broadly liberal ideological values. Furthermore, featured in photos or videos, skateboarding can also assume aesthetic dimensions of the beautiful (or of the sublime), depending of course on the aesthetic qualities of the medium. Barrow, however, denies skateboarding the possibility of being an aesthetic language, seeing it instead as "a language that is spoken for and amongst ourselves. Whereas other art is designed to communicate to the outside world, skateboarding is actually inward-looking". In a reified world, skateboarding (as

Games must be evaluated according to specific judgement criteria. This means that the criteria used to evaluate competitors must be established in advance in order to prevent any surprises that would emerge from free and uncalculated movements: a free and uncalculated movement is by default an 'error'. Pre-established criteria serve to quantify everything of relevance to the activity and thus depend upon a pre-established conception of the sport, its competitors and their limits.[3] What are the comparable criteria that could be used to quantify art? What criteria are to be used to quantify skateboarding? Were such criteria established, they would impede skateboarding from evolving as a living and always newly created art form, since they would ascribe to skateboarding a specific terrain, a specific relation to time, a specific ranking system and specific competitors willing to execute specific tricks in a specific sequence in order to be placed in a specific ranking. Presently, in competitive contexts, such specifics serve as the rational limits by which the winners and losers of skateboarding are determined, something that is incompatible with the idea of skateboarding as an art form. It has always been possible to fail at skateboarding, just as one can fail to adequately render form and meaning in a work of art. But with the acceptance of skateboarding as an Olympic sport, skateboarding has changed (yet again) and is being showcased for the first time as a true organized sport – with far-reaching consequences: the official sport of skateboarding is now to be, ironically, 'played', just as athletes 'play' games of football or hockey in professional, competitive formats.

To explain this 'consecration', the following discussion will first examine the dialectical process that led skateboarding to become an organized sport (i.e. a 'sport of competitive skateboarding'). This process is of significance, because the Olympic Games represent the third rational moment in a process that inures identification with the current ideology. Drawing upon a discussion of Sartre's existentialism – with a nod to Kant's categorical imperative – I will then suggest that skateboarders in this third moment are in the process of losing their auton-

---

well as other art forms such as postmodern music) cannot help but adopt an inward-looking stance as a means of resisting reification, a positioning which does not impede it from transmitting meaning that transcends skateboarding itself.

3   Professional skateboarder Neil Blender questioned these exact limitations of the competition format at a skateboarding contest in 1986 in Tempe, Arizona. During his timed run, he only performed rather basic maneuvers, but spent the majority of the time limit painting an image of an oversized grimace on one of the wallride obstacles with a spray can. Should the judges evaluate his performance according to creative instead of athletic criteria? And how many points can be attributed to a work of art?

omy. Finally, I will discuss the future possibility of having two parallel cultures – the culture of skateboarding and the culture of the sport of competitive skate-boarding – and the viability of each element within this inevitable relationship.

This article ought not to be understood as a form of protest against the inclu-sion of skateboarding in the Olympics. Rather, it is a critical rendering of how skateboarding is to become a sport, how skateboarders lose their negative free-dom and how two cultures related to the skateboard have become intertwined, for better or worse.

A DIALECTICAL PROGRESSION TOWARDS THE SPORT OF COMPETITIVE SKATEBOARDING

In the effort to understand philosophically how skateboarding has become an Olympic sport, I will not proceed via a detailed reconstruction of its history. Rather, I will show the main articulations of its progression in order to demon-strate how skateboarding has followed a rational progression in the process of becoming the sport of competitive skateboarding. Becoming an Olympic sport is the rational conclusion of a dialectical cycle whereby the sport of competitive skateboarding almost inevitably had to emerge as an end product. It was by this logic that skateboarding inevitably became an end product ready to be consumed by a general and impersonal public.

The dialectical cycle in itself was best analyzed and implemented by Hegel. Very early in his thought, Hegel had tried to conceptualize the Absolute as "the identity of identity and non-identity; being opposed and being one are both to-gether in it" (Hegel, 1977, p. 156). The Absolute, better known as the Idea, be-comes the Absolute through several dialectical cycles that force the Absolute to risk itself into otherness as a means of making sense of the otherness which it becomes a part of. Philosophy is where only the Absolute can reveal itself com-pletely, because philosophy's concept "is *the self-thinking* Idea, the truth aware of itself, – the logical system, but with the signification that it is universality *ap-proved and certified* in concrete content as in its actuality" (Hegel, 2007, § 574, p. 275). Philosophy is where the logical determinations of the Idea are finally verified in reality and where the Absolute can be said to have achieved freedom, as there is nothing that has resisted its understanding. As the young Hegel wrote: "The need of philosophy can satisfy itself by simply penetrating to the principle of nullifying all fixed opposition and connecting the limited to the Absolute" (Hegel, 1977, p. 112).

Every dialectical cycle is precisely the identity of identity and difference. This second identity is offered rationally, as rationality for Hegel is expressed via its capacity to produce true form from itself. Reason [*Vernunft*] needs otherness, the difference, that is offered by intellect [*Verstand*] when truth is posited against something else that resists it. This truth must then be sublated [*aufgehoben*] through reason, as the opposition must be part of the whole and free truth, and the activity of the intellect is accepted only in regards to the fact that its oppositional stance was a step into a rational progression (cf. Hegel, 2007, § 467, p. 204-205).

Hegel sees this reason as operational in history. "The only thought which Philosophy brings with it to the contemplation of History, is the simple conception of *Reason*; that Reason is the Sovereign of the World; that the history of the world, therefore, presents us with a rational process" (Hegel, 2001, p. 22). From a standpoint of positive dialectics, nothing resists reason, and everything in history has served reason as something to identify and reunite with its opposite in a more profound and concrete truth. In this context, rationality must be understood as attached to an ideology, an ideology that organizes all differences within its unity, just as in Hegel's dialectics rationality serves the progression of the Idea.[4]

How might this apply to skateboarding? What ideology has been at work in the dialectic cycle of skateboarding? To put it bluntly: Liberalism, in its moral and economic meaning. By ascribing economic value to everything, Liberalism insures that everything is comparable and ascribed some form of moral meaning, since it is the manifestation of individual choice. However, Liberalism encourages choices of a certain type: choices in consumerism, choices in entertainment, and choices in terms of lifestyle, all of which have to be protected by rights. In this sense, choices such as these are not meant to produce creative activities; rather, as Nietzsche so succinctly claimed, Liberalism means "*herd-animalization* [...]" (Nietzsche, 1997, p. 74). The inherent logic of Liberalism demands that all individual choices be useful to oneself and to others according to a Utilitarian rational of global well-being, rendering every choice that does not proceed in this same direction suspect and dangerous. Skateboarding was, for a moment in its history, highly suspect to Liberalism with regard to its economic and moral sense: Liberalism could hardly ascribe a clear value to the activity in itself, much less a commercial and/or Utilitarian value for the benefit of society as a whole. Skateboarding represented a challenge to the goal of Liberalism itself, as it re-

---

4   As Adorno puts it: "Identity is the primal form of ideology. We relish it as adequacy to the thing it suppresses; adequacy has always been subjection to dominant purposes" (1973, p. 148), and thus has always had a repressive political and social effect.

sisted the aim of making man a "function, unfree, regressing behind whatever is ascribed to him as invariant" (Adorno, 1973, p. 124). It is easily apparent then that Hegel's dialectical philosophy comes with a unified social program gained through differences, differences that must contribute to this unity rather than being disharmonious or motley. Thus, if reason was to find a way to make skateboarding fit into this dominant ideology, it had to be formatted in such a way that it could be sold, appreciated and practiced in a safe and controlled environment in accordance with another of the most basic principles of Liberalism: 'One person's freedom ends where another's begins'. The Olympic Games embody this format, the format of all formats. But how did skateboarding arrive at this point?

(a) *Identity*: the skateboard was first created as a toy, without any claim to depth of meaning other than being a consumerist object, a simple imitation of a surfboard to be used on asphalt. Skateboarding was initially an instrument of leisure, and only later became a sport that would draw from gymnastics and alpine skiing (Schäfer, 2018. pp. 47-49). This period ran its course roughly from 1960 until the late 1970s.

(b) *Difference*: soon enough, however, people began to perceive something else in the skateboard and sought to project onto it, or rather through it, a way of life, a 'Dasein', that philosophically transformed the skateboard into an object of expression and resistance. This started at the beginning of the 1980s when skateboarding assumed a vertical dimension through the adaptation of such new terrains as ditches and dried out Californian pools. Skateboarders subverted the skateboard by diverting its original entertainment function to become a means of reshaping the way we could look at urban environments and ourselves. This Dasein was thus resisting the authority of the institutions of public order and offering a strong moment of opposition, especially when, in the early 1990s, skateboarding began to implant itself directly in the urban landscape after having left the pools and vertical skateparks, that had by then become legitimized, to enter into the streets (ibid., pp. 53-54). It was street skateboarding, as the creator of a subculture, that would then carry the differentiation of this 'Dasein' in contrast to a form of vertical skateboarding that had found legitimacy as a measurable and legitimate sports format (ibid., pp. 52-53).

(c) *Identity of identity and difference*: currently, rationality is finding a way to use this differentiation and opposition to its advantage: it has produced a form of skateboarding that now includes the moment of opposition, thereby allowing it to assume dimensions of the first identity of the skateboard (a consumerist and sportsmanship object) by adding to it the sense of an entire way-of-life. A way-of-life pacified of course, devoid of any real struggle, an image/imitation of this way-of-life, but nonetheless just enough to give traction and depth to the initially perceived skateboard.

Let us present the second and third moments of this process in greater depth. In the moment of opposition, or difference, the second moment of the dialectical process, there were of course other dialectical cycles at work. It is thus impossible to say that every skateboarder embraced this oppositional stance to ideology. Rodney Mullen, for example, arguably the best skateboarder of all time, has entertained a career, mostly in its early stages, participating in contests in controlled environments. These competitions offered no resistance to the liberal forces at work. And based on this state of affairs, skateboarding has always in some way been divided: skateboarders wanted to earn a living doing what they loved, but what they loved was an act that could exist without the interference of a rational ideology. However, in this second moment of the process, the negation towards rationality was not sublated into a higher unity. There was no unification of the dialectical tension between the creative and destructive impulse behind skateboarding, behind 'Skate and Create' and 'Skate and Destroy'. In this dialectical moment, skateboarding was difficult to define and skateboarders were the actors of their own plays. Along those lines, they were also the creators and the destroyers of the 'institutions' which they themselves had created to serve the needs of skateboarders.

This rational progression continued unabated, however, as interests derived from the skateboard industry grew in size, with ideological actors reaping what they did not sow. Reason works as if it were incapable, in its primal rage disguised as logical reasoning, to leave anything aside (cf. Adorno, 1973, pp. 22-23): reason must assign everything within it a value and a place; unassigned elements are perceived as a menace that challenges its absoluteness. So skateboarding had to be introduced to the general public with only two possible outcomes: either ideological actors could wager selling it to the general public with the intentions of gaining money on their bet, or they could lose their bet and sacrifice skateboarding altogether while taking it with them to their demise.[5] This is the bet ESPN took in 1995 when it introduced to the world the first X Games contest to showcase skateboarding and other 'action' sports. Marketeers of the X Games, focusing on key demographics, were able to generate public interest. Similarly, it was on the back of one key skateboarding figure that the video game *Tony Hawk's Pro Skater* was first introduced in 1999 to great commercial suc-

---

5   This second outcome is exactly what happened to skateboarding in its 1965 crash. What had been considered only one year earlier as an interesting new activity became overexposed and subsequently perceived as a menace to orderly society.

cess, resulting in a very profitable franchise. Tony Hawk was exactly the type of personality that the ideological actors needed to profit from skateboarding; he was a halfpipe skateboarder who had gained an enormous public profile after landing a 900-degree aerial at the X Games in front of a live TV audience. So he was already practicing skateboarding in an audience-friendly format in a controlled and non-threatening environment (a specifically built halfpipe) and was able to express a positive and rational message about skateboarding to the general public. Metaphorically speaking, he was the lion that voluntarily put itself into a cage so that people, from a safe distance, could look at him in awe.

By 2010, the commercial interest in skateboarding had mostly died down. Vertical skateboarding (halfpipe) especially had lost the broad public's favor, simply because it seemed too monotonous to non-initiated viewers. And even street skateboarding seemed to have been milked dry from a consumerist standpoint, as John Riccitiello, former chief of EA Games (responsible for the 2010 video game *Skate 3),* confirmed in an interview: "At least for the level of excitement out there, skateboarding seems to have run its course as the representative example in that broader genre [of action sports]" (Totilo, 2010).

So how was skateboarding to reinvent itself (or how could some outside influence repackage skateboarding) as a means of forestalling disappearance as a (morally and economically) valued activity at risk of relapsing into otherness? Street skateboarding had to be the key because it was more exciting, more dangerous, and more subversive, thus more seductive. In 2010, the first edition of Street League Skateboarding (SLS) emerged, an international competitive series of professional skateboarding. During the invitational series, professional competitors battle for ranking points and a championship title at a final event that would end the season. The SLS works with a ranking system used by professional judges to grade routines performed by skateboarders in a controlled course and in a controlled time frame. SLS was founded by skateboarder and entrepreneur Rob Dyrdek with a specific goal: "foster growth, popularity, and acceptance of street skateboarding worldwide" (Streetleague.com, 2018). SLS also operates its own foundation (SLS Foundation) to support public skate parks (Street Plazas) with the help of donors including Nike SB, Kraft, Sony, Microsoft, 7 Eleven and many more. The mission statement is as follows:

"Assist municipalities, non-profits, and private donors with the design, development, and construction of legal and safe skate plazas, as well as assists with educational programs that both increase understanding and encourage the participation in skateboarding." (Streetleaguefoundation.com, 2018)

The SLS Foundation breeds future skateboarders who have been trained in safe and legal skate plazas (conforming to notions of rights and security, cornerstones of liberalism) and who perhaps one day will be able to enter the SLS big league to compete for big prize money and international recognition. This development is similar to professional hockey, where teams provide arenas to municipalities to promote the recognition of hockey as a sport. The X Games were the progenitor of SLS, but SLS provides an official and rational structure that goes beyond organized competitions, ensuring that skateboarding finds a place in cities through plazas and skateboard workshops: skateboarding is thereby contained and appreciated in its legitimate limits at the same time. It is exactly at this point that skateboarding ceases to exist as an autonomous activity to become the sport of competitive skateboarding instead.

As the prerequisite for acceptance as an official Olympic discipline, every sport needs an international federation. For the sport of competitive skateboarding, this was until recently the FIRS (Fédération Internationale De Roller Sports), a Swiss-based association founded in 1924 that had already been recognized by the International Olympic Committee (IOC). The FIRS wanted to become the acting body for organizing international skateboarding competitions that serve as Olympic qualifiers but stood in direct competition with the International Skateboarding Federation (ISF) founded in 2004. Both associations lobbied the IOC to be recognized as the official global federation of skateboarding. In order to establish skateboarding as a structured sport, Gary Ream, the President of the ISF and owner of the mythical Camp Woodward (primarily a gymnastics camp, but also a BMX and skateboarding camp), has worked directly with SLS – and successfully so: the SLS competition series was sanctioned as the official world championship series of street skateboarding in 2014. From the IOC's perspective, the ISF seemed less established and credible than the FIRS but enjoyed a tremendous level of credibility within the ideological world of skateboarding (not to be confused with the world of skateboarding as a whole, as numerous skateboarders remain ignorant of the existence of the ISF and its goals). Skateboarding then received official recognition as an Olympic discipline in 2015, forcing the two competing associations to align their goals: in 2017, the ISF and FIRS jointly created the new World Skate association in order to provide a structured foundation for skateboarding as an Olympic discipline. Among other things, World Skate has worked towards recognizing SLS as the official Olympic qualifying format. This recognition arrived on April 16, 2018, when World Skate and Street League Skateboarding (SLS) announced the SLS World Tour and Super Crown World Championships as the official world championship series and the accredited format for qualifying for Olympic street skate-boarding.

As is thus apparent, the consecration of the sport of competitive skateboard-ing did not occur in the absence of obstacles (Smith, 2016): it needed an outside ideological actor and partner to succeed. This is a good example of what Hegel called the "cunning of reason [*List der Vernunft*]" (Hegel, 2001, p. 47). This, of course, is not to say that reason is some kind of overseeing God that has already decided the fate of human beings, but that reason – meaning human reason and the reason of a people – always finds a way to reconcile the irreconcilable when a true will to indentify the difference is present. With the World Skate associa-tion and Gary Ream as chairman of the board, the sport of competitive skate-boarding is presented as an organized sport: training in a municipal skatepark that has been built in accordance with the highest international standards, a skateboarder can then participate in different official competitions and become an internationally recognized professional athlete. By comparison, a skateboard-ing performance by an outcast in an eccentric white jumpsuit at a Museum, as Mark Gonzales did in 1998,[6] is now to be seen as anarchic, a farcical affront to the standards of the polished sport of competitive skateboarding.

Could this historic development have gone any differently? Perhaps, but ra-tionality had its eyes on the skateboard from its very beginning as it first emerged from out of ideology, and was unwilling to allow it to linger out of sight. Even if not inevitable, the result was nonetheless highly predictable.[7]

EXISTENTIAL FREEDOM AND THE OLYMPIC GAMES

Skateboarders, in skateboarding, have experienced a negative freedom that can also be called a form of existential freedom in which "man first exists: he mate-

---

6   This work of performance art was called 'Backworlds/Forwords'. It was conceived by Johannes Wohnseifer in collaboration with artist and skateboarder Mark Gonzales at the Museum Abteiberg in Mönchengladbach, Germany in 1998.

7   Ideology does not always have to work from outside, often its rationality is acknowl-edged by alienated individuals. David Carnie, for example, offers a clear example when he states that "Skateboarding is going to be in the Olympics whether we like it or not. I don't like it. But NBC and the IOC want it. And they're going to get it one way or another. If it isn't done by skateboarders, it will be done by one of a handful of other groups out there claiming to be the official governing body of skateboarding" (Brixey, 2012). Skateboarders then, of their own accord, acknowledge reason.

rializes in the world, encounters himself, and only afterwards defines himself" (Sartre, 2007, p. 22). There is no essential achievement that has been set prior to the actions taken; there is only the necessary condition of building a life through projects that are creatively realized. The culture of skateboarding operates according to a system of 'belonging' in which one has to earn the respect of others before one can fully enter the culture. This is no different from other sports. However, to earn respect in the past, skateboarders did not always have to put their athletic skills forward. A lot of meaningful actions in skateboarding are assessed according to criteria of style and attitude; thus, some skateboarders have earned renown despite the absence of the kind of athletic skills required to win contests or even face other professional skateboarders in a friendly sport competition (as in a game of SKATE). And this form of recognition must continuously seek renewed validation, because the culture of skateboarding lacks the kind of system of official recognition present in organized sports. To use the terms of existentialism, skateboarders have always known that "existence precedes essence" (Sartre, 2007, p. 20) and that they can never stop creating and inventing, and thereby reinventing themselves in the process. Skateboarders could feel that "We are left alone and without excuse. That is what I mean when I say that man is condemned to be free" (ibid., p. 29). Nothing can be seen as insuring everlasting perseverance, and nothing can be used to justify cessation of the process of creation. Skateboarders set goals for themselves, but these goals are always chosen and never imposed from a realm external to the essence of the skateboarder or of skateboarding itself. To live without any excuses is freedom.

Sartre separates the phenomenological world into two poles: the in-itself [*en-soi*] and the for-itself [*pour-soi*]. The in-itself is a thing that has been given a clear function through its essence in the whole of the actual (liberal) world. The for-itself is the conscience that is always conscious of things or itself, but can never fully be an essence, as it must time and again project itself in the world and be the whole of its actions. Sartre states clearly: "being in-itself is what it is", and conscience in its being "*has to be* what it is" (Sartre, 2003, p. 21). The for-itself is nothingness, a void of being, an existence that is always opened and directed towards the in-itself. Others (other for-itself) are, for the for-itself, constant reminders of its own void; that is why Sartre says, in the fifth scene of his play *No Exit* [*Huis clos*], that "Hell is other people"[8], as others always under-

---

8   Skateboarders certainly understand the phrase 'Hell is other people' every time they have to earn the respect of a skate shop employee who is, for instance, "vibing" them (Barrow, 2018, p. 18), or generally every time they have to prove their dedication to the culture of skateboarding in their attitude, style, wit and creativity in order to con-

mine the attempts of the for-itself to constitute itself as an essential being. The for-itself is thus presented with two dispositions: good faith [*bonne foi*] or bad faith [*mauvaise foi*]. Sartre presents bad faith in those terms: "If we define man's situation as one of free choice, in which he has no recourse to excuses or outside aid, then any man who takes refuge behind his passions, any man who fabricates some deterministic theory, is operating in bad faith" (Sartre, 2007, p. 47).

Bad faith consists in a self-deception in order to try to become an in-itself, something stable, established with a clear value, without having to project itself into the world time and again, or trying to project the same image of itself to become this projection. This behavior inevitably fails as the for-itself can never be the in-itself. Good faith is to accept this fate of the for-itself by accepting that "On all sides I escape being and yet – I am" (Sartre, 2003, p. 84). However, many people place themselves in a position of bad faith and chose to declare that "I am bound to uphold certain values" (Sartre, 2007, p. 48) as if they preceded human existence. Every time the for-itself attempts to posit values that purportedly come before itself and that thus consecrate it as something being, as in-itself, the for-itself exerts bad faith. The ideological progression of skateboarding towards the sport of competitive skateboarding is symptomatic of this; ideology forces the individual into a position of bad faith, as the individual is compelled to submit to values that claim precedence over him.

It is possible to compare the existential freedom skateboarders enjoyed and generally want to preserve with Sartre's refusal of the Nobel Prize of literature in 1964. Sartre refused this consecration because the writer, he says, must resist transformation into an institution, even if this happens under the most honorable circumstances (see Sartre, 1964). To become an institution is to be 'made'; the for-itself acts as if it were a thing. When a culture organizes contests solely within itself, the consecration is minimal, and actors must act on the win to prove their creativity again and again. The consecration offered by skateboarding is fragile. It needs to always be regained and may never be achieved through simple repetition. However, when the consecration comes from an institution bigger than the culture itself, the culture must bow down to this institution and acknowledge a hierarchical relationship that instills pre-decided values into the smaller culture. This cuts freedom at its roots, since actors are now given an aim that does not always follow the culture itself, and this aim becomes a positive freedom, a freedom to choose the right or wrong path, since a path as been set.

---

tribute to its reinvention, or at least its perpetuation through a cycle of actions that never really permits an essential determination of the for-itself projected in the urban landscape.

Winners can no longer reinvent themselves, since they are now part of a larger institution that wants to ideologically protect and preserve itself.

The Olympic Games are surely one of those institutions. And in the Olympic Games, there are also national ideologies that have precedence over athletes. It seems that the Olympic Games are not fully aware of who they are inviting when they invite skateboarders. Because the individuals from the culture of skateboarding who might participate in the Games have not – except for a few exceptions such as participants in SLS and X Games – been groomed to fulfill the demands placed on the behaviors of normal athletes. I do not anticipate that these skateboarders will have problems with performance-enhancing doping, as this practice is largely absent from skateboarding as opposed to other competitive sports. However, there will inevitably be clashes as the competing skateboarders will contradict the aims of the Olympic Games and/or the national ideology they are supposed to incarnate. The main operative reason here is clearly the bad faith instilled in those institutions. Of course, this will likely only happen in the beginning stages of the introduction of skateboarding into the Olympic Games. In an analogous situation, snowboarders as Olympic athletes have learned to follow a regimented system of training, just as normal athletes do, in order to be able to perform professionally. Many observers also argue that in doing so, snowboarding has lost its rebellious image. But in competitive skateboarding, participants in X Games and SLS have learned already how to act like professional athletes in front of a TV audience. Perhaps this is the preliminary step towards meeting the demands of the Olympic institutions and progressively reifying the culture of skateboarding.

Upon conforming themselves to Olympic culture, skateboarders will become progressively more objectified for the sake of the success of the institution. This would seem to touch on Kant's categorical imperative. The second formulation of Kant's categorical imperative posits that no rational being, as being an autonomous being, can become an object for itself or treat others as objects.[9] This goes beyond consent: a rational being cannot accept being treated as an ob-

---

9   Kant's second formulation is "Act in such a way that you treat humanity, whether in your own person or in the person of any other, never merely as a means to an end, but always at the same time as an end" (Kant, 1993, p. 36). Kant is a thinker of positive freedom since rational actors are to follow their duties according to the categorical imperative understood and deduced from out of their own rationality. However, even if there is for Kant a positive path to follow, and in existentialism there is not, the end result is the same: free actors can never be objectified and reified in values that are posited before, and externally to, their own actions.

ject, as this would suggest submission to our affective side, that side that we cannot trust with morality according to Kant. There is of course a lot of affectivity in skateboarding: the entire aspect of 'belonging' rests on a sense of acceptance and joy, and skateboarders are surely not always pure rational actors. However, affectivity in itself never implied the distortion of the culture of skateboarding. So how did affectivity come to desire objectification and bad faith? The main spaces of skateboarding are cities, and, in particular, architectural structures that are not meant for skateboarders but that have been reshaped by skateboarders' activities.[10] Skateboarders are amongst the groups that challenge the very welcoming mask liberal cities have tried to put on in commercializing themselves to the world. This is because skateboarders have never been welcomed in the heart of the liberal city – neither in the past, nor the present – except for when fenced-in pens known as 'public skateparks' have been created for them.

The affectivity of skateboarders which leads to willingly acting against authority and ideology has exposed the rational contradictions in the liberal ideology. But this comes at a price: living on the margins and exposed to exclusion and punishment is a difficult life, as ideology will always deny recognition to individuals who do not accept its rules.[11] It is precisely here that the problem arises: the emotiveness of skateboarders, wounded in their inability to fully achieve recognition, directs them to adopt those traits that they have in common with respected athletes, for instance athletic skills that can be measured. In so doing, they themselves become rationalized objects and, as such, rational contradictions. Just as snowboarders compare each other to professional hockey players in order to explain to the public their rankings, skateboarders will objectify

---

10 Craig Stecyk, the author who put into perspective the Z-Boys' approach to skateboarding, has insisted on this idea of treating architecture with decisive terms. The problem with Stecyk's writings is to know whether they are intended to serve as marketing tactics or a true description of negative freedom.

11 In the *Dogtown and Z-Boys* documentary from 2001, there is much insistence on how the 'original seed' of skateboarding, Jay Adams, has led a life of drugs and alcohol leading him to prison. Stacy Peralta, director of this documentary and also a Z-Boy, tries to show how Adams did not take the chance 'to make it' as a glorified and accepted skateboarder when the time came. Perhaps having not been able to fit in is not Adams fault, perhaps he did *not* go wrong in being a poor promoter of his self, perhaps it is the whole promoting side of skateboarding that was the problem. There is a structural problem at work in the understanding of what 'making it' means in skateboarding.

themselves consciously to serve the institution of organized sports and, in turn, become institutions themselves.

Two Parallel Cultures?

Is it possible for the two cultures of skateboarding to coexist simultaneously? Is it possible to have skateboarding as an autonomous activity and the sport of competitive skateboarding as parallel manifestations of the use of a skateboard? As of now, skateboarding and the sport of competitive skateboarding seem to share a common fate. If the sport of competitive skateboarding were to crash, skateboarding would not be able to sustain itself either, since it depends on a lot of sponsors and supporters to live. Nike SB and Adidas, for instance, are sponsors that are working in accordance with the promotion of the sport of competitive skateboarding, but also have enough reason to support the skateboarding ethos in movies or skatepark projects that still allow skateboarding to shine and keep its inner and negative drive alive. Without the ethos of skateboarding, the sport of competitive skateboarding would only be a sport and would lose an edge that is very important to those companies and to skateboarders as well. To the general public, the sport of competitive skateboarding must appear as a credible form of skateboarding to entice curiosity by permitting voyeurism into a culture that usually, as the general public thinks, happens in the dark corners of the liberal world. Viewed in a soberer light, the appeal of skateboarding does not come from its physical danger: alpine skiing is more dangerous than skateboarding but is not seen in the same way, because alpine skiing is not (or perhaps it was but is not anymore) considered in terms of a critical engagement with the architectural space where it manifests itself. The sport of competitive skateboarding still needs the ideological resistance of skateboarding so that athletes can still impersonate something that was absent from the Olympics before and that offers better representation, especially of a younger audience. But in return, the ideology of sports helps to bring to skateboarding a generally better recognition and helps small companies owned and operated by skateboarders to keep the drive alive. Thus, it does not seem that two truly parallel and separate skateboarding cultures can exist independent of each other as they are necessarily intertwined.

However, we must also keep in mind that skateboarding has survived numerous previous crashes. Thus, should the principle animating the sport of competitive skateboarding lose its viability, it seems unlikely that skateboarding's reawakening or renewal will originate from the sport-oriented side of skateboarding. The past has shown that it is always from the skateboarding side of things that skateboarding has been able to reinvent itself while finding an ethos consonant with that of skateboarders. And this is no surprise, as the crash always happens from the competitive side of things and skateboarding once again faces the consequences of having trusted ideology. The negative force of skateboarding is the phoenix that rises from the ashes of the sport of competitive skateboarding as its ruins provide excellent material for a creative process that allows for the reshaping of the ethos of skateboarding.

Skateboarding is fundamentally a struggle, or the manifestation of a struggle, and needs as fuel a countervailing ideology that can act as a foil. Thus, if something was to go wrong with the model of the sport of competitive skateboarding and/or in the dialectics between skateboarding and the sport of competitive skateboarding,[12] of the two it is skateboarding that will survive and strive. Adorno writes: "Nonidentity is the secret *telos* of identification. It is the part that can be salvaged; the mistake in traditional thinking is that identity is taken for the goal" (Adorno, 1973, p. 149). Skateboarding as the non-identity can be salvaged as it will always to some extent resist its identification with a dominant ideology, an ideology that is a myth of unity and standardization, estranged from any real human experience wherein the telos is constant projection, a constant negative activity.

IN CONCLUSION: THE MEANING OF THE SPORT OF COMPETITIVE SKATEBOARDING

Every game has a life of its own. A game has its own rules, its own goals and its own elements of surprise. To partake in a game is to exercise free choice, and a game can be constantly reinvented, but in entering the game one must understand it before being able to contribute to it and partake in its reinvention. As Gadamer puts it: "Every game presents the man who plays it with a task. He cannot enjoy the freedom of playing himself out without transforming the aims of his purposive behavior into mere tasks of the game" (Gadamer, 2004, p. 107). This happens on a given terrain, a terrain that becomes sacred, and that clearly

---

12 It is of course impossible to know whether the future holds problems for the sport of competitive skateboarding or for the dialectical relation described here, as "the owl of Minerva begins its flight only with the onset of dusk" (Hegel, 1991, p. 23). Philosophy cannot be a prophecy. However, since the Olympics will require changes from the inside of skateboarding, this form of competitive skateboarding might have a longer run than other previous attempts.

separates this world of the game from the usual world of meaning. That is why playing a game is a very serious activity. If it is seen only as a game, it cannot be played, because it becomes an object included in a vaster web of values. For example, it is possible to say that playing hockey contributes to healthy living, but it cannot be played for this reason, it has to be played for itself, or else it becomes inauthentic and a burden to the falsely playing players. Gadamer is right in saying that "Someone who doesn't take the game seriously is a spoilsport [*Spielverderber*]. The mode of being of play does not allow the player to behave toward play as if toward an object" (Gadamer, 2004, p. 103).

Organized sports are often referred to in terms of 'play'. It is important to keep in mind that in adopting a format as a sport, the game has already undergone a process of objectification and institutionalization. The actors of those sports are still referred to as players: amateur players and professional players, the distinction lying in the fact that amateurs play the game for itself, internally, while professional athletes play the game yes internally, but with an ulterior motive as well; they play to earn a living, often a very luxurious one for that matter. Amateur players are dedicated to the seriousness of the game itself and thus their relationship to the game may be characterized in terms of good faith, whereas professional players are dedicated to something other than the sport itself and their relationship closer to one of bad faith.

It is interesting to remember that the Olympics were initially dedicated to amateur players in order to celebrate the importance and the diversity of the games played. But this is no longer the case: many sports are played in the Olympics by professional players and they cannot limit sponsors' exposure. The sport of competitive skateboarding is no exception: there will be professional athletes representing their countries and their brands, some brands that were not first associated with skateboarding.[13] It bears noting, moreover, that skateboard-

---

13 For example, it was announced that Nike SB will be the official shoe sponsor of at least all of US skateboard athletes at the Olympics, and probably of many other countries as well. Shoe companies that have evolved from within skateboarding culture are not receiving recognition, even if they were essential to the development of skateboarding. This is how a rationalization process works from the ideology standpoint, or, in Ed Templeton's words, how "Nike won": "There are Nike and Vans as far as big money goes in skateboarding shoes, and everyone else lost. Everyone else is hanging by a thread, if you're not one of the big companies like New Balance or Adidas that subsidizes skateboarding through a global running shoe or basketball shoe business. Skateboarding as a whole never stood up to that, and the concept is that in the long-term, Nike doesn't care about skateboarding" (Senrud, 2017).

ing also makes a distinction between amateur and professional skateboarders. However, and as I have tried to show in this article, skateboarding does not offer enduring recognition. As a result, the professional status attained by skateboarders is very fragile and ultimately functions as a motivation to participants to keep on creating, just as artists need their 'benefactor' to be able to carry out their projects. It is only when ideological sponsors come into play that professional skateboarders may be considered as reified professionals, the same as other professional players.

Overall, it is thus another ideological trick of reification to pass off professional and organized sports as games and to ascribe a Utilitarian value to the dimension of play in these activities. Skateboarding, in contrast to the sport of competitive skateboarding, is truly a freer and more authentic game. Locations in the city that engender repeated surprises for skateboarding become sacred as they become the theatre of great tricks and styles that occur only for the sake of the continuation of skateboarding itself and its progression. When the performance of a trick has been concretized, it can be felt as a relief, not won without effort but without strain, as the game in itself is the goal, a constellation that denies the player self-justification in terms of liberal (moral and economic) values. The sport of competitive skateboarding, on the other hand, attempts to sacralize formatted skateparks as its sites of worship, to groom individuals into ideological career paths via regulated competition milestones that can lead to ideological consecration. The acceptance of the sport of competitive skateboarding within the Olympics will prove that a skateboard can be used for athletic performance and that the athletes can become things, billboards on which patriotism and consumerism can place their branding. In trying to restrict the freedom of skateboarding, by appropriating the creative, playful aspect of skateboarding, the sport denies the liberating qualities of the skateboard by subverting it into a tool of subjugation.

REFERENCES

Adorno, T. (1973). *Negative Dialectics*. New York, London: Continuum.

Barrow, T. (2018). Vibeology. *Transworld Skateboarding*, 394, 9-10, 2018.

Barrow, T. (2019). *Hot Take: Skateboarding is not Art*. http://www.jenkemmag .com/home/2019/01/07/skateboarding-not-art/ (Consulted on 17.01.2019).

Brixey, W. (2012). *Skateboarding VS. the Olympics: A Brief History*. http://www.jenkemmag.com/home/2012/09/04/skateboarding-vs-the-olym pics-a-brief-history/ (Consulted on 15.02.2018).

Cantin-Brault, A. (2015). The Reification of Skateboarding. *International Journal of Science Culture and Sport* 3, 1, 54-66.

Gadamer, H.-G. (2004). *Truth and Method.* New York, London: Continuum.

Hegel, G. W. F. (1977). *The Difference Between Fichte's and Schelling's System of Philosophy.* Albany: SUNY.

Hegel, G. W. F. (1991). *Elements of the Philosophy of Right.* Ed. A. W. Wood. Cambridge: Cambridge University Press.

Hegel, G. W. F. (2001). *The Philosophy of History.* Kitchener: Batoche Books.

Hegel, G. W. F. (2007). *Hegel's Philosophy of Mind.* Ed. M. Inwood. Oxford, New York: Oxford University Press.

Kant, I. (1993). *Grounding for the Metaphysics of Morals.* Indianapolis, Cambridge: Hackett.

Marx, K. (1955). *The Poverty of Philosophy.* Moscow: Progress Publishers.

Nietzsche, F. (1997). *Twilight of the Idols.* Indianapolis, Cambridge: Hackett.

Sartre, J. P. (1964). *Sartre on the Nobel Prize.* Sartre's letter transl. by R. Howard. https://www.nybooks.com/articles/1964/12/17/sartre-on-the-nobel-prize/ (Consulted on 18.12.2018).

Sartre, J. P. (2003). *Being and Nothingness. An essay on Phenomenological Ontology.* London, New York: Routledge.

Sartre, J. P. (2007). *Existentialism is a Humanism.* New Haven, London: Yale University Press.

Schäfer, E. V. (2018). From Record to Ritual. Outlines of an "Effective History" of Skateboarding. In Butz, K. & Peters, C. (Eds.), *Skateboard Studies* (pp. 44-63). London: Koenig Books.

Senrud, C. (2017). *"Selling Out" with Tony Hawk, Jeff Grosso and Ed Templeton.* http://www.jenkemmag.com/home/2017/05/22/selling-tony-hawk-jeff-grosso-ed-templeton/ (Consulted on 18.12.2018).

Smith, B. (2016). *How Olympic Skateboarding almost didn't happen.* https://sports.vice.com/en_ca/article/53xd88/how-olympic-skateboarding-almost-didnt-happen (Consulted on 03.13.2018).

Streetleague.com (2018). http://streetleague.com/about/ (Consulted on 01.29.2018).

Streetleaguefoundation.org (2018). http://streetleaguefoundation.org/about/ (Consulted on 01.29.2018).

Totilo, P. (2010). *Skateboarding has run its course as a top video game format.* https://kotaku.com/5703454/skateboarding-has-run-its-course-as-a-top-video-game-format. (Consulted on 03.13.2018).

Skateboarding in Pedagogical Production

Tim Bindel & Niklas Pick

Youthful, cool, creative and lively – skateboarding can be associated with attributes which can also evoke institutional-pedagogical desires. This is especially interesting in sports didactics, a field that is not merely limited to a canon of classical club sports. Motoric learning and creative space appropriation automatically become objects of teaching, whilst lifeworld orientation (cf. Zander, 2017) exists in any event, because skateboarding is considered to be a youth movement *par excellence*. Similar to taking rap from its origins to the cultural stage of school for English lessons, it is also possible to adapt skateboarding as a teaching subject, despite it being considered as a "wild, adventurous and often forbidden art of movement" (Ehni, 1998, p. 121). The concerns of dealing with an orchestration of youth culture and the domestication of the free spirit can be countered by two developments. First, in Germany, skateboarding has developed into an established sport within a little over 40 years and it can now be imagined as institutionally organised in view of the Olympic Games 2020. Second, today, some of the once youthful skaters of the 1990s and 2000s work as established teachers in schools and they are glad to pass on their passion to the next generation by offering skateboarding in physical education.

Out of this complex set of conditions, this paper explores a post-critical moment and ties the question of the 'whether' with that of the 'how' of a pedagogical orchestration of skateboarding. Several reconstructions become necessary *en route* from the streets to the school, which inevitably changes the nature of skateboarding. Scholastic as well as Olympic skateboarding will subsequently differ from the original street sports. We aim to reveal the pivotal challenges resulting from the educational processes of skateboarding. Following a discursive positioning of skateboarding into the context of physical education, we present findings from interviews in which experts reveal their insights and practical experiences. The analysis of six expert interviews results in three essential topics: the involvement of teachers in the skate scene, the teaching-learning complex and the matter of space.

SKATEBOARDING IN A SPORTPEDAGOGICAL DISCUSSION

Four step-by-step defining reference frameworks are available to classify the skateboarding phenomenon in a discourse of sports education. We shall initially consider the youth phenomenon and subsequently integrate it into the structures of informal sports (Bindel, 2008) before we address the discourse of alternative sports (as a trend) and ultimately concede that skateboarding is an activity with inherent logics.

To understand skateboarding as a 'leisure sport' means to stage the compulsory physical education as a counter pole. In the process, the phenomenon moves to one side with all sports activities outside of the classroom, i.e. those which young people perpetuate of their own accord. In the past, this extremely broad comparison was of particular quantitative relevance; it is commonly known that sports as leisure activity are highly relevant for children and young people, also in the digital era. The field of sports education moves toward educational areas for young people that also exist beyond the context of school (cf. Neuber, 2010). This goes for the swimming association as well as for skateboarding, as long as the sport at hand provides experiences which introduce personal, social or motoric challenges. From a didactic perspective, the potential to enrich classes can be accredited to skateboarding as well as to all other forms of leisure sports. Therefore, most current syllabi reference to leisure sports. In this context, the question arises as to whether the capacity to act and competencies – which currently seem to be the most popular objectives of the curricula – can also be related explicitly to skateboarding. In short: what is the extent to which lessons contribute to the act of skateboarding? Until now, the topic appears in some curricular concepts in the field of "gliding – driving – rolling" (for example, in North Rhine-Westphalia, Germany), which focuses on cross-motoric abilities. This does not include skateboarding as a culture.

The peculiarity of skateboarding compared to club sports, which are still paramount in sports-scientific youth research, can be identified when positioning it as an 'informal sport'. Bindel (2008) defines informal sport as a sport whereby the three activity roles – exercising sport, imparting sport and organising sport – appear symbiotically. Thus, any institutionally organised sport – i.e. in schools and clubs – becomes the antithesis of informal sport. In the case of informal sport, the active youths themselves are responsible for the participation as well as for the organisation. Although this provides particular learning opportunities, also for the informally organised skateboarder, it also introduces social patterns which complicate the participation for individuals or groups. In this context, the under-representation of girls in skateboarding must be discussed. A pedagogical-institutional assumption of the organisation by the teacher in schools or skate-parks is more conducive to correspond with the inclusive idea rather than the in-formal youth sport (cf. Bindel & Erdmann, 2016). Particularly interesting from the perspective of teaching-learning models is the fact that the participation in informal sports is not administered or checked by external authorities. Instead, various methods are established, from observation and learning-by-doing to mentoring by way of active participants with the advantage of knowledge or ex-pertise. The curriculum of skateboarding consists not only of standard tricks, but also concerns style and norms (cf. Bindel, 2008). Contrary to club sports, not the concept of a "correct" sport dominates (Bindel, 2015). Rather, individual solu-tions assert themselves. The transfer of expertise to a teacher in a school or skatepark is one of the most significant changes, because it gives up the informal character of skateboarding. This creates the risk of adapting the sport to tradi-tional role distribution, as it can be seen at Olympic skateboarding, for example.

A further specification of sports educational classification supplements the characterisations above. Skateboarding can be classified as a trendy '(alterna-tive) sport'. However, the term trend has not been associated with skateboarding for quite some time, since the practice has long since exceeded the zenith of a trend. Almost as the mother of all other trend sports, skateboarding still provides the pivotal characteristics specified by Schwier (1998) and subsequently by Laßleben (2009). On one hand, the 'trendiness' of skateboarding has to be found in its alternative patterns, compared to competitive sports. In order to avoid du-plication, we would like to discuss the aspect of stylisation. In short, we argue that skateboarding has the potential to not only unfold as a sport, but also as a lifestyle: One can be a skater! Political attitudes and models of lifestyle form skateboarding and can be outwardly displayed by apparel, among other things. Freedom and the focus on flow and experience are the adolescent leitmotifs of the lifestyle. They can be found in the sportive action itself and are translated to interpretational sovereignty and process orientation. Skaters see the city as an exercise space. They usually don't only train for competitions, but also search for current experiences, as per the sport-sociological theory. In reality, one has to assume a post-trend sport where the borders between present and future orienta-tion are as blurred as they are between freedom and standard. The current fitness and health trends clearly show that standardised actions and clear expertise can be integrated into lifestyle-relevant sports practices. Also, sports trends are displayed in social developments. While skateboarding in the alternative sport discourse of the 1990s and 2000s was discussed as street, style and fun sports, the current fitness trends arise from the discourses of a performance society, which focusses on third-party knowledge and allocates one's own actions to the social design of a good life. Most of the young people will hardly find it remarkable that skateboarding is externally organized, because the current alternative youth sports pushes interpretational sovereignty into the background. Although, according to Laßleben (2009), the application of non-traditional sport can be based upon the characteristics of the (old) alternative sports, he also leaves space for new approaches.

Our fourth sports educational attempt of indexing is basically a capitulation. One cannot allocate skateboarding in its entirety to one category; skateboarding is *skateboarding*. There is no other sport with the same past, the same present and future. This is a unique, movement-cultural phenomenon which is not just an example of non-traditional sport (within the context of schooling), as it does not represent just one of many informal acts which are more than a sportive leisure option. But what represents the soul of skateboarding? This question can possibly only be answered individually and subjectively. However, all will agree that skateboarding in Germany has become a part of the urban environment which is attempting to assert itself in neoliberal displacement scenarios (cf. Peters, 2016). In education contexts, this sport can not only be adapted as a movement practice, but as an example for subculture. In this context, the topic not only contains the practice of skating, but also the theories of power, culture and space.

SKATEBOARDING AT SCHOOL – REGARDING THE STATE OF RESEARCH

A state of research in the proper sense cannot be reported. There are no explicit sports-didactic papers and we do not possess empirical data to address skateboarding in the context of classrooms. The extremely nominative conducted discourses regarding the consideration and mediation of action sports or the addressing of informal sport should be illustrated here briefly with a focus on skateboarding.

Bindel and Balz (2014) derive the value of educational consideration of the informal sport from the interpretational sovereignty taken up by the activities compared to the matter of sport. They also consider the assignment of school sports in assuring young people that they are allowed to co-design and change the sports culture. This, in turn, also legitimises skateboarding and moves the self-determination and self-development of the pupils into focus. The papers by Schwier (1998), Stern (2010) and Peters (2016) confirm that skateboarding demands approaches which could also be expressed as educational objectives in accordance with Klafki (1997), particularly self-determination and co-determination.

Laßleben (2009, p. 18 cont. and 57 cont.) recently summarised arguments for the integration of alternative sports: *proximity to life, culture critique, promotion of independence and athletic capacity to act, support of regular exercise and equal opportunity access to non-traditional sport, differentiation options, satisfaction of the need to present, and the promotion of self-controlled learning.* In view of skateboarding, the arguments weigh in with varying significance. The extent to which a beginner would feel comfortable in demonstrating their abilities on the skateboard in front of others could be questioned. Equally, the actions would not indicate a proximity to life, as the distribution of skateboarding is not comparable to many traditional sports. Furthermore, the topic will not be raised in athletic leisure times of most girls. However, this illuminates the potential indicated in the previous chapter to provide access to the sport for a clientele which would otherwise not be encouraged in the informal sector.

It is the achievement of Laßleben (2009) that he did not stay within the well plausible arguments for the integration of the alternative sport. He develops a concept which sensitively searches for characteristics of a successful implementation based on the ambivalent character of the action sport. He clearly illustrates that one has to reflect on the general conditions when addressing alternative sports – and that also goes for skateboarding. This concerns elementary questions, e.g. is the subject offered in class or as extra-curricular sport? At which school level can the subject be offered? Etc. The teacher turning skateboarding into a school subject will have to take preliminary decisions. Also, this means that the status of personnel, material, space and time has to be worked out. In short: It is an effort to establish a subject such as skateboarding in school; the extent of the integration will be a matter of the commitment of the individual teachers.

We shall only comment rudimentarily on the specific implementation in this paper. We select on three mediation references of Laßleben, all of which suit skateboarding. The inclusion of "pupils as experts" (Laßleben, 2009, p. 99) can facilitate the specific learning methods in skateboarding. In addition, it is important to "discover exercise space and make it available" (ibid. p. 101) and "[to] discuss aspects of stylisation" (ibid. p. 99).

All in all, we are looking at good arguments for skateboarding in school sports and are able to specify plausible characteristics for teaching. However, there is no normative overload without empirical insight into class reality and explicit teaching-learning discourses. We anticipate practical key issues for the teaching environment and verification of the norms. We consider a qualitative survey among experts as a particularly suitable research method.

EXPERT SURVEYS REGARDING THE TOPIC – THE RESEARCH DESIGN

Our research design addresses the following issues:

Why should skateboarding be discussed during physical education or extra-curricular activities and what are the specific issues of this subject? This didactic approach of the subject could indicate a normative or discourse-analytical strategy in connection, for example, with discourses to alternative sports during physical education in accordance with Laßleben (2009). However, as the topic of skateboarding cannot (no longer) be easily classified among the rather simplified concept of alternative sports, the empirical approach should lead to an explicit debate.

Expert interviews were chosen and the focus was placed on the intention with which the selected teachers broach the subject of skateboarding. However, next to the positive aspects considered by the skateboard savvy teachers in their teaching subject, the problematic in the transition from the informal cultural environment to externally controlled education should also be scrutinised. In the process, the limited exercise space in schools is a particularly interesting factor.

Teachers as well as skateboard trainers who are experts in skateboarding in physical education were approached for interviews.

The survey of six male experts (4 practicing physical education teachers, 1 former skater who offers university seminars on the subject, 1 physical education teacher with scientific expertise of the subject) based on the method of problem-centred interviews, whereby the execution of the interviews ultimately shows features of the narrative method (cf. Mayring, 2016). An informal discussion on the topic of skateboarding in physical education at school proved to be a guideline.

The analysis of the expert interviews was based on the qualitatively structured content analysis of Mayring (ibid.). The following results were systematised in three central categories.

SCENE AFFILIATION OF THE TEACHERS

The reasons why the interviewees teach skateboarding are located in their passion for this subculture. Some of the teachers were skating for many years and are still active. It is assumed that skateboarding has a great potential to promote personal development and 'works' beyond youth:

"Skateboarding still plays a very important role in my life and I know that it harbours potentials and is also somehow suitable for lifelong exercise." (GL, 2017, p. 1)[1]

The passion of skateboarding, as emphasised by CP in the interview, is a prerequisite for the authentic performance of the subculture and the authenticity of the teacher. The involvement in the community as well as the expertise on the skateboard promotes the motivation of the pupils.

"Well, I believe that the fact that the teacher himself is a part of the community and able to skate is a necessary prerequisite for the ability to offer it authentically as a teacher. Naturally, this also has a stimulating effect, which is a motivation for the pupils when they realise: wow, he can do this." (CP, 2017, p. 15)

This non-typical expectation for physical education can be substantiated by the subculturally relevant function of role models. In the skate scene, newcomers often approach a good skater with whom they can identify and whom they can look up to. The school environment would therefore require something like a 'skater sports instructor' who not only demonstrates how to perform a trick, but is also able to inspire the pupils with their artistic movements.

"I always had someone to look up to. I was able to identify with him. Therefore, if there is cool physical education teacher, and he does not even to look cool, he just has to be able to do something." (DH, 2017, p. 16)

Based on the description of the interviewees, we could think that pupils consider it 'cool' if the physical education teacher can master a sport which is normally exercised during one's youth.

---

1   Initials for experts, year of interview, location in transcript; transcripts can be requested by contacting the authors.

However, this claim of a native 'skater sports teacher' is not shared by all experts, as is evident from the conversation with TD.

"At the university seminar [T. B./N. P.: TD conducts university seminars on skateboarding] I couldn't care less how well the up and coming sports teachers are able to ride a skateboard during the exam. It is even cooler for kids if the teacher is bad at it, because then they have the additional sense of achievement of being better than the teacher." (TD, 2017, p. 5)

According to TD, skateboarding is a "movement-oriented youth culture". While growing up, young people come into contact with the scene and their motivation for skateboarding is fed by the fact that they are able to achieve something, which is not possible for everyone (cf. Hitzler & Niederbacher, 2010). In view of the school, TD – in contrast to the interviewed practitioners – believes in success if the teacher is not scene savvy. Thus, the motivation of the pupils increases due to a sense of superiority.

It is becoming evident that the interviewed experts are not united in the view as to how deeply the teacher has to be involved in the scene in order to discuss skateboarding and motivate pupils. External and internal views are in contrast. While TD eliminates competency barriers in his lessons at the university the teachers are only able to argue from their own standpoint. A former or active skater is sooner likely to exude their passion in class than someone who is inexperienced and underwent neither training nor advanced education. So far, the prerequisite of including skateboarding in class seems to be the scene affiliation. Ultimately, it is not clear whether competence is at the core of the success. Being involved can therefore not be unequivocally termed a condition, but rather the reality.

THE TEACHING-LEARNING ISSUE

Skateboarding is a subculture, defining itself through self-efficiacy which is now finding its place within physical education (Borden, 2001; Lombard, 2016). The teaching-learning process of skateboarding in the street, in the park or at the gym functions according to the *trial & error* motto. Adolescent skaters use the affordance of their environment to acquire new forms of movement on the boards. In the scope of school, this type of learning is difficult to establish, as physical education is ruled by system-inherent limitations. Furthermore, the path of teaching-learning in class is typically determined by methodical-didactic schedules, thus jeopardising the self-efficacy of the pupils by way of heteronomy.

The discourse as to whether skateboarding should also be determined externally under methodical-didactic planning or whether the pedagogic virtue of self-efficiacy will thus be lost becomes clear in the statement of TD.

"I caution against and say hands off of these standard methodical-didactic rows. It breaks the pedagogic virtue of skateboarding, because self-determined skating is once again determined externally." (TD, 2017, p. 17)

The afore-mentioned "virtue" of skateboarding to confront standards and develop freely represents the core of the culture. As a skater for many years, DH attempts to bring his pupils closer to the different options of skateboarding to enable them to translate the subcultural versions of leisure and sport into other situations of their lives. In this context, for example, it seems to be important to look at skateboarding from another perspective as that of the performance aspect (Laßleben, 2009; Peters, 2016).

The intergenerational relationship seems to be more recalcitrant than the idea of a flexible sports depending on motives and sense integrated in many sports curricula. In the context of school, teachers have exactly that which skaters rebel against: authority. According to the statement of practitioners, pupils therefore have to be provided with the space to deal with the skateboard themselves. In order to provide pupils with this space, one has to depart from the concept of a typical hierarchical classroom. Essentially, the teacher has to rethink or even turn his back on the syllabus and allow the skateboard to take effect (cf. Lange & Sinning, 2012). TD recommends occasionally retreating as a teacher and merely taking on the role of an observer. Not all experts share the belief that skateboarding can only be taught in an environment without hierarchy. GL finds a compromise in this matter: The teacher formulates the objectives, the pupil decides on the leaning path.

"[...] I had developed or designed some sort of skateboard driving license and there were several stations for the completion of which one could collect a stamp; thus, everyone was principally able to initially advance at their own pace and time [...]" (GL, 2017, p. 22)

Furthermore, the informal character of skateboarding does not have to be considered a hook of the lesson, but rather a non-traditional sport with new movement experiences. Contrary to TD's opinion, AH has even established a series of exercises for his sports lessons to learn the basic moves (starting, stopping, accelerating, mastering tight and wide corners) of skateboarding. Therefore, skateboarding is definitely taught by external determination; this is how MJ operates in the eight grade. He uses the technical similarities to snowboarding and introduces skateboarding as a preparation for the snow sports trip (Lange, 2009). MJ teaches the afore-mentioned five basic abilities by way of various exercises. How skateboarding is ultimately implemented in class differs greatly and sets fundamental positions against each other.

Skateboarding is a rather complex type of sport, which intrinsically motivates practitioners and is learnt with much creativity. During physical education, some pupils experience an externally determined teaching-learning process. In order to meet this problem, physical education is designed more individually by the experts. Practice does not reveal any ideal solution for the inclusion of skateboarding in physical education at school.

THE ISSUE OF SPACE

The area of street-oriented skaters mostly evolves from the opportunities of urban space (cf. Borden, 2001). In contrast, the sports hall at school is rather limited and predefined. At first glance, there seem to be only the gym, the school yard or sports grounds. Physical education at school is usually taught in the gym. Sport types, such as gymnastics and swimming are exercised in predetermined sports venues. If one were to transmit this to skateboarding, including the space within the proximity of the school, this means that spaces that are not defined as sports grounds would have to be used as well (cf. Bindel & Schwarz, 2017). Lessons at non-standard, unofficial areas bear safety concerns. The interviewed experts report that the first attempted lessons were therefore conducted in gymnasiums. The good floors were also highly interesting for the first rolling attempts. Due to the smooth surface, the rolling phase lasted longer and the risk of a stone being in the way is eliminated (cf. Hauer & Zimlich, 2012).

However, schools also have access to defined spaces outside of their direct property (cf. Bindel & Schwarz, 2017). DH is skateboard teacher at a skating hall, available to school classes with his expertise and knows that a skating hall has an extremely challenging character for the pupils in addition to the opportunities of performance differentiation:

"I have several areas where people can subdivide. For example, I am only on the flat with those yet unable to do anything. I subsequently move to the smaller ramps with those who know a little more. And with those who are really good, I naturally skate in the pool etc."(DH, 2017, p. 2)

Depending on the structure of the school area, it is not always possible to teach in a skating hall. Therefore, the interviewed teachers rather use the available options at school and in the vicinity to offer greater variety. It is difficult to teach an informal type of sport within a predetermined space such as a gym. Although the smooth surfaces at gyms are perfect for skating, there is often only one third of the hall available, thus limiting the scopes for movement. There are waiting periods because all of them cannot skate at the same time, which means a loss of learning time compared to informal opportunities. The gym seems more suitable for initial steps on the skateboard than for teaching advanced pupils.

CONCLUSION

According to our research, the three identified challenges emerging for teachers are the question of relevance of scene affiliation, teaching-learning and space issues. The problem of authenticity can be expressed as transcending all issues – initially a typical problem for action sports. The practices of youth culture are naturally subject to a multi-faceted filtering process. Even if one were to find clever ways according to Laßleben (2009) to broach action sports in physical education at school, the scope of class is always artificial. However, this is a problem arising in physical education at school per se. Yet, skateboarding cannot be considered to be a random informal sport or action sport, but should be seen in its own right. As such, it is particularly unwieldy, because the activity is extremely charged with meta-sportive dimensions of meaning, which also transport attitudes that contradict the authoritarian world of school. Just imagine: a scene affiliated skater would be graded for his action by an adult…

There will always be an interpretation of skateboarding which shall resist institutional occupation. Correctly so, some skaters will not leave 'their' sport for commercial events, high-performance sport or school. However, our research also shows that there may already be hybrids beyond the positions that can possibly be described as idealistic. Wherever (former) skaters work as teachers at schools, they will take their passion and attempt to pass it on. The above-mentioned filter processes are then accepted as a matter of fact and traversed rather pragmatically. The committed practitioners are surely capable of ignoring the culturally critical view of social scientists on the matter. Ergo: skateboarding at school is – albeit rare – a reality; unfortunately, we only know little about it.

It is surprising that experts are not able to agree on what remains on the way from road to school due to the filter. From practicing via the skateboard license through to free exercising, we have already found many variations of teaching and learning even during this small random test. One cannot assume that a general didactic of skateboarding would be in their interest because 'skater teachers' appear with individual solutions and strong positions. In a classroom situation, skate biography and teaching profession merge to a unique path which – according to our interpretation – has to fit the type. One is more of a teacher at school, the other remains a skater while, another one mixes both quite contrasting professions to create something entirely new.

The question as to whether only skaters can give skateboarding lessons would have to be answered in the negative from a profession-theoretical aspect. Scene affinity or affiliation would not be required if one looks at the profession of a sports teacher. Just as it is with football, dancing or parkour, professional action or strong involvement is not necessary. Skateboarding appears to be a particularly unwieldy enterprise in this instance as well. Due to the fact that the practice of skating is strongly involved, a teacher who stands on the board with great effort and precariousness would be difficult to imagine. It is particularly the casualness, the effortlessness and the easiness which are embedded in the movements. It is doubtful whether the subject can be offered regardless of scene affinity. However, we are lacking case studies to continue the discussion.

Least problematic seems to be the issue of space; possibly because it only impacts on the skating and not the interaction on a social-hierarchical basis. Skateboarding in a gymnasium is possible for pragmatic reasons. In addition, the flooring of the hall seems to be suitable for beginners. However, with the retreat of skating into the hall – be it in the skatepark or at school – a significant dimension is lost which can best be described with terms such as space appropriation and assertion in a public space. Here, it is possible to link up with Laßleben, who recommends seeking out facilities outside school. From a sports-didactic perspective, this is recommendable. However, which 'true' skater would like to see 25 beginners together with teacher in the cityscape? It may therefore be best if scholastic as well as Olympic skateboarding were to be established as a special discipline.

REFERENCES

Bindel, T. (2008). *Soziale Regulierung in informellen Sportgruppen (Social regulation in informal sports groups)*. Hamburg: Czwalina.

Bindel, T. (2015). *Bedeutsamkeit und Bedeutung sportlichen Engagements in der Jugend. (Relevance and significance of athletic commitment during adolescence)* Aachen: Meyer & Meyer.

Bindel, T. & Balz, E. (2014). Informeller Sport in der Schule (Informal sport at school). *Sportpädagogik (Sports education) 38,* 1, 2-6.

Bindel, T. & Erdmann, M. (2016). Stottern und außerschulisches Sportengagement in der Jugend – eine exemplarische Ergänzung der Inklusionsdebatte (Stuttering and extra-scholastic sports engagement during adolescence – an exemplary supplement of the inclusion debate). In *Zeitschrift für Inklusion, 3* (2016) (in Journal for inclusions).

Bindel, T. & Schwarz, R. (2017). Sport-Räume: Entwicklungspotenziale, Problematiken und pädagogische Möglichkeiten. (Sport facilities: development potentials, difficulties and pedagogic options). *Sportpädagogik (Sports education) 41,* 2, 2-7.

Borden, I. (2001). *Skateboarding, space and the city: architecture and the body.* Oxford, New York: Berg.

Ehni, H. (1998). Den Skatern auf der Spur. (Tracking skaters) In Schwier, J. (Ed.), *Jugend, Sport, Kultur.* (Youth, sport, culture). *Zeichen und Codes jugendlicher Sportszenen* (pp. 109-124). (Signs and codes of adolescent sports scenes). Hamburg: Czwalina.

Hauer, J. & Zimlich, M. (2012). Zwischen Szene, Spektakel und Erziehung.: Skateboarden in der Schule. (Interim scene, spectacle and education: skateboarding at school). *Bewegungserziehung, 66,* 2, 52-59 (Movement education).

Hitzler, R. & Niederbacher, A. (2010). *Leben in Szenen: Formen juveniler Vergemeinschaftung heute* (3. vollständig überarbeitete Auflage). (Life in scenes: Shapes of juvenile communitarisation today - third revised edition). Wiesbaden: VS Verlag.

Klafki, W. (1997). Die bildungstheoretische Didaktik im Rahmen kritisch-konstruktiver Erziehungswissenschaft. (Education-theoretic didactic in the context of critical-constructive educational science). In Gudjons, H. & Winkel, R. (Eds.), *Didaktische Theorien,* 9. Aufl. (pp. 13-34). (Didactic theories). Hamburg: Bergmann + Helbig Verlag.

Lange, A. (2009). *Erfolgreiche Spiele für Rollen, Gleiten und Fahren: Fahrrad, Rollbrett, Inliner, Skateboard, Skier, Schlitten und Schlittschuhe (Successful games for skating, gliding and driving: bicycle, roller board, inliner, skateboard, skiers, sled and ice skates)* (1. edition) Wiebelsheim: Limpert.

Lange, H. & Sinning, S. (2012). *Neue Sportarten und Bewegungsfelder für den Sportunterricht: innovatives Lehren und Lernen im Lichte der Themenkonsti-*

tution. (New types of sport and movement areas for physical education at school: innovative teaching and learning in light of theme construction). Baltmannsweiler: Schneider Hohengehren.

Laßleben, A. (2009). *Trendsport im Schulsport: eine fachdidaktische Studie. (Non-traditional sport in physical education at school: a subject-didactic study).* Hamburg: Czwalina.

Lombard, K.-J. (Ed.). (2016). *Skateboarding: subcultures, sites and shifts.* London, New York: Routledge.

Mayring, P. (2016). *Einführung in die Sozialforschung: eine Anleitung zu qualitativem Denken.* (Introduction in social research: instructions for qualitative reasoning). (6. revised edition). Weinheim [and others]: Beltz

Neuber, N. (Ed.) (2010). *Informelles Lernen im Sport.* (Informal learning during sport). *Beiträge zu einer allgemeinen Bildungsdebatte.* (Contributions for general education debate). Wieskateboardingaden: VS.

Peters, C. (2016). *Skateboarding: Ethnographie einer urbanen Praxis. (Skateboarding: ethnography of an urban practice).* Münster, New York: Waxmann.

Schwier, J. (1998). Stile und Codes bewegungsorientierter Bewegungskulturen. (Style and codes of movement-oriented movement cultures). In Schwier, J. (Ed.), *Jugend, Sport, Kultur.* (Youth, sport, culture) *Zeichen und Codes jugendlicher Sportszenen* (pp. 9-29). (Signs and codes of adolescent sports scenes). Hamburg: Czwalina.

Stern, M. (2010). *Stil-Kulturen.* (Style cultures. *Performative Konstellationen von Technik, Spiel und Risiko in neuen Sportpraktiken. (Performative constellations of technology, game and risk in new sports practices).* Bielefeld: transcript.

Zander, B. (2017). *Lebensweltorientierter Schulsport. (Life-world oriented physical education at school) Sozialisationstheoretische Grundlagen und didaktischer Perspektiven.* (Socialisation-theoretical principles and didactic perspectives) Aachen: Meyer & Meyer.

Lords of the Rings: Reasserting the Skateboarding Art at the Olympic Games

Tait Colberg

Marten Persiel's film 'This Ain't California' (2012) inserts a fictional story of brash young skateboarders into the real, brutal context of Communist East Germany during the last years of the Cold War. Some of the footage is genuinely archival, other images are made to appear so with the use of vintage cameras, costumes, and props. The funniest on-screen moments include shots of wholesome young comrades in track-and-field-style uniforms performing stiff and strange maneuvers on their 'rollerboards' against austere geometric backgrounds, clips attributed to some East German Ministry of Sport. Whether the footage is authentic or fabricated by the filmmaker, skaters of any era can enjoy a laugh at such a ridiculous effort to sportify and nationalize their anarchic activity and subculture. Thank God – or hail, Skatan – we can all sigh with relief that outside forces with self-serving motives never succeeded in athleticizing and subjugating skateboarding; not in Cold War East Germany, and certainly not in the liberal, democratic West during the years since!

Or haven't they done so already, to some degree? Large corporations began penetrating the skateboarding scene in the United States during the mid-1990s through events like the X Games, then the Dew Tour, and lately Street League Skateboarding. In the process, prize money and endorsement deals for participating pro riders have risen astronomically. Have skateboarding's fundamental virtues of personal expression, do-it-yourself initiative, and anti-authoritarianism declined at the same time and as a direct result? Skateboarding appears more popular around the world today than ever before, but has it also become tamer and more homogenous, especially among top-earning pro skaters and the youngest riders who idolize them? And will the inclusion of skateboarding in the Olympics, beginning with the 2020 Summer Games in Tokyo, only hasten the transition and solidify the transformation of skateboarding from a wild, fertile art to a sterile, domesticated sport?

As a skater who first stepped on a board in the 1980s, when skateboarding remained a small, but vital subculture even in the United States, I fear that the answer to these questions may be yes, at least within shortboard street and vert riding. I have argued broadly against the trend toward sportification in my book, *The Skateboarding Art* (2012). Here I aim to address the Olympic issue specifically. What follows is a description of the attitude, behavior, and misbehavior that I would like to see among pro skaters attending their first Olympiad.[1] The scenario that follows may be no more than a fantasy; it may never reach the eyes of pro riders heading to the Games, and the strict regulations thrust upon all Olympic 'athletes' may render any rebellion among skaters impossible without serious legal and financial consequences. Nevertheless, the image of pro riders reasserting the virtues of the skateboarding art at the 2020 Olympic Summer Games in Tokyo, however idealized, may open the minds of other skaters and the non-skateboarding public to alternative ways of living, at any moment, over and above the sporting outlook.

Travel Plans

Long before Olympics-bound pro skaters board their planes to Tokyo, they do their homework. From behind their laptops and on their smartphones, they study the skate scene of the host city and the whole of Japan. Locating Tokyo's skate shops, especially the independent operators, is a top priority, since they function as key points of information and connection within any local skate network.[2] Pro skaters plan casual visits to each of these shops – no pre-arranged crowds, no hundreds of hasty autographs – where they expect to meet the owners, employees, and local riders in person, many of whom they have come to know already from a distance through the wide range of unique and astonishing Japanese skate videos. Visiting pro skaters plan to post a few pictures on their social media outlets encouraging their followers to patronize each shop, and they themselves an-

---

1   'Pro' meaning any skater selected and scheduled to compete at the Games, whether or not he, she, or they earn a living by their riding ordinarily. Small countries may send skaters to the Olympics who otherwise do not hold professional status.

2   Despite the International Olympic Committee's recognition of World Skate as some kind of global governing body, skateboarding remains a patchwork of local scenes, each with its own special qualities.

ticipate purchasing some local goods as souvenirs. No visiting pro skater makes arrangements to attend any Olympic sporting event before making the rounds of the local skate shops to thank and support them as centers of the art.

Pro skaters heading to the Olympics also go online to locate the skateparks in Tokyo and throughout Japan. They shake their heads with disappointment, but not surprise, when they read that the host city recently demolished its most popular park to make way for an Olympic stadium. They plan to skate the remaining parks in Tokyo and its environs at special sessions during the later days of the Games. Scrutinizing local skate blogs and other chat sites helps visiting pro skaters find other prime spots that lie outside the boundaries of designated parks.

In all of their online preparations, Olympics-bound pro skaters aim to make personal contacts with their Japanese brothers and sisters. In addition to new friendships, these fellow skaters can offer guidance around the city and beyond, both geographically and culturally. Visiting pro skaters realize that they cannot rely upon the official translators and handlers provided by Olympic authorities. These personnel, while friendly and knowledgeable about the city and the Games, are unlikely to have a deep understanding of the skateboarding art, and they are sure to discourage skaters' natural instincts to roll past or pop over any rules and regulations handed down from the Olympic Committee. Only fellow skaters of any status and skill level – the shared experience of riding cuts across the artificial distinctions of pro and amateur – can show the true bounty and boundaries of their city and country.

Olympics-bound pro skaters also prepare to document their stay carefully. Before departure to Tokyo, individual pro riders or 'national teams' collectively make all of the arrangements to bring along a trusted photographer and/or videographer. This filmer is ideally a skater too, with experience capturing others in action and on the move.[3] While still at home, pro skaters demand full Olympic credentials for their filmers so that they may follow their subjects everywhere they go: into the Olympic Village, to and from the various sports venues, and onto the floors of the official skate courses. To gain this level of access, pro skaters are willing to identify their filmers as 'trainers' or 'coaches' rather than photographers and videographers. The camera is just an incidental training tool, they tell Olympic bureaucrats, used to record images at practice sessions for later re-

---

3   An older photographer, who may capture beautiful images from a fixed position with carefully positioned lights, is less desirable than a younger, more social-media-savvy person who is ready to skate into and out of a shooting situation without interrupting a pro rider's flow and without falling into the hands of disapproving property managers and security guards.

view, so that riders can adjust their performances accordingly before the official competitions begin, as many athletes do. Pro skaters and their filmers also make certain that any footage they create together, within the Olympic complex or outside, remains their property and does not fall into the ownership of the Olympic Committee or any of its agents.[4] And pro skaters more flush with cash and connections are also prepared to direct their filmers toward the riding of their less privileged peers; everyone who rips makes the cut.

Finally, pro skaters attending the Olympics make a few material preparations. Riders with high-profile sponsors ship packages of extra boards – at least a dozen decks, pairs of trucks, and sets of wheels; plus griptape, bearings, and hardware – directly to their rooms in the Olympic Village or to other team facilities at the Games. A pro skater may expect to break one or two decks during the weeks of the Games; bringing so many complete boards will prepare them for another contingency. Pro riders also pack stashes of paint markers in their bags, since pressurized spray cans cannot travel aboard airplanes, with a special purpose in mind…

ON THE SCENE

As soon as pro skaters arrive at the Olympic Village, they begin to apply the 'skater's gaze' to their new surroundings: They assess every stairway, rail, ledge, bank, bench, planter, outdoor sculpture, and other paved feature for its creative potential, just as they do in every other town and city that they visit on sponsored tours or during personal travels. Wherever and whenever some riders find a skate-worthy spot in the Village, they spread the word to their peers and session it together. Likewise, pro skaters scan the Olympic sports venues for elements worthy of a slap, pop, or flip. Sometimes they hit spots outside the arenas after hours to make big tricks that require a great number of attempts and long run-ups free of foot traffic. But pro riders also put their mark on Olympic sports venues in broad daylight when they are buzzing with spectators and athletes.

Skaters also make themselves visible by refusing to walk or ride shuttle buses to sports events that they might like to watch. They roll on their boards from one venue to another and within the foyers and hallways inside the arenas. As a

---

4   In this way, today's pro riders continue the long tradition of skaters documenting their own activity and creating the kinds of original photo and video artworks that they themselves value, free of any sporty 'call of the game', meaningless statistics, and vapid interviews with sports journalists.

general rule, pro skaters take their boards everywhere they go and put them to use at every chance they get. No admittance with a skateboard? Pro skaters record the refusal on video, share it online, and take their business elsewhere. At all times and in every space, they remain identifiable to spectators and athletes as skateboarders by putting the tool of their trade to use, not by any particular fashion choices or media reputation. Pro skaters feel shame at the thought of anyone catching a glimpse of them merely strolling around in their 'just-chillin'' shoes.

By these actions, and from the day they arrive until the moment they depart, pro skaters show all of the visiting athletes, spectators, and their Olympic and Japanese hosts that skateboarding, first and foremost, is the art of repurposing under-utilized spaces and structures to create new experiences and spectacles. Pro skaters at the Olympics make clear that no one can contain any rider within a designated park, no matter how lavish, and only during certain hours of the day or night.[5]

And images of off-limits skateboarding at the Olympics begin circulating around the world immediately. Filmers go to work at every session, large or small, inside the Village or at the various sports venues. They shoot every skater at the spot, not just their assigned riders. Throughout the Games, pro skaters post a steady stream of still pictures and video clips to their social media outlets: sometimes footage of themselves, more often shots of others, and always images of actual skating, not tourist pictures of someone's first time eating sushi or spotting a passing sports celebrity. And filmers regularly upload all of their recordings to secure devices or online sites for future editing and release. As an additional precaution, filmers carry multiple cameras – just as pro skaters hold extra boards in reserve – in case of damage from wayward boards or confiscation by disapproving authorities.

Filmers do not share their footage, captured exclusively by skaters for skaters, with mainstream media channels covering the Olympics. Nor do pro skaters perform for any TV cameras that point their lenses toward a session in progress; they drive them off, render their footage unfit for broadcasting with foul language and other bad behavior, or simply skate away and return to the spot later, after the TV cameras have moved on to some sporting event. Only amateur photo snappers and video dabblers, excited by the sight of skaters in action, are welcome and likely to receive some personalized pictures with pro riders, always

---

5　By acts of trespassing and the vandalism of adding wear and tear to street obstacles, skateboarding often is a crime and riders are proud of it. Skaters of all levels abandon or break customs of civil society that are no more than customary whenever and wherever there are opportunities for art-making.

with a board in the shot. Cutting out mainstream media middlemen aiming to monetize their art, pro skaters at the Olympics do not grant interviews to sports journalists; they speak only to representatives of the skate press, especially small, local channels, who may attend the Games or meet visiting pro riders at more hospitable locations in Tokyo proper.

ONE TRIBE

On video and in person, pro skaters at the Olympics consider their appearance an important part of their performance art. They do not make their clothing into patchworks of all their sponsors' logos, like NASCAR drivers or professional cyclists.[6] Pro skaters, therefore, are equally wary of the official apparel of the Olympic Games, national uniforms, and flags of both sorts. Skateboarding, like all robust arts, is supra-national; anyone, anywhere who rides a skateboard joins the club. Often its members, though separated by great distances and diverse cultures, have more in common with one another than with their nearest non-skating neighbors, including their fellow 'national teammates' and other Olympic athletes. Shared experience unites skaters, and national origins do not divide them.[7] Surely, there are skaters from France or Brazil or Japan, each with a distinct riding style and subculture based on their local terrain and customs, but the longer they practice the art, the more they become skaters first. In public statements at the Olympics pro riders call themselves 'skaters from France' or 'skaters from Japan' rather than 'French skaters' or 'Japanese skaters'.

Like most young people with access to the powerful information technologies of the internet and mobile phones, skaters of all levels recognize the broad

---

6   The transparent labeling and product placement in the attire and on-camera poses of pro skaters at corporate mega contests, especially ads for products that are not essential to riding a skateboard, have already become an embarrassment. After all, no respectable skater dresses like a corporate billboard in the streets or when filming a proper video part. Skaters find ways to promote the companies that genuinely help them and others to ride their best with some moderation and style.

7   The positive experience of riding forms the strongest bond. Many times, though, skaters from different parts of the world also share encounters with derision and persecution by the common people, sports authorities, and the broader governments of their homelands; skaters often have to look elsewhere for support and to build transnational and trans-cultural ties of their own. Skateboarding becomes the community that they have chosen, beyond the accidental surroundings of their birth.

trend toward globalization and the softening of national and cultural boundaries.[8] So pro skaters at the Olympics resist efforts to separate their ranks too strictly by country of origin and to create competition for national glory. Nor do they participate naively in the Olympic myth of nations setting aside their differences and allowing good sportsmanship to unify the globe for the duration of the Games.[9] Pro skaters may choose to represent certain aspects of their native lands and cultures at the Games, but they do not allow themselves to be chosen by the Olympic Committee or national governments to endorse their policies or conceal their crimes.

As practical strategies, pro skaters at the Olympics eschew national uniforms and the official apparel of the Games entirely, or modify their text and imagery to better suit the larger cause of skateboarding itself. They also deface other official merchandise and signage bearing the words 'Olympic Skateboarding' or 'Nation X Skateboarding'. A quick swipe with a paint marker crosses out the proper adjectives, and with them, outsiders' false claims upon the art. Likewise, skaters strike through the words 'athlete' or 'competitor' wherever Olympic signs or print materials aim to describe them with these misnomers, and they scribble 'skater' or 'artist' or some other punchline in their place. Wherever skaters encounter the Olympic Rings, they fill in the last circle with the Skater's Anarchy, updating the time-honored icon with a small 'rt' inside the circle be-

---

8   Like other artists, skaters help drive this movement by touring the world in person and by disseminating videos, marked geographically mostly to alert other riders to the choicest skate spots in every region; the curious onlookers, distracted drivers, and irritated security guards in the footage are the same the world over. International travel is one of the leading incentives and chief indicators of top pro riders. The skateboarding art, like others, is portable and transferrable with little need for translation. The sight of a fellow human being boardsliding a long rail or blasting a tweaked air high above a ramp's coping is striking to an onlooker anywhere, without any verbal explanation or commentary. Spotting even a novice skater carving down a hill or popping an ollie over a pothole may be a magical experience for a citizen of any nation in the world.

9   The Olympics, even the ancient ones, have never been free of social, economic, and political agendas, and often nations have used them explicitly to advance themselves and hinder their enemies. Like all artists, skaters reserve the right and take every opportunity to expose, ridicule, and replace the hypocrisies of the powerful and the masses who follow them blindly. Skate magazines, videos, and board graphics have done so for decades, targeting brutal police departments, unchecked military aggression, corrupt politicians, wealthy elites, ignorant mobs, shallow celebrities, pompous academics, self-righteous religious leaders, and so on.

side the capital 'A'. Pro riders carry flags of their own making, as they roll from one sports venue to another, so that they might attract fellow skaters from among the Olympic spectators.

OUT OF BOUNDS

Although individual skaters are able to modify Olympic merchandise and signage on the sly, larger numbers of riders and the noise of their unsanctioned skating in the Village and at sports venues are bound to attract the attention of curious spectators and, just as often, irate security guards. When these officers arrive and attempt to shut down a session in progress, pro skaters deploy all of the countermeasures that they have developed in the streets. Sometimes they play dumb: 'We can't skate here? I don't understand', they say, and with a flash of their Olympic identification cards, the only official items of the Games left undefiled by paint markers, they point out, 'we have *these*!' On other occasions, pro skaters scold meddlesome security guards, waving the same credentials: 'We are Olympic *athletes*, and you are interfering with our *training*!' In both cases, skaters happily turn the tokens and terms of the sports world against its authorities. Sometimes playing nice with security guards becomes the most effective strategy for prolonging a session, or at least escaping without any serious consequences: 'We're glad you're here; can you help us keep everyone safe by holding back pedestrians and re-directing vehicles for a few minutes? Thank you!' Once filmers have captured the last trick, smiling skaters pose for smartphone selfies with the security guards holding or standing upon boards themselves, creating a warm Olympic memory for all.

Some encounters play out less smoothly. A few of the most aggressive guards seize boards shot out from under riders' feet after bailed tricks. The aggrieved skaters put up no fight to reclaim their equipment – they have dozens of replacements stashed back at the Village and elsewhere just for this contingency.[10] With a quick trip to the board depot, any rider is ready to take the best revenge: he, she, or they continue skating. Pro skaters at the Olympics step back from security guards and civilians who become physically aggressive. They allow filmers to capture belligerent behavior on video, and they play back the

---

10 The board supply is communal: no matter who brought this one or that one from home to the Games, any skater who has lost or broken a board receives a new one, especially if the skater in need comes from a developing nation where boards are scarce or exorbitantly expensive.

footage to the bad actors' superiors, the local police, and the world at large over social media.

The conflict between Olympic security personnel and pro skaters cuts both ways, however. Some guards pass verbal complaints and their own video footage of skaters operating outside of the competition zones to higher ranking Olympic authorities, who then send official statements of disapproval to national team leaders and to specific skaters, warning them of disciplinary actions for further violations. Offending skaters post these statements to their social media outlets for laughs and mostly ignore the warnings, unmoved by the inevitable outcome: The first riders disqualified from competition, thrown out of the Village, and banned from attending any Olympic contest as a spectator receive the highest praise from fellow skaters, both pros on the scene and everyday riders around the world. Mock medals for these achievements begin circulating online. The winners do not leave Tokyo immediately, though. Instead, banned riders capitalize on their connections to local shops and skaters and spend the remainder of the Games exploring spots and parks in the city and the surrounding areas, always with Japanese guides in tow and couches to surf. Soon, they will rejoin the rest of the pro riders for special sessions.

SPORTSMANSHIP

The reactions of other Olympic athletes to the sights and sounds of unsanctioned skateboarding in the Village and at sports venues are mixed. Some, accustomed to years of training and competition within highly specialized, tightly regulated facilities, are simply baffled: 'What are *they* doing here? This can't be the skateboarding competition?!' A few others, who participate in the most well established and highly esteemed events of the Summer Games, mutter their disapproval to one another. They correctly identify the official skateboarding events as short-lived gimmicks for drawing younger audiences to the Olympics, but they entirely miss the counterpoint of skateboarding out of bounds, and they dare not confront sessioning skaters directly.

Many more athletes, though, are excited to come across pro skaters practicing the art on their own terms. The strength and coordination of skaters, and the countless hours of practice necessary to develop them, are familiar to these elite athletes, yet the particular movements and skills of skaters appear radically different and fascinating. The same athletes are also shocked by the immediate danger into which skaters routinely place themselves, especially when they see riders suffer hard falls, only to rise, and try again, and again, and again, each time without any safety measures or medical personnel on the scene. And many athletes quickly discern the degree of independence and even outright defiance that skaters must summon to create a session outside of the skatepark: 'They don't care what anybody says…!' flashes across the minds of onlooking athletes.

The individualism of skateboarders, without any loss of camaraderie, impresses many athletes as well; without any explicit coaching and free from common uniforms, each skater appears to have has his, her, or their own way of speaking, acting, and dressing in addition to a unique riding style. In these ways, the most astute Olympic athletes begin to recognize that skaters are similar to the musicians, comedians, filmmakers, and other professional creatives whom they themselves admire; in a word, they acknowledge that skaters are *cool* in ways that they aspire to be. And so, some of the world's finest athletes, gathered for the globe's most prestigious competitions, approach skateboarders as they hammer away at off-limits spots for smartphone selfies to share with millions of sports fans. Pro skaters happily oblige friendly, supportive Olympic athletes, insisting – to the horror of trainers and coaches – that the athletes step on boards themselves for pictures. Skaters and filmers also give athletes chances to participate in their artworks, inviting them to strike poses in the background as skaters bust tricks and to join celebrations that follow 'makes' of big tricks. Amiable Olympic athletes even use their celebrity status to help deter aggressive authorities who would otherwise shut down skate sessions outside of prescribed areas.

Yet pro skaters do not chase down superstar celebrity athletes at the Games and take wide-eyed selfies standing beside them. Pro riders abstain from this kind of fawning for two reasons: First, there are no athletes, Olympic or otherwise, more impressive in their physical performance than the most skilled skateboarders.[11] And second, superstar celebrity athletes have reached the peaks of their professions and the public's attention with the support of robust cultural

---

11 Many athletes are considerably less versatile in their skill set, since they are such narrow specialists; some train their bodies and minds to execute a single physical task, like throwing the javelin, for example. Ball players have a wider range of skills, sports fans may argue, but they do not risk placing their entire weight, and their fate, upon their playthings as skaters do; the stakes for mishandling the ball are much lower than missing a board. Gymnasts risk life and limb in comparable ways, and the creativity of their routines approaches the level of skaters' lines, sports fans may retort. This observation may be true, but the apparatus of each gymnastic event remains fixed to the ground and unchanging from one competition to another. Skaters adapt their riding to the constantly shifting terrain of new cities, parks, and ramps. As a result, they have no athletic superiors to whom they might bow.

networks.[12] Skaters, on the other hand, typically do not enjoy the same cultural support structures, even in today's boom times, when pro contests appear on television during the summer months with heavy commercial endorsements, and when the Olympics have decided to include skateboarding for the first time.[13]

In fact, skaters often find cultural forces and institutions arrayed against them, especially when they ride outside of the Olympic arena, the courses of corporate contests, and even the local skatepark. Parents, teachers, police, civic and religious leaders threaten skaters in vain with punishments at home, visits to the principal's office, jail sentences, and eternal damnation for these transgressions. When skaters fall, onlookers laugh, and when they arrive at hospitals, doctors and nurses add insults to injuries. Skate shops struggle to remain solvent, factory sponsorships are few, and pro careers even fewer, brief, and seldom profitable enough to pay the rent or support a family. And the perks of pro status disappear immediately, as soon as skaters step out of the contest environment; back on the street, even the highest-earning skaters still have to tolerate, escape, and physically defend themselves against finger-wagging pedestrians, aggressive security guards and police, and distracted drivers. If skateboarding has ladders,

---

12 Humble as their beginnings may have been, they soon found sports facilities at local parks and schools. Family members, teachers, coaches, religious and civic organizations encouraged their athletic development and dreams. They passed through recreational, high school, and collegiate leagues into the professional ranks with the assistance of sports agents, attorneys, players' unions, and specialists in sports medicine. And they can look forward to a lifetime of financial stability, at the very least, as multimillion-dollar endorsement deals for all manner of products and services supplement already hefty salaries. Certainly, superstar celebrity athletes have worked hard physically, emotionally, and psychologically to climb the ladders of their respective sports. But all the while there was a ladder to climb, a system to navigate, a network to exploit. The price for players is the conformity that they accept and the control that they cede at every stage of their progress. Even athletes in less popular sports enjoy the lower tiers of cultural networks, though they may never reach levels of international fame and fortune.

13 The construction of skateparks, many of them municipal, may have increased significantly in recent years, but their total number is still likely to fall well below the amount of basketball courts, soccer fields, and other sports facilities that local governments routinely include in their budgets and that parents take for granted as available to their children. And parks can never fully contain the skateboarding art; it must commit the trespassing, vandalism, and other violations of community norms necessary to explore and exploit the full range of paved surfaces.

they are scarce, short, and rickety. Hence, its rewards are not chiefly fame and fortune, but hard-won freedom for the individual and solidarity within the tribe.

Surely, athletes who have reached the highest levels of play and pay erected by the larger culture possess certain kinds of toughness. But they are not skatetough enough to battle against the powers-that-be and build their own structures, however makeshift and fleeting. So pro skaters at the Olympics show respect for the achievements of superstar celebrity athletes that they encounter on the sidelines, in the stands, or at parties during the Games, but they do not fall at their feet. Superstar celebrity athletes may receive more money and more of the world's attention, but skaters of every level are more often masters of their own fates. Accordingly, pro riders at the Olympics spend more time taking pictures with their brothers and sisters in skateboarding, especially those at the bottom of society's usual scale, than with celebrity athletes at the top.

No Warm-Ups

Like the planners of corporate mega contests, organizers of the Games assign skateboarders certain days and times to practice on their designated courses before the official competitions begin. Pro skaters take full advantage of the offer, but not in the manner that Olympic authorities expect.

On practice days, pro skaters do not arrive individually at their venues, insert their earbuds, and go 'into the zone' to develop and rehearse winning runs, occasionally glancing sideways to measure the competition. The reason is simple: they do not skate this way in the wild. Even when skaters concentrate intensely and work hard to build the best possible video parts, they still operate in collaboration with filmers and usually with the support of a small crew of fellow riders and other homies. After a long, painful battle against a particular obstacle, everyone cheers the victorious skater on and rushes towards the filmer to watch a replay on the camera.

Pro riders at the Olympics work together in similar fashion to turn their 'practices' into open, raucous skate jams. They arrive together as early as possible, and they skate all day, ignoring Olympic personnel who tell them that their time has expired, and making no effort to clear the area for the BMX riders who might follow them. Skaters leave one course only to check out the action on another, and no one pays any attention to their official classification as a 'Street' or 'Park' specialist. Each course is fair game for every rider, as terrain to ride or as a place to take a break and admire the riding of others. Skaters also ignore gender on the days designated for 'Men's Skateboarding Practice'. Male riders invite all of their female and non-binary peers to join them.

From beginning to end, 'bust or bail' is the rule; no one skates conservatively, holding tricks in secret reserve for the official competition. And no one spends the entire session chillin' on the sidelines or in the stands; skate tough or go home. To keep everyone's energy up and to add another layer of creative collaboration, skaters take turns connecting smartphones or laptops to the venue's sound system and blast tunes of their choice. No one interrupts the flow of the skating and tries to become the voice of authority, even as a joke, by grabbing a microphone and delivering some corny commentary over the action. Filmers detach themselves from the specific skaters who brought them to the Games and record everyone's riding. No sports journalists are allowed entry into the venue or access to the footage. From the ramps' platforms and the sidelines, skaters themselves snap pictures with old friends and teammates from across the globe whom they seldom see and with new ones whom they have met for the first time. Throughout each jam, the pros skate *with* one another, as skateboarders of all kinds do almost instinctively, and not *against* one another, as corporate sponsors, government officials, and common sports fans would prefer.

The activity differs in some ways, though, on days that Olympic officials set aside for 'Women's Skateboarding Practice'. Even though male riders welcome their sister skaters to join their jams, they are reluctant to invade the women's scene. Male riders acknowledge that every aspect of building a life in skateboarding is more difficult for women, from acquiring their first boards, to making their first public appearances at parks and in the streets, to finding other female skaters like them, to gaining the attention of sponsors and the skate press. And women, on board and off, face issues that their male counterparts seldom encounter, if ever: a whole range of shaming, harassment, and even assaults aimed at their abilities, body types, sexualities, and more. As much as skaters have to be tougher than athletes, so skater girls have to be much tougher than the boys. By the 2020 Olympic Summer Games, the world of women's skateboarding still remains small and deserves special discretion and support.

So rather than charging into the women's practice sessions, even with the best intentions, male riders first ask their female counterparts what sort of presence, if any, they would prefer. Some may permit none at all; a large crowd of dudes, either in the stands or on the courses, may inevitably alter or interrupt the women's ownership of the space and their experience skating together. Other women may allow a male audience, but prohibit male riders on the courses. Even if a few women encourage the men to skate alongside them, the men probably do better to decline this minority's invitation. Whatever the consensus of the female skaters, the men honor their decision. If male skaters fill the stands, they cheer the women's riding as vocally as they celebrate one another's. With the women's permission, they capture and share just as many pictures and clips to their social media channels. And if female filmers also agree, the photographers and videographers who usually follow the men take positions on the courses and cover the female riders with the same enthusiasm.

When the practices-turned-skate-jams have finished – when Olympic staff, weary of chasing stubborn skaters around the courses, finally decide to turn off the lights – all of the pro riders leave the venues together and find places to unwind and socialize casually in the Village and elsewhere in the city. None party so hard on any night of the Games, however, that they cannot skate the next day fully.[14] And pro skaters at the Olympics do not embarrass themselves and the wider community of riders by posting clips of their drunken stumbles and baked rambles on their social media outlets. No glory attaches to any skater tossed out of Tokyo night spots, the Village, or the entire Olympics for bad behavior while inebriated or stoned. Pro skaters allow sports journalists to save their favorite 'wild and crazy, hard-partying' characterizations for the snowboarders of the Winter Games. Riding skateboards, the pros demonstrate, is the true rebellion.

THE MAIN EVENT

After days of hit-and-run skating in the Village and at the various sports venues, and after practice sessions on the skate courses that turned into all-day jams, the moment of the first official Olympic skateboarding competition finally arrives. Security guards open the venue, maintenance crews put the final polish on the floors and ramps, and sports journalists test their equipment and rehearse lines of pseudo-skatespeak. Crowds of spectators and panels of judges shuffle into the arena and find their seats.

And nothing happens. None of the pro riders appear. The courses sit empty. As the crowd becomes confused, then bored, then irritated, Olympic officials

---

14 Pro riders at the Olympics do not fall into the trap, laid by aging executives at multi-million-dollar tobacco and liquor companies and by the leaders of murderous drug cartels, that getting high on smokes, booze, and dope are the strongest acts of teenage and twenty-something rebellion. Nor do they perpetuate the myth that boozing and smoking are somehow integral parts of skateboarding. Anyone who cannot ride without a bottle or a blunt in hand belongs in a rehabilitation program, not at the Olympics or elsewhere within the pro scene.

make frantic calls to the Village in search of the skateboarders. They receive no replies. When security guards rush to the Olympic dormitories, they find the skaters' quarters abandoned, but without any signs of accident or foul play; all of the dresser drawers are empty, the beds made, and every appointment and decoration rests in the same place as it did when the pro skaters arrived. They have packed, cleaned their rooms, and left *en masse* and without any notice or indication of their whereabouts.

Organizers and sponsors of the Games soon become furious, as television networks cut away to other sporting events in progress, and as spectators begin grumbling about refunds for the price of their tickets. The winners' podiums stand vacant, and the medals lie untouched. The Olympics will have no skateboarders, on this day or any other, to draw young viewers to its corporate advertisers; there will be no reflected glory for patriots and politicians who show little more than contempt for skateboarding during the years between the Games.

But pro skaters have not left Tokyo entirely, since they have not finished their business 'at' the Olympics. The night before the first official skateboarding competition, they quietly left the Village and disbursed to other area hotels and the homes of Japanese skaters whom they befriended in the previous weeks. The next morning, pro riders spread themselves out across the city's and the suburbs' skateparks, and they begin blasting messages to their followers on social media that skate jams are going down at every site: all day long, free of charge, and open to all riders. Tokyo skate shops and prominent local skaters echo the invitations on their own online channels. Soon every park in the city and some in nearby areas fill with skaters, both native Japanese and foreign visitors, including many who have raced from the stands at the abandoned Olympic skateboarding venue. Pro riders give away surplus boards and other swag and take pictures or sign autographs for anyone who lost money on tickets to the Olympic skateboarding events.

Everyone skates together at these park jams, without any separation between pros and ordinary riders. There is mutual celebration of everyone's skating, regardless of age, experience, gender, nationality, or any other distinction. A few megaphones and makeshift sound systems at each location build hype and provide basic crowd control. The same filmers who covered the pros in the days leading up to their exodus from Olympic competition now cover everyone, and they send out a steady stream of images over the internet all day and into the night. Taking their lead from the pros, skaters at the jams largely ignore any sports journalists who straggle over to the parks. Sometimes skaters spill out of the parks onto sidewalks and streets, overwhelming police, pedestrians, and vehicles with their numbers and energy, but always in the spirit of creative play rather than genuine hostility. At the end of the day's sessions, visiting skaters of all ranks make special shows of praise and thanks to their Japanese hosts without any mention of the Olympic Games. At night, small bands of skaters break away from the crowds for some after-hours street sessions, while others enjoy the last parties of their stay in the island nation.

AFTERGLOW

When pro skaters finally board their planes home, exhausted, they feel pride and satisfaction that they have brought the genuine skateboarding art – creative, vital, and communal – rather than some lifeless parody to the Olympics. In every deed and misdeed at the Games, pro riders pushed skateboarding itself into the spotlight, not their 'personal brands', not the products and services of advertisers, not divisive nationalism, not overblown sports. And the Olympics are never likely to invite skateboarding to return as a result. Mission accomplished.

In the aftermath of the Games, pro skaters receive some hostile receptions when they arrive home. A few politicians and sports authorities describe pro skaters and their behavior at the Olympics as 'insulting', 'disappointing', and even 'traitorous'. Pro skaters pay little mind. Artists of all kinds are accustomed to these charges; they grow to accept them as the price of doing business and even welcome them as signs that their work is successfully provoking audiences. Family members and other people closest to pro skaters are more understanding, since they have developed some familiarity with the art by years of association. Local skaters are certainly supportive of the pros' conduct at the Games. Watching the trials and triumphs of top riders, as they dodged and defied Olympic authorities, reminded amateurs of similar experiences skating at home. Pro riders practicing the genuine skateboarding art throughout the weeks of the Games also produced far more photo and video footage for viewers outside of Japan than a few days of official competitions might have generated. Skaters of all levels can direct any non-skating countrymen, disappointed or angered by the absence of network television coverage of Olympic skateboarding, to this abundance of online material.

Some sponsors, especially mainstream brands operating outside of the skateboarding industry proper, express their disapproval with pro skaters' disappearance from Olympic competition and its global television broadcasts. The time has come for pro riders to reevaluate their arrangements with these companies: Do they have a deep understanding of skateboarding after all? Is supporting the skateboarding art and its artists at the top of their priorities, or are they more interested in breeding some gross mutation to serve their own profit motives? Companies that are genuinely invested in skateboarding identify themselves by recognizing the value of staging a much larger, longer-lived, and more authentic event than any Olympic authorities or sports fans could have imagined.

Pro skaters escape from any disapproval into the piles of footage they have brought back from the Games. They assemble scattered clips of themselves into full video parts, and they share footage of everyone else, so that skaters around the world can create, release, and remix an entire library of Tokyo 2020 riding by themselves. Occasional shots of baffled sports journalists and seething Olympic officials add some extra laughs.

In the end, skaters of all levels rejoice at the sabotage and failure of the Olympic skateboarding experiment. They have bitten hard one hand that might have fed and tamed them. Without this distraction, we skaters may continue building a world of our own, one that properly reflects and supports us, and the only one that has any chance of inspiring others to do the same for themselves.

Authors

Beal, Becky (Ed.D.), is a Professor of Kinesiology at the California State University, East Bay, Hayward, CA, where she teaches courses in the sociology and philosophy of sport and has been active member of the Center for Sport and Social Justice. For nearly thirty years she has researched the cultural and political dynamics of skateboarding.

Bindel, Tim (PhD), is a Professor/Head of Department of Sport Pedagogy at the Johannes-Gutenberg-University Mainz. His interests include sport pedagogy, ethnographic strategies in the study of youth cultures, sport and social responsibility, intergenerationality.

Bock, Katharina (PhD), is a Sociologist, Linguist and Communication Scientist. She works as a Research Assistent at the Department of Social Sciences, University of Hildesheim. Her interests include youth research, interaction research, knowledge and media sociology.

Borden, Iain (PhD), is a Professor of architecture and urban culture at The Bartlett School of Architecture, University College London (UCL). Iain's research focuses on social and cultural experiences of cities and architecture, and his most recent book, Skateboarding and the City: A Complete History (2019).

Cantin-Brault, Antoine (PhD), is a Professor of Philosophy at the Université de Saint Boniface Winnipeg. His research focus includes German Philosophy, Greek Philosophy, Metaphysics, Ethics and Politics as well as the philosophical study of musics.

Colberg, Tait, has been riding skateboards of various sizes and shapes for more than thirty years. He is the author of the book 'The Skateboarding Art' (2012), and he has contributed to The Skateboard Mag, The Skateboarder's Journal, and Monster Skateboard Magazine. He skates goofy and always with a horizontal split-line in his griptape.

Ebeling, Kristin, holds an undergraduate degree in History from University of Washington and is a lifelong skateboarder. She currently serves as Executive Director of Skate Like a Girl, a non-profit organization that reaches 7,000 skaters in Seattle, Portland, and San Francisco Bay each year. Her experience as a youth mentor, skater, and activist, informs her unique approach to improving equity in access in skateboarding, inspiring nontraditional skaters globally. Kristin also contributes to The Skate Witches, Vent City Podcast, and Skateism.

Kilberth, Veith, blends his Sports Sciences diploma from the University of Cologne with experience as a former professional skateboarder. Currently a doctorate candidate at the Europa University Flensburg, he plans and realizes skate park projects as a partner in design office Landskate. Veith specializes in the field of youth marketing, action sports, skateboarding and skateparks.

Pick, Niklas, received his Master degree (Physical Education, Mathematics) from the University of Wuppertal. He is an experienced skateboarder and his research focuses on the integration of skateboarding in physical education.

Schäfer, Eckehart Velten (PhD), works as a journalist, sociologist, and historian in Berlin. In 2017 he completed his dissertation on the history of body, space, and signification in the practice of skateboarding since the 1960s at the Carl von Ossietzky University Oldenburg. His interests include social theory, the relation of sport and society, the city and urbanism, as well as political and cultural movements in the twentieth century.

Schweer, Sebastian, is a Sociologist and Literary Scholar. He is a Member of the PhD-Net "The Knowledge of Literature" (Humboldt University Berlin) and Author of the book 'Skateboarding zwischen urbaner Rebellion und neoliberalem Selbstentwurf' (2014). Sebastian's research focuses on political theory, subcultural studies, urban studies, contemporary literature and the culture of remembrance.

Schwier, Jürgen (PhD), is a Professor for Kinesiology and the Sociology of Sport at the Europa-University Flensburg. From 1998 to 2009, he served as Professor for the Sociology of Sport at Justus-Liebig-University Giessen. His research focus includes sports communication, physical education, cultural studies, youth (sub) cultures, as well as the development of alternative sports.